ORIENTALISM

◆ DELACROIX TO KLEE ◆

ORIENTALISM

◆ DELACROIX TO KLEE ◆

ROGER BENJAMIN
Curator and Editor

MOUNIRA KHEMIR
Guest curator and contributor Photography

URSULA PRUNSTER
Guest curator and contributor Australian Art

LYNNE THORNTON
Contributor

THE ART GALLERY *of* NEW SOUTH WALES

Published by The Art Gallery of New South Wales, 1997

© The Art Gallery of New South Wales

National Library of Australia
Cataloguing-in-publication data:
Art Gallery of New South Wales
Orientalism: Delacroix to Klee

Includes index
ISBN 0 7313 1344 5 (softbound)
ISBN 0 7313 1356 9 (hardbound)

1. Art Gallery of New South Wales – Exhibitions.
2. Auckland City Art Gallery – Exhibitions.
3. Exoticism in art. 4. Islamic countries in art –
Exhibitions. 5. Middle East in art – Exhibitions.
6. Africa, North, in art – Exhibitions. 7. Art,
Modern – Exhibitions. I. Benjamin, Roger, 1957 – .
II. Title.

709.03074

Editor
Angela Gundert

Catalogue and exhibition design
John Spatchurst, Spatchurst Design Associates

Compilation
Fiona McIntosh

Transparencies
Diana Curtis

Word processing
Leanne Primmer and Debbie Spek

Filmwork
Response Colour Graphics Pty Ltd, Sydney

Printing
Samhwa Printing Co. Ltd, Korea

Softbound distributed by
The Art Gallery of New South Wales
Art Gallery Road, The Domain
Sydney NSW 2000 AUSTRALIA

Hardbound distributed by
Thames and Hudson Ltd
30–34 Bloomsbury Street
London WC 1B 3QP, UK

Thames and Hudson (Australia)
11 Central Boulevard, Portside Business Park
Port Melbourne, Victoria 3207 AUSTRALIA

Exhibition dates
The Art Gallery of New South Wales
6 December 1997–22 February 1998
Auckland Art Gallery
20 March–7 June 1998

* Works for Sydney only
ⁿ Work for Auckland only

CONTRIBUTORS

ROGER BENJAMIN **Co-ordinating curator and editor**
Roger Benjamin is Senior Lecturer in the Department of Fine Arts at the University of Melbourne, He publishes on Matisse, Fauvism and Aboriginal art, and has been researching and teaching the history of French Orientalism since 1990. He co-curated the retrospective 'Matisse' for the Queensland Art Gallery in 1995.

MOUNIRA KHEMIR **Guest curator Photography**
Mounira Khemir is an independent scholar and freelance curator of photography based in Paris. Her *L'Orientalisme: l'orient des photographes au XIXème siècle* was published by the Centre National de la Photographie in 1994. She has curated exhibitions and lectured widely in Europe and the Middle East.

URSULA PRUNSTER **Guest curator Australian Art**
Ursula Prunster works as a curator and public programmes co-ordinator at the Art Gallery of New South Wales. In 1994 the Art Gallery and Beagle Press published her *Legendary Lindsays* to accompany the exhibition.

LYNNE THORNTON **Adviser to the exhibition**
Lynne Thornton is a saleroom expert and authority on Orientalist painting based in Paris. Since 1983 she has edited ACR Edition's series 'Les Orientalistes', in which she has published several volumes. Her *Du Maroc aux Indes: souvenirs d'orient* is to appear in early 1998.

CATALOGUE CONTRIBUTORS

SUSAN AYKUT's doctorate on images of the hammam is in progress in the departments of History and History of Art at LaTrobe University, Melbourne. She lectures regularly on Orientalist painting.

CAROLINE JORDAN was awarded her PhD for 'Pilgrims of the Picturesque: The Amateur Woman Artist and British Colonialism' (University of Melbourne, 1996). She has published several articles on women and modernism in Australia.

ALISON INGLIS is Lecturer in museum studies and 19th-century art in the Department of Fine Arts at the University of Melbourne. Her PhD on Edward Poynter's decorative work is nearing completion. She is a regular contributor to Australian art journals.

JOHN PIGOT's doctoral thesis on Hilda Rix Nicholas was completed at the University of Melbourne in 1995. He curated 'Capturing the Orient: Hilda Rix Nicholas and Ethel Carrick in the East' at Waverley City Gallery, Melbourne, in 1993.

PETER RUDD's doctoral thesis on Emile Bernard's career after Pont-Aven is in progress at the University of Sydney. His article on Manet's *Little cavaliers* appeared in the *Burlington Magazine* for November 1994.

MARY ROBERTS lectures in art theory at Canberra School of Art. She gained her PhD with 'Travel, Transgression and the Colonial Harem', on John Frederick Lewis (University of Melbourne, 1995). She is co-editor of *The Opacity of Vision*, essays on Michael Fried (Power Publications, 1998).

NOTE ON TRANSLATION

Peter Rudd translated all texts by Mounira Khemir, including the essay, 'The Orient in the Photographers' Mirror', photography catalogue entries and the photographers' biographies. Unless otherwise noted, all translations for the painting catalogue entries are by their respective authors.

Front cover
Lucien Lévy-Dhurmer, *Evening promenade Morocco* c. 1930 (detail)
Private collection (cat. 97)

Front jacket flap
Henri Béchard, *Great Pyramid, eastern view* c. 1875 (detail)
Bibliothèque des Arts Décoratifs, Paris (cat. 140)

Frontispiece
Clérambault, *Untitled (drapery)* photograph
Collection Musée de l'Homme, Paris (cat. 174)

Back cover
Clérambault, *Untitled (drapery)* (detail) photograph
Collection Musée de l'Homme, Paris (cat. 174)

Back jacket flap
Henri Béchard, *Interior of the Amrou mosque* c. 1870
Collection Claude Philip, Orange (cat. 125)

CONTENTS

ACKNOWLEDGMENTS

Realising this exhibition on the theme of Orientalism is the fulfilment of a long-held ambition. It was not, however, until we were able to secure the services of Dr Roger Benjamin of the University of Melbourne as curator that the project became possible. We have all been inspired by his very individual enthusiasm for the subject and guided by his knowledge. The resultant exhibition and this splendid publication are very much the consequence of his imagination and his dedication. He has been ably assisted by Ursula Prunster of this Gallery, Mounira Khemir, a freelance curator of photography in Paris, and Lynne Thornton, the respected Orientalist specialist in Paris, all of whom have made substantial contributions to the curating of the exhibition and to the preparation of this catalogue. We are also indebted to Peter Rudd, John Pigot, Lara Smith, Mary Roberts, Alison Inglis, Caroline Jordan and Susan Aykut for their co-operation with Roger Benjamin, and to Brahim Alaoui of the Institut du Monde Arabe in Paris for his support and advice.

Public and private collections around the world have made works available for the exhibition and we are much indebted to the lenders for their generosity and co-operation. From the very outset the project received, through the most helpful and supportive role of Brian MacDermot of the Mathaf Gallery in London, a commitment to lend from the distinguished Nadj Collection of classic Orientalist paintings. Without this group of crucial works we would have found it immeasurably more difficult to achieve such a rich and glowing panorama of Orientalist paintings. I must express my special thanks to Henri Loyrette, Director, and Caroline Mathieu and Geneviève Lacambre, of the Musée d'Orsay in Paris for agreeing to lend so many highly significant works, and to Arlette Sérullaz and Jean-Pierre Cuzin of the Musée du Louvre for their support. Thanks are also due to Josiane Sartre, Director at the Bibliothèque des Arts Décoratifs, and Jacqueline Dubois and Christine Barte at the Musée de l'Homme, who helped Mounira Khemir with the selection of photographs. We have received assistance from many sources in securing loans for this exhibition and I express my particular thanks to Peter Nahum at The Leicester Galleries in London; His Excellency John Spender, Ambassador, and Harriet O'Malley of the Australian Embassy in Paris; His Excellency Ashton Calvert, Australian Ambassador to Japan; and His Excellency Dominique Girard, Ambassador, and Laurent de Gaulle of the French Embassy in Canberra.

Here in the Gallery the management and co-ordination of the exhibition has been in the ever-capable hands of Anne Flanagan, along with Anna Hayes, Fiona McIntosh and the staff in the Exhibitions Department. To Angela Gundert my thanks for her meticulous editing. John Spatchurst has designed the catalogue and the presentation of the exhibition with his usual flair and refinement.

I would also like to record our appreciation of the Director, Chris Saines, and his colleagues at the Auckland Art Gallery who are participating in the tour of this exhibition.

Regular and reliable corporate sponsors of art exhibitions are as rare as they are treasured. Over the years Louis Vuitton has supported many of our most successful and enjoyable exhibitions. With their trademark and distinctive product the coincidence of Louis Vuitton and Orientalism seemed to us to be a natural one. Once more they have provided their generous financial support and we are again delighted to be working with such a valued and constant sponsor. As I have so often done before, I thank Julia King, Chief Executive of Louis Vuitton Australia, and in doing so record our appreciation, and indeed that of all those who visit and enjoy this exhibition, for making it possible.

Finally to Channel 7, Qantas and the Hotel Inter.Continental Sydney, our renewed thanks for their wonderful and continuing support. ◆◆ EDMUND CAPON

SPONSOR'S STATEMENT

Louis Vuitton is once again proud to be able to sponsor an exhibition at The Art Gallery of New South Wales, and *Orientalism: Delacroix to Klee* is a particularly appropriate exhibition of paintings and photography for our partnership with the Gallery.

The exhibition covers the work of artists who found the mirage and the mystery of the Orient irresistible and who travelled to Egypt, Turkey, Morocco, Algeria, Palestine and Syria to capture its mood.

Orientalism is about travel, and it was during the period 1830–1930 that the means of travel changed dramatically. Coaches became more luxurious, and steam-trains and steamships – and later the motor car and the aeroplane – became fashionable ways to seek adventure. Travel became the dream of educated Europeans.

When 19th-century Europeans spoke of the Orient, they envisaged romantic images of horsemen with flowing robes, of falconry and women exotically dressed. It was in reality a harsh landscape under vivid blue skies whose strong light created unfamiliar colours.

The fashion for Orientalism provided Louis Vuitton with his opportunity. He began business in 1854, and in 1869 was making trunks and packing crinolines, hats and uniforms for Napoleon III and Empress Eugénie for their voyage to Egypt for the opening of the Suez Canal.

The new modes of transport demanded new types of luggage, and the Louis Vuitton company has always been at the forefront of innovation. An English gentlewoman travelling to Turkey in search of Noah's Ark, for instance, had a carriage designed by Louis Vuitton which could be disassembled to fit into three trunks.

Louis Vuitton Australia has had a long and fruitful partnership with The Art Gallery of New South Wales and we are delighted to help bring this exhibition to Sydney. ◆◆

Julia King, Chief Executive, *Louis Vuitton Australia Pty Ltd*

DIRECTOR'S INTRODUCTION

This, the first exhibition on the theme of Orientalism to be held in Australia and New Zealand, is a revelation of the colours, shadows, contrasts, mysteries and unfamiliar faces of the artists' views of the European encounter with the Islamic worlds of North Africa and the Middle East. It is, as Roger Benjamin says, an exhibition about the aesthetics of travel; but within that single notion there lie a myriad of different experiences and responses: from the romantic bravura of Delacroix's clashing Arab cavalry, Gérôme's powerfully sensuous realism, Guillaumet's view of the epic desert horizon, to the delicate reminiscences of Paul Klee and the colourful seductions of Matisse's odalisques of nearly 100 years after Delacroix. It is also an exhibition that inevitably raises questions about the very nature of this firmly Occidental view of an equally firmly Oriental world. The question is whether the classic Orientalism of Delacroix's candescent visions of despotism and Arab fury, or of Gérôme's sensuously perfumed parlours, or Dinet's fascination with atmosphere and local detail are lordly demonstrations of cultural superiority or excited responses to the mysteries and seductions of the exotic and the unfamiliar. While there is indisputable evidence that all these artists were inspired by their fascination with the subject and its seen and unseen opportunities it is equally true that, with some exceptions – Dinet for example – their encounters with the Oriental world were generally vicarious. That, it might be said, was in itself a process of the imagination – just as our imagination too is surely driven by the experience of these richly patinated paintings.

The European mind is a naturally inquisitive one, but one less inclined to actual involvement. The theme of Orientalism is a perfect demonstration of that sensibility touring the Orient, forever watching, recording and absorbing Delacroix's romantic opportunity: 'the picturesque is plentiful here. At every step, one meets ready-made paintings that would bring twenty generations of painters wealth and glory'. Perhaps it was that view which sustained the tradition throughout the 19th century, but in the era of the Impressionists and after, the division between 'seeing' a picture and 'making' a picture increasingly placed the subject as little more than pretext. When we come to the Orientalist works of Matisse and Klee, for example, it is undeniable that it is the artist's vision and emotion that is the guiding creative initiative, and yet the model, the subject, was by no means a matter of indifference to them. The 'picturesque' and modern painting may not seem to be compatible but that in no way invalidates later Orientalist works, because Matisse, Klee and their 20th-century colleagues were less travelling pictorialists than they were artists of the modern era responding to a fresh and tantalising range of colours, textures, decorative effects and experiences.

Exhibitions on the theme of Orientalism have been held in the recent past in both Europe and the United States. Inevitably our view of the tradition from this part of the world is different, and that difference is manifest in the selection of works. Never before have Australian artists – Conder, Roberts, Streeton and Carrick for example – been included in such exhibitions; and yet they too worked in the heat, the clamour and the calm, and the dusty evocative haze of the streets and kasbahs of Tangier, Algiers or Cairo. Furthermore, works by artists from the region have seldom been included, but here we can see, in the essentially European panorama, paintings by Hamdy Bey from Turkey, and Mammeri and Racim from Algiers, working in a manner that suggests a certain European aspiration, but one tempered by their own traditions. Such an exhibition is also an opportunity to view certain works from this collection, and indeed other Australian collections, within the enlarged but specific context of a special exhibition. We have not, for example, ever had the opportunity to see two of this Gallery's most substantial and colourful 19th-century works, Poynter's epic *The visit of the Queen of Sheba to King Solomon* and Dinet's splendid *The snake charmer*, so convincing in atmosphere in their Orientalist context. The overall scope of the exhibition, from the work of Delacroix and Ingres to the more avant-garde aspirations of Matisse and Klee, gives a much fuller picture than the traditional view of the theme. Seldom are the works of the so-called French 'colonial art' movement seen in this context, but here we include Orientalist subjects by Besnard, Dufresne, Suréda and Marquet. Similarly, the art of photography has generally been excluded from such surveys, and yet here is an extraordinarily rich and poignant visual record of encounters, experiences and travels through those then remote and mysterious places. The absence of colour is more than compensated for by the profound nuances of tone and texture which inspire these images, perhaps less dramatic than their painted counterparts, with a powerful combination of intimacy and reality.

In its vision, its embrace and its scope this must surely be one of the most inclusive exhibitions on the art of Orientalism ever held.

Orientalism is not a movement or a style; it is more in the nature of a tradition with its base in a common fascination and, uniquely, that common factor is the place. Generations of artists have been engaged by such themes as the still life, the portrait, the heroic figure, but never has a loosely defined cultural region proven such a sustained (well over a century) source of inspiration as the 'Orient'. As such the theme became another, but less obvious, medium for charting the progress of artistic style, from Ingres and Delacroix in the early 19th century to Klee and Kandinsky in the 1920s and 1930s. Into this pattern, even within the confines of the subject, we can place the Australian Orientalists; indeed it is asserted that Roberts's ability in handling the effects of dazzling light was first gained in the heart of Moorish Spain, in Granada. ◆◆

Edmund Capon, Director, *The Art Gallery of New South Wales*

THE ORIENTAL MIRAGE[1]

Roger Benjamin

THIS EXHIBITION IS ABOUT THE AESTHETICS OF TRAVEL. IT IS ABOUT PAINTERS AND PHOTOGRAPHERS RENDERING THEIR ENCOUNTERS WITH PEOPLE AND PLACES WHICH, INITIALLY AT LEAST, WERE STRANGE TO THEM. FOR MANY THAT PLACE WAS THE 'ORIENT', A LOCATION WITH ALL THE ALLURE AND RESONANCE OF MYTH, A PLACE FABULOUS BECAUSE FEW HAD VISITED IT. YET WE CAN BE PRECISE ABOUT ITS LOCATION: WHEN WESTERN EUROPEANS OF THE 19TH CENTURY SPOKE OF THE 'ORIENT', THEY MOST OFTEN MEANT THE HOT COUNTRIES OF NORTH AFRICA AND THE MIDDLE EAST, DESERT COUNTRIES THAT HAD LONG KNOWN THE IMPRINT OF ISLAM, AND WHICH HAD LONG BEEN CLOSED TO THE EUROPEAN TRAVELLER.[2]

In discussing the work produced by artists who visited this Orient, the word 'mirage' presents itself as a useful key to understanding. A mirage is an optical phenomenon of the desert, whereby light refracted through layers of super-heated air produces a reflection of the blue sky on the sandy surface, which thus appears as an illusory sheet of water. Derived from the French word for mirroring or reflection, 'mirage' is a properly Orientalist term, taken up during the Napoleonic era to describe a 'phenomenon…which [the French] army had daily opportunities of seeing, in their march through the deserts of Egypt'.[3]

Fig.1
EUGENE DELACROIX
Scenes from the massacres at Chios
1824
oil on canvas
419 x 353 cm
Musée du Louvre, Paris

The 'Oriental mirage' is thus a phrase that captures an important principle, a metaphor for the way travelling artists always have an unstable view of their subject. In general, imitative painting of any sort is an approximation of the scene before an artist, given the vagaries of technique, personal interpretation, and the deliberate adjustment of a random view. Even the practitioner of the 'objective' art of photography will personalise a scene by selecting a subject, framing it in certain ways, and printing it as desired; subjectivity necessarily enters every stage of the process. Orientalist painters or photographers are in addition faced with the obstacle of cultural misunderstanding when depicting other peoples. Try as they might to produce a mirror or reflection of the scene before them, Orientalists, like ethnographers, are limited by their ethnocentrism in attempting to gain knowledge about other cultures;[4] whatever their expertise, the artists' own culture invariably skews the image. The 'Oriental mirage' in this sense is the impossibility of any artist obtaining full knowledge of the cultural Other that forms his or her subject.

On the other hand, mirages most certainly attract: 'The thirsty traveller in the desert pants to attain the cooling stream in the far distance. Alas! 'tis but a mirage'.[5] The mirage of life in the Orient has stood before countless travellers from the West as an enticement, an escape from the routine and the familiarity of a modern life that had become, for a Gustave Flaubert in 1850, stupefying in its banality. Escapism and sexual adventure has fuelled many an artist's voyage,[6] as it may do the tourist's today. The parallels between the Orientalists and modern tourists are many, key among them being the impulse to document one's experiences of the extraordinary with the drawing or the written account (in the 19th century), or the snapshot and video today. The mirage of the exotic which travellers of yesteryear sought to confirm by experience has today been reduced to a name for a tropical resort.[7]

DELACROIX'S EXAMPLE

For many artists the image of the East could in fact be seized, richly, through their brushes; it did not slip like dry sand between the fingers of the traveller. Here are the limits of the mirage as a metaphor: despite its fleeting character, the Oriental mirage could be converted to gold. The great example of this is the painting of Eugène Delacroix, the artist with whom this exhibition begins. What Delacroix saw on his overland journey through Morocco in 1832 provided him with subjects for the rest of his life. In a moment of prescience he wrote in a letter from Meknès: 'The picturesque here is in abundance. At every step one sees ready-made pictures, which would bring fame and fortune to twenty generations of painters'.[8]

Delacroix's Orientalism introduces concepts and images that link many works in this exhibition. His voyage to Morocco became the archetype of the Orientalist experience, the one that set the agenda. Major artists such as Eugène Fromentin in 1846, Auguste Renoir in 1881, and Henri Matisse in 1912 made their own voyages South and East in deliberate emulation of the romantic master. Delacroix's very predisposition for the East became symptomatic: well before his departure, Oriental themes provided subjects for paintings at the State Salon. *Scenes from the massacres at Chios*, 1824 (fig. 1) was based on the Greek war of independence against the Ottoman Turks which drew European sympathy and the active fighting of liberals such as Lord Byron.[9] With its image of a Greek family facing death, enslavement or rape at the hands of gorgeously clad Mameluke horsemen, Delacroix gave currency to violence in an exotic frame that remained one of the mainstays of Orientalist art.[10] Delacroix's partiality – his 'reportage'

Fig. 2
EUGENE DELACROIX
The death of Sardanapalus
1827

oil on canvas
392 x 496 cm

Musée du Louvre, Paris

staged to maximise sympathy for the Greek victims of the Islamic forces – is an early example of the phenomenon that Edward Said sees as characterising the discourse of Orientalism as a whole: a subtle and persistent Eurocentric (and Christian) prejudice against Arabo-Islamic peoples and their culture. This was less a matter of racism (although racism did play a part), than of the aggressiveness necessitated by the colonial expansion of the European powers, France and England, in Africa and the Near East throughout the 19th century.[11]

One such prejudice – that the natural political order of the East is despotism – is given powerful expression in Delacroix's *The death of Sardanapalus,* 1827 (fig. 2). Inspired by a play by Byron, this riot of bloodletting and sensuous excess is premised on the eastern (but here pre-Islamic) ruler's brutal control over the destiny of the people, beasts and treasures of his household, which he destroys rather than have fall into enemy hands. Despotism and violence linked to sex continued to fuel certain inflammatory Orientalist images of the Islamic world, especially those of later neo-Romantic painters such as Regnault, Dehodencq, Clairin and Benjamin-Constant (qq.v.).

Yet *Sardanapalus* was strictly a work of imagination, not powered by any direct encounter with its subject. This is true also of the celebrated series of odalisques[12] by Delacroix's aesthetic alter-ego, J.-A.-D. Ingres. These works, which posit the East as the place where western erotic imagination found its home, began in earnest with his coolly seductive *Grand odalisque* of 1814 (fig. 3). Ingres's painted replica of the *Grand odalisque*'s head is one of the key images in this exhibition (cat. 12). The *Grand odalisque* was succeeded by the 1839 *Odalisque with slave* which, while ethnologically more precise, was, like it, painted in Rome from European models and Turkish studio props (see cat. 14). If Delacroix had been inspired by Byron's writing, Ingres's imagery of the harem and bath was fuelled by travellers' accounts such as the *Turkish Embassy Letters* of Lady Mary Wortley Montagu. Yet Rome was the furthest limit of Ingres's actual travel, and his erotic Orient remained a mirage of nudes beyond his grasp and multiplying in his imagination in works like the *Turkish bath* (see fig. 9).

Fig. 3

JEAN-AUGUSTE-DOMINIQUE INGRES
The grand odalisque
1814
oil on canvas
91 x 162 cm
Musée du Louvre, Paris

Fig. 4
EUGENE DELACROIX
*Collision of
Arab horsemen*
1843–44

oil on canvas
81.3 x 99.1 cm

The Walters Art
Gallery, Baltimore,
Maryland, no. 37.6
(cat. 10)

Delacroix, on the contrary, seized the opportunity for travel East when invited in 1832 by the Comte de Mornay to act as the artist accompanying his diplomatic mission to the Sultan of Morocco. For centuries Morocco, like most of the Maghreb (the Arabic word for North Africa),[13] had been closed to most Europeans. That changed with the French capture of the corsair capital of Algiers in 1830, and subsequent invasion of the vast Algerian hinterland. France was obliged to send an emissary (de Mornay) to seek an alliance with the ruler of neighbouring Morocco.

Thus Delacroix's journey was only possible with diplomatic intervention and travel under guard. As Said showed in the case of writers, European painters could only travel in territory made secure by military expeditions and, later, colonial settlement; as in the Australian experience, the art is indelibly a cultural legacy of the colonial process. Delacroix's group was given safe-conduct by successive warrior tribes from Tangier south to Meknès, providing an unending stream of martial subjects for this most able of draughtsmen (fig. 4). His documentary procedure was typical of later Orientalists, if exceptionally rich: Delacroix filled some seven notebooks with hundreds of pencil or pen drawings (replete with annotations and watercolour highlights); his transcribed comments have been published as his 'journal'; and he sent numerous letters home.

Fig. 5
EUGENE DELACROIX
*Women of Algiers
in their apartment*
1834

oil on canvas
180 x 229 cm

Musée du Louvre,
Paris

Most 19th-century paintings were executed after the journey on the basis of such documents (in the 20th century, with its emphasis on spontaneity, this was less the rule).[14] For the famous *Women of Algiers in their apartment*, 1834 (fig. 5) Delacroix sat French models, dressed in Maghrebian costumes, in the poses he had sketched in Algiers (where he had been given the rare opportunity of observing the womenfolk of a somewhat equivocal Islamic household).[15] Although this painting has become an icon among Orientalist harem interiors, when first exhibited it was praised less for its sensual subject than its high colour, its detachment, the art of 'pure painting' that it seemed to propose.[16] This exclusively aesthetic response mirrors Delacroix's own Moroccan writing in seeking to define the visual parameters of the scene: how the light differed from that of the North, how colours in the locals' costumes were bleached, or line clarified. The Orient was early on linked with the formalist aesthetic – and such aestheticising supplanted any consciousness of a subject's political dimensions.

THE EXPANDING EAST

Fig. 6
ALEXANDRE
DECAMPS
*Turkish
guardhouse
on the Smyrna–
Magnesia road*
1833

oil on canvas
91 x 155 cm

Musée Condé,
Chantilly

Travel to Morocco was exceptional; the usual destinations of Orientalists in the 1830s and 1840s were Turkey and Egypt. The diminished control that the Ottomans, based in Constantinople, had over the Eastern Mediterranean enabled Alexandre Decamps to visit Asia Minor and Syria in 1828. Famous for peaceful genre scenes that were enamel-like in their lustrous colour, Decamps explored the 'everyday life' of Turkish citizens under Islam (fig. 6). In Egypt the French presence was gradually replaced by an English colonial primacy; British painters such as John Frederick Lewis (q.v.) and Edward Lear took advantage of this in the 1840s, and French landscapists such as Prosper Marilhat and, later, Jean-Léon Gérôme and Léon Belly (qq.v.) travelled there regularly. Egypt's combination of grandiose antiquity along the Nile, and the Islamic splendour of caliphate architecture in Cairo, made the country irresistible to painters, to photographers such as Maxime du Camp and Roger Fenton, and to writers such as Gustave Flaubert and Gérard de Nerval.

Algeria only became marginally safe for French painter–travellers with the surrender in 1847 of the Emir Abd-el-Kader, a brilliant military and religious leader who for fifteen years had led a jihad or declared holy war against the French invaders. The key battles of that war were painted on a giant scale by Horace Vernet, whose *Taking of the smalah of Abd-el-Kader* of 1843 presented an enthralled French public with an Orientalism of cinematic proportions. The first outstanding easel painter in Algeria after such events was Théodore Chassériau (q.v.), who in 1846 worked in the French-controlled stronghold of Constantine. An old Roman town, Constantine was a melting-pot of different communities, in particular the Kabyls, the autochthonous Berber people, Arabs descended from the great religious invasions begun in the 8th century, and Jews whose ancestors were expelled (along with the Andalusian Moors) from the Iberian Peninsula during the Catholic 'Reconquest' of Spain in 1492.

This panoply of ethnic identities came to constitute the key pictorial subject for Orientalists such as Chassériau, Dehodencq, Matisse and Suréda. The ethnic groups perceived by the Europeans had their 'mirage' aspect: categories such as the 'Moors' for instance, were inexact if not fictitious.[17] The Jews of North Africa provided more fixity and, as Delacroix had discovered, were more willing to act as sitters for figure or portrait paintings than most Muslims, for whom a long-standing interpretation of religious texts forbade the representation of the human figure.[18] Chassériau's lost *Sabbath of the Jews of Constantine* and Dehodencq's *Jewish bride in Morocco* (cat. 59) expressed a fascination with these most direct descendants of the biblical peoples.

Chassériau's *Combat of Arab horsemen* of 1856 (cat. 16) is indebted to images such as Delacroix's *Collision of Arab horsemen* of 1843–44 (cat. 10). It has often been asserted that the horse was essential to the romantic sensibility because it could symbolise extremes of passion in a creature nevertheless subject to the rational rule of mankind. For Delacroix, Chassériau and Fromentin, the ideal riders were Arabs rather than modern French soldiers in their constricting uniforms. While the French admired their feats of horsemanship and their courage as military opponents, the Arabs, with their loose-fitting robes and scimitars, were also eminently 'pictorial'. The horsemen of Delacroix and Chassériau never fight on specified occasions (as in true military painting); their rage is ubiquitous, as if nothing else happened in the chaos of unending tribal warfare. That is the image French writers often gave of Maghrebian politics before European intervention.[19]

THE AESTHETICS OF ORIENTALISM: FROMENTIN AND GAUTIER

Eugène Fromentin is a crucial figure for this exhibition: this 'brilliantly gifted' artist, 'with his fantasias, his falconry hunts, his nervous, swift little horses' won many admirers from the 1850s to the 1870s.[20] Fromentin was also an articulate aesthetician who put forward the first clear view of the problems that painting in exotic climates presented to European artists. A gifted novelist as well as painter, Fromentin had travelled extensively in Algeria from the late 1840s, and a decade later conveyed these memories in two influential travel books, *A Year in the Sahel* and *A Summer in the Sahara*. Given the breadth of experience recounted in these books, the narrowness of Fromentin's painting is striking: his most abiding theme is the 'noble' Arab pastime of falconry – riders seen up close at full gallop, or groups of horsemen trotting under immense skies. He believed that North Africa presented great problems for the painter:

> *[The Orient] is exceptional...it escapes general laws, the only ones which are worth following...Even when it is very beautiful, it retains a certain modicum...of exaggeration, of violence that renders it excessive. This is an order of beauty which, having no precedents in either ancient literature or art, immediately strikes us as appearing bizarre.*

Fig. 7
LEON BELLY
*Pilgrims going
to Mecca*
1861

oil on canvas
161 x 242 cm

Musée d'Orsay,
Paris

*All its features appear at once: the novelty of its aspects, the singularity of its costumes,
the originality of its types, the toughness of its effects, the particular rhythm of its lines,
the unaccustomed scale of its colours.*[21]

For Fromentin the 'bizarre' character of the Orient calls into question the task of representation, an anxiety which recalls the metaphor of the mirage as unstable reflection:
how was it possible to produce an image of something that was, if not in principle unrep-
resentable, then beyond the limits of beauty? The European eye was dazzled by unfamiliar
costumes, ethnic types, gestures – details of a kind Fromentin called 'documents'. An
over-documented painting, in this sense, leads to 'pictures composed like an inventory,
and the taste for ethnography will eventually be confused with the feeling for beauty'.[22]

Similar problems faced the painter of landscapes in the East. In Fromentin's estimate the
Oriental landscape:

> *inverts everything, it reverses the harmonies which have organised landscape
> for centuries...It is the land...of inflamed landscapes under a blue sky, that is to say
> brighter than the sky, which constantly leads...to reversed paintings: no centre, because
> light flows all around; no moving shadows, because the sky is cloudless.*[23]

Despite these reservations, at the height of his powers Fromentin did attempt certain
paintings of this harsher, more 'bizarre' East. Two of his greatest achievements are
exhibited here: the *Street of Laghouat* and the *Land of thirst* (cats 17, 19). The first was
directly observed, the second inspired by travellers' tales he had heard in the Sahara. The
Land of thirst functioned, a little like Delacroix's 'massacres', as a disaster-painting that
would agitate the imagination of comfortable visitors to Parisian Salons.

Fromentin's success contributed to the vogue for Orientalist painting during the 1850s.
One prescient commentator saw new patterns in travel and technology behind this
fashion. Théophile Gautier, the celebrated romantic novelist and critic, was the most

persuasive supporter of Orientalism in these decades. He had travelled in Spain, Algeria, Turkey and Egypt, and used this first-hand experience to judge the authenticity of the painter–travellers he singled out in his entertaining reviews of the annual Salon.

By 1859 Gautier saw this great movement of artists as being facilitated by the new technology of *La Vapeur* – steam-power – which drove the trains on the many lines opening up in France and beyond (including Algeria), as well as the steamships plying the sea-lanes across the Mediterranean. For Gautier, as for J. M. W. Turner, their smoke-stacks and fireboxes, rather than killing off the artistic subjects of bellying sails and galloping horses, actually ushered in new subjects – in this case by enabling travel. Gautier wrote:

> *Today Nature has replaced the historical landscape, and painters realise that studio models are not the only species of mankind. Steam-power, so often belittled as bourgeois and prosaic, has carried them off with the spin of a propeller or a wheel, with more speed than the legendary hippogriff. Today the Sahara is dotted with as many landscapists' parasols as the Forest of Fontainebleau in days gone by.*[24]

There was a whole world awaiting discovery. In his famous *Abédécaire du Salon de 1861* Gautier welcomed a veritable 'caravan' of Orientalist painters whom the Parisian art-lover could accompany on 'this voyage of the eye which costs nothing, and involves no fatigue'.[25] The time was fast approaching when the Orient would challenge Italy as the arbiter of modern aesthetics: 'The voyage to Algiers is becoming as indispensable for painters as the pilgrimage to Italy; they go there to learn of the sun, to study light, to seek out unseen types, and manners and postures that are primitive and biblical'.[26]

Fig. 8
HENRIETTE BROWNE
*A visit
(harem interior;
Constantinople,
1860)*
oil on canvas
86 x 114 cm
(present where-
abouts unknown)

In the opinion of Gautier, Léon Belly rivalled Fromentin at the head of the Oriental contingent in 1861. He had the success of his career with his *Pilgrims going to Mecca* (fig. 7). Belly's preferred painting-ground was Egypt – not the Egypt of the Pharaohs or the bazaars of Cairo, but that of agriculture along the Nile, and the nearby desert (cat. 22). Gautier's appreciation of the grandiose *Pilgrims* also applies to the more lyrical *Gazelle hunt* (cat. 21): 'In it the varied types of Islam are represented with their characteristic costume and gait…in an atmosphere whose heat one can feel, on sand which burns the feet, in the heart of a land which seems dream-like by the sheer force of its reality'.[27]

Fig. 9
JEAN-AUGUSTE-
DOMINIQUE INGRES
Turkish bath
1862

oil on canvas
diam. 110 cm

Musée du Louvre,
Paris

Gautier's admiring passages on the British painter Henriette Browne drew attention to the unusual fact of her being a successful female exhibitor (see cat. 32). Browne's *A visit* (fig. 8), which showed women in a Turkish harem, led Gautier to reflect on the restrictions he had felt as a male traveller to Turkey. 'Only women should travel to Turkey', he concluded: '*A visit* indeed shows us the interior of a harem by someone who has seen it, a rare if not unique thing, for although male painters often do odalisques, not a single one can boast of having worked before the model'.[28] Browne's sober vision of the scene (reproduced here in colour for the first time), where all the women are fully clad and greet each other with grave gestures worthy of a diplomatic reception (if not a convent – Browne's other speciality), highlights the phantasmagoric character of most male visions of the harem, which are mirage-paintings as a matter of principle.

In fact the octogenarian Ingres was elaborating his celebrated *Turkish bath* (fig. 9) at this very time. Ingres was the quintessential armchair Orientalist: his harem imagery was drawn from disparate sources, from anonymous travellers' woodcuts to the 18th-century writings of Lady Mary Wortley Montagu, friend of Alexander Pope and witty epistolarian who had visited the women's baths at Adrianople. Ingres's *Turkish bath* projects the women's bath as an erotic site of unrelieved intensity, suggesting the full gamut of sexual dispositions, from the implied lesbianism of several foreground figures, to the dominating masculine voyeurism suggested by the construction of the picture as a peep-hole view onto a zone forbidden male access. Although the *Turkish bath* was kept from public view until the year 1905 (when it was studied by the Fauve avant-garde and engraved by Coraboeuf, cat. 15), Ingres's earlier more decorous odalisques had helped legitimise a vast series of female nudes in exotic surroundings which included those of Gérôme (cats 41, 43) and Débat-Ponsan (cat. 50) right through to Matisse's odalisques of the 1920s (cat. 124).

Nudity of the kind seen in the Parisian Salons would have been unacceptable in Victorian London: witness the works of John Frederick Lewis, 'the greatest of the immense number of British painters of desert, bazaar and harem subjects'.[29] Lewis was probably more familiar with the life of women under Islam than any male European painter before Etienne Dinet: from 1840 he lived for a decade in Cairo, seeming to adopt the life-style of an Oriental dignitary. Lewis's large private house, replete with

Fig. 10
JOHN FREDERICK
LEWIS
The hhareem
1849

watercolour
and body colour
88.6 x 133 cm
Private collection
(cat. 24)

intricate decorative *mashrabiyyas* or lattice balcony windows, was the décor he adopted for many of his interior scenes.

A painter of immense application in the difficult technique of watercolour, Lewis achieved effects of ornamentation that become almost psychedelic in their complexity. Already in his own day Ruskin and Gautier compared this sensibility to that of Islamic art,[30] especially in the infinite variations of the decorative motif which had inspired Lewis in the Alhambra in Spain and again in Old Cairo architecture. Yet Lewis's preoccupations with depicting light and shade, diaphanous materials, reflections and limpid colour meant he found a way of preventing that detail from becoming heavy; indeed, a certain gaiety of visual atmosphere attends his images of women in their interiors.

In Lewis all is decorous behaviour and sartorial propriety. He was a student of daily life, a genre painter with a very reserved sense of the anecdote. His masterpiece, *The hhareem*, here exhibited in context for the first time in many decades (fig. 10), in fact inscribes a complex interpersonal intrigue which only a familiarity with contemporary European perceptions of Egyptian manners can help to decode (see cat. 24).

THE GEROME PARADIGM

Lewis's counterpart in France, although very different in temperament and public profile, was Jean-Léon Gérôme. A brilliant technician, Gérôme more than anyone else was responsible for establishing documentary realism as the norm for Orientalist painting in the second half of the 19th century. Gérôme's vision of the East was disseminated widely for a number of reasons: his position as a long-serving professor at the Ecole des Beaux-Arts meant that he influenced many students, among them the Turkish painter Osman Hamdy Bey (q.v.) and the American Frederick Arthur Bridgman (q.v.); his paradigm of academic realism also inspired others, such as the Austrian artists Ludwig Deutsch and Rudolph Ernst (qq.v.). In addition, Gérôme's work was widely distributed in photo-engraved form, and his paintings sold exceptionally well, especially in the United States (Gérôme had married into the Goupil family, which had a dealership in New York).

From the 1850s Gérôme travelled extensively in the Near East and Egypt, often in the company of artist colleagues. He refined procedures for the documentary preparation of painting, utilising pencil drawings and precise oil sketches of landscape, and also pioneered putting the new technology of photography to use in his painting. His wealth helped Gérôme amass a vast collection of Oriental artefacts, which he used as studio props.[31] With such resources Gérôme executed, in his Paris studio, oil paintings which achieve an almost hallucinatory visual perfection, at the same time as they marshal an iconography of eastern sexuality that can at times go beyond the heterosexual norm of the bath scene (see *The snake charmer*, cat. 40).[32]

However earnest the endeavours by which Gérôme sought to authenticate his pictures (for example in his meticulous copying of Arabic inscriptions), and however influential the model of Orientalism he proposed, his success with critics has always been uncertain. Gérôme represented the pinnacle of power in the art establishment and was often identified as the enemy of the Impressionist movement. Many romantic critics, although supporters of Orientalism, found his visual approach too static, his figure painting 'wooden'. A leftist such as Jules-Antoine Castagnary could impugn Gérôme's morality as well as his commercial success, writing in 1864 that Gérôme was:

> *selling off the notes he's made during his voyage to the Orient. His Almeh is a note he should have kept in the portfolio. It is of a coldly calculating indecency, and I recoil from describing it. A crabbed technique in any case, mean, unpleasant, boring in the extreme.*[33]

Gérôme continues to excite controversy. Linda Nochlin, the first art historian to comprehend Edward Said's critical analysis of Orientalism as a cultural phenomenon, in 1983 read in Gérôme's work signs of a Eurocentric arrogance that inscribed commonplace prejudices against his Arabo-Islamic subjects: the idea of Oriental decay, the subjection of women, an unaccountable legal system. Nochlin also cleverly analysed the minutiae of Gérôme's painting as an example of pictorial rhetoric that served a subtle imperialist agenda.[34]

Although such arguments have been influential in academic circles, their continued viability is called into question today by the popularity of Gérôme and his disciples with the very people – in particular, art collectors from Saudi Arabia and the Gulf States – his pictures were said to denigrate (see the essay 'Post-Colonial Taste: Non-Western Markets for Orientalist Art' in this catalogue).

THE REALIST CRITIQUE OF ORIENTALISM

Castagnary's harsh words formed part of the first sustained critique of Orientalist painting to challenge the enthusiasm of Gautier and the Romantics. It came from the quarter of young Realists, left-leaning peers of Gustave Courbet who opposed the art establishment and the broader social order. Their socialist position on colonisation held that capital in the international framework had as little right to exploit workers in the colonies as it did the European proletariat. Many French royalists and republicans also felt that after the 1870 defeat in the Franco-Prussian War, France should concentrate its military resources along the border with Germany, rather than spreading them thinly in far-flung colonies which cost more to administer than they returned.[35]

Thus the realist Castagnary called on French artists to occupy themselves with the problems of modern life on French soil, arguing the case against Orientalism from 1857 until 1876, when he effectively declared the movement dead and buried. Castagnary may be credited with popularising the term 'Orientalism', which he used in a pejorative sense to help him isolate and decry what he considered a negative tendency in art.

Rather like the fretful Fromentin, Castagnary claimed that the strangeness of the Oriental scene meant that it was out of harmony with the average Frenchman:

> *I love the Nature which surrounds me because, being born into it, used to seeing it, I feel an intimate relation to it…it has helped form my very personality, and wherever I go I carry it with me. Now your desert, your palm trees, your camels, they may dazzle my mind, but they will never give me the sweet and peaceful emotion I have at the sight of cows in a meadow bordered by poplars…*[36]

Castagnary not only condemned those artists who 'rush into the distant Orient following the botanists and geographers', but also the exponents of the meticulous painting that sought to recover the lost traditions of the ancient East, like Alma-Tadema with his *Egyptians 3,000 years ago* (cat. 35). He showed a profound lack of sympathy for the goals of this 'archaeological' movement which forms an important aspect of Orientalism, especially in the hands of the British 'Victorian Olympians' Alma-Tadema, Edwin Long and above all Edward Poynter.

Poynter's masterpiece, *The visit of the Queen of Sheba to King Solomon* (cat. 34), was purchased by the then National Art Gallery of New South Wales in 1898. Driven by a particular kind of historical imagination, Poynter sought to furnish his images of the ancient Orient with items from the latest archaeological finds. In a century obsessed with unearthing and appropriating the buried treasure of ancient Mesopotamian and Egyptian civilisations, painting and archaeology became a synthesis in which the artist's concern for strict historical accuracy was less important than arriving at a visually arresting Oriental décor.[37]

Castagnary was typical of progressive French critics in attacking the high finish and elaborate detail of such works. This after all was the moment of the rise of Manet and early impressionist painting, where a broad vision of the ensemble and a liberated technique were sought. Such goals clashed with the 'scientific' concern for archaeological exactitude and its accompanying detail.[38]

It is not surprising that a brilliant young painter such as Henri Regnault (q.v.), who threw off the constraints of his early Beaux-Arts training to achieve a much more painterly technique, could attract the interest of the critic. Looking back at the Orientalist movement in 1876, Castagnary saw that: 'Regnault could have been a useful recruit. His stay in Spain and Tangier, his grandiose imagination, the verve and the brilliance of his execution might have done more for the doctrine than twenty years of camels and desert'.[39] However, Regnault's death in the Franco-Prussian War cut short this potential exoticist revival, as did the social changes wrought by the war and the Paris Commune. Castagnary sensed that:

> *the taste for foreign things is diminished amongst us…and as time passes and as the Republic establishes itself, each Frenchman feels he is becoming more French. Let us abandon this movement, and let history be its judge. In a few years' time we will be able to set up a stone, and engrave upon it these consoling words: Orientalism was once alive and well in French painting.*[40]

Fig. 11
HENRI REGNAULT
Summary execution under the Moorish kings of Granada
1869

oil on canvas
302 x 146 cm

Musée d'Orsay, Paris

ORIENTALISM REVIVED

Despite his definitive tone, the critic had it wrong. Regnault might have died, but the Orientalist movement did not perish with him. In the later 19th century it regained momentum, in new directions that corresponded to the diversification of aesthetic concerns following the breakdown of the academic system. Regnault's own legacy was encapsulated in his *Summary execution under the Moorish kings of Granada* (fig. 11), which spread the shock-waves of its theatrical violence through the Musée du Luxembourg, and in his more intimate masterpiece, *Hassan and Namouna* (cat. 61).

Regnault's example galvanised the work of his two followers, Georges Clairin (who had worked with him in Tangier) and Benjamin-Constant (qq.v.). All three can be usefully described as neo-Romantics. Benjamin-Constant was a highly visible figure in the official Salon, where paintings such as his *Entry of Mohammed II into Constantinople*, 1876 or *The sherifs*, 1884 were controversial for their bloodthirstiness, epic scale, and too obvious a debt to Delacroix.

A second impetus to the movement came from a new generation of French artists dedicated to living for extended periods in North Africa and acclimatising themselves to local conditions. The key figure here is Gustave Guillaumet (q.v.), a painter already successful in the Salons of the late 1860s with works such as *The desert* (fig. 12). More than anyone else it was Guillaumet who rose to Fromentin's challenge to paint the 'dangerous novelties' offered by the desert scene. Living in the regions traversed by Fromentin two decades earlier (and by the writer Isabelle Eberhardt two decades later), Guillaumet attempted to represent the extraordinary visual conditions he saw there:

> *The decomposition and bleaching of tones in light, the coloration and transparency of shadows, the unpredictable play of reflections, the envelope of beings and things in this palpitating atmosphere that, in great bright landscapes such as these, bathes the dryness of lines as if in an imperceptible and vibrant fluid...*[41]

Virtually the painting of a mirage, Guillaumet's *The desert* is astonishing for the painter's willingness (like a French Turner) to make light and the degradation of colour the

Fig. 12
GUSTAVE GUILLAUMET
The desert (The Sahara)
1867

oil on canvas
110 x 200 cm

Musée d'Orsay, Paris

subject of the painting. More characteristic is *The seguia, Biskra* (cat. 66), in which his close observation of ethnic types is alleviated by a feathered brush technique that avoids the visual freezing of Gérômesque detail. A similarly impressionistic sensibility animates the series of Guillaumet's eloquent literary sketches, entitled *Tableaux Algériens* and published posthumously in a deluxe volume illustrated with the artist's prints and drawings.

Guillaumet's new naturalism and his commitment to living a desert life was an inspiration to a group of young academically trained painters, among whom Etienne Dinet became the pre-eminent figure. Dinet owed his early encounters with the Orient to a new scheme of travelling scholarships introduced by the government of Jules Ferry, which for the first time gave artists free rein to travel not only beyond Italy, but Europe itself. Ferry was responsible for an aggressive new push for colonial possessions, gaining a protectorate in Tunisia (1883), the conquest of Tongking (1884–87), as well as campaigning in Madagascar (1885). The Committee for French Africa, founded by Ferry's colleague Eugène Etienne, understood the potential of Orientalist painting and sculpture for popularising the colonies, and in the 1890s began generous government funding. Government money supported Orientalist painting displays in the colonial pavilions at the Universal Exhibitions of 1889 and 1900. In 1893 a new artists' society set up by a group of Guillaumet's followers under the presidency of Léonce Bénédite (curator of the Luxembourg Museum), was equally significant: the Société des Peintres Orientalistes Français held a large annual Salon of Orientalist art in Paris for the next forty years, and administered numerous scholarships in what amounted to a movement of State-funded exoticism and colonial art.

Dinet was the most dedicated exhibitor among these 'French Orientalist Painters', having already emerged as a leader at the Salon of 1890 with his *Snake charmer* (see cat. 69), purchased on the spot by representatives of the National Art Gallery of New South Wales. In the marketplace at Laghouat, wrote Bénédite:

> *a numerous group of Arabs, who have come from all points of the desert, surround the old conjurer…They observe, with the most varied expressions of indifference and disdain, naive admiration or astonishment…the snake charmer, an old fossil of bizarrely mixed blood, who makes bracelets and necklaces with his trained reptiles. Here again, the new element…is the dimension of the extraordinary in these figures, expressed in their state of exasperation with the light.*[42]

Dinet's concern with the ethnic specificity of his models bespeaks the intimate knowledge of the desert towns this cultural emigré began to develop: learning fluent Arabic, making a permanent home at Bou Saâda, working closely with the M'Zabite writer Sliman ben Ibrahim, and converting to Islam in 1913. Dinet painted the religious life, daily habits, and fables dear to the desert people with a familiarity and sympathy unrivalled in the history of Orientalism.

THE IMPRESSIONIST ORIENT

The third great diversification of Orientalism at this time was among artists in the broad Impressionist movement. Only one painter from the original impressionist group, Auguste Renoir, travelled to and painted in the Orient, working in Algiers in the springs of 1881 and 1882. In view of the distaste of realist critics for Orientalism, it is surprising to see an orthodox 'painter of modern life' like Renoir make such a move. But Renoir was also a fervent admirer of Delacroix, early on exhibiting a splendidly steamy *Odalisque*, 1870 and making a masterful copy of Delacroix's *Jewish wedding* in 1875. He finally travelled to Algiers during a hiatus in his career, partly to recuperate from a recurrent illness.

In Algiers Renoir painted outdoors at a number of picturesque sites already favoured by more conventional Orientalists, such as at the mosque of Sidi Abd er Rahman and the Jardin d'Essai, the botanical garden at nearby Hamma, where he made several canvases of the luxuriant tropical vegetation. His major Algerian canvas has always been considered the *Arab festival* (cat. 71), which appears to represent a religious concert and surrounding crowd on the outskirts of the kasbah. Scholarship's very inability to define the event or its participants indicates Renoir's departure from the ethnographic norm of Orientalism. His stated concerns in Algeria seem to have been primarily aesthetic; he was later to say: 'Everything is white: the burnouses they wear, the walls, the minarets, the road…And against it the green of the orange trees and the grey of the figs'.[43] In this comment people are reduced to a problem of the palette – the colonised people are aestheticised, treated as pure spectacle by the visiting colonial tourist.

Renoir's is above all an approximation, an *impression*, of the exotic subject in which, like Belly or Guillaumet, he attends to visual conditions but employs the high tone and blonde coloration of the impressionist palette to render the heightened colour of the scene. In this he was not alone: in the decade of the 1870s the painter Albert Lebourg, a technical experimenter whose works paralleled those of the Impressionists, made numerous views of the kasbah and port of Algiers while recuperating from a chronic chest complaint.[44]

As Impressionism increasingly became the *lingua franca* of international modernist painting from the 1890s onwards, so more painter–travellers employed its visual strategies. A key figure at this juncture is Albert Besnard, less a true Impressionist than a virtuosic academic draughtsman who had caused a storm of controversy by exhibiting society portraits whose excessive colour was said to be licensed by Impressionism.[45] A popular artist who won many official mural commissions, Besnard painted in Algeria in the winter of 1893–94, and exhibited his Algerian canvases to acclaim at the new Salons of the Orientalists and the Société Nationale. His sonorous *Port of Algiers at dusk* (cat. 98) was acquired by the State for the Luxembourg Museum, and became one of the best-known Orientalist pictures of the early 20th century.

Besnard extended his interest in the exotic by travelling through India for half of the year 1911. The display of the resulting pictures proved to be *the* event of the mainstream art calendar for 1912. Although they take us beyond the geographical confines of North Africa and the Near East that are the focus of this exhibition, such brilliantly coloured and executed works as Besnard's *Fruit merchant at Madura* (cat. 99) are a reminder of the much expanded scope of European Orientalism around 1900. The British had a long-established tradition of painting in India, and by the late 19th century a new indigenous School of Calcutta was beginning to emerge.[46] French artists were painting in Japan and China, as well as in the French possessions in Indochina and Oceania (notably Tahiti, where Paul Gauguin lived). Just as French artists were now living in such colonies, so British painters had long since emigrated to the far-distant colonies of Australia and New Zealand.

It is a measure of the extent to which Australian artists could join the Euro–American cultural fraternity that significant numbers of them painted in North Africa around the turn of the century (see the essay 'From Empire's End' in this catalogue). In every case, patterns of travel to the metropolitan capitals of London and Paris from the Antipodes enabled their Orientalism, as it did that of an American artist such as Henry Ossawa Tanner or even the professional Orientalist Frederick Arthur Bridgman (qq.v.). Although both American artists were better established professionally in Paris than the Australian artists there, they still had a secondary cultural relationship to the metropolis.

The first group of 'Heidelberg School' artists from Melbourne – Tom Roberts, Charles Conder and Arthur Streeton – passed through North Africa rather adventitiously; the second group of primarily female artists – Hilda Rix Nicholas and Ethel Carrick – made a more sustained contribution just before the First World War. The highly attractive works by these Australian artists, 'Orientalists' of the moment, are small but exemplary *plein air* paintings, employing the general visual language of a cautious, draughtsmanly Impressionism learned at a remove from the centre. The temporary nature of their visual tourism did not allow these artists the time to work up major studies, as did their British exemplar Frank Brangwyn, who painted some large canvases in Morocco, the favourite winter 'sketching-ground' of British artists.

SYMBOLISTS

It is after the turn of the century that the painterly contributions of progressive modernists to the old traditions of Orientalism become more widespread. At the root of the new aesthetics lay the ideas of Symbolism, in particular that it was no longer necessary for a painter to try and literally transcribe a scene, but that the pictorial elements of line, colour, shade and light would help evoke the idea independently. More radically, in the wake of Mallarmé's concept of the self-sufficient sound in modern poetry, such pictorial elements came to be regarded by artists such as Matisse, Kandinsky and Klee as no more than general symbols for the observed world which had their own autonomous pictorial life in increasingly abstract painting.

The links between Symbolism and Orientalism are a focus of this exhibition. At least two noted Symbolists of the 1890s, Lucien Lévy-Dhurmer and Armand Point, were born in French Algeria and began their careers with Orientalist landscapes. While both turned to an esoteric symbolist subject matter once based in France (Point for good), Lévy-Dhurmer after 1900 began treating eastern scenes with greater frequency and regularly returned to Algeria and Morocco over a thirty-year period. His chosen medium was pastel, the pale, crumbling colours of which uniquely suited the atmosphere of lyrical introspection he attained in his best works. Lévy-Dhurmer's *Evening promenade Morocco* (cat. 97) is an image of womanhood exceptional among Orientalists in that it both respects the traditional veil of the North African woman, and plays on that covering-up of the visage to develop an aura of mysterious beauty, hinted at only by the gaze of jewel-like eyes.

Emile Bernard, famous in the history of modernism as the collaborator of Gauguin in founding the School of Pont-Aven, was an exponent of the new symbolist aesthetics around 1890. Doubtless following the example of Gauguin, he fled France in 1893 for Cairo, where he lived for the next decade, assuming the life-style of an Arabophile cosmopolitan gentleman, like a latter-day J. F. Lewis. In that decade Bernard's painting went from a Pont-Aven primitivist reinterpretation of the Egyptian fellah (whom he treated visually as he had done the Breton peasants, cat. 90), to an idiosyncratic rendering based on his admiration for the Venetian Old Masters Tintoretto and Veronese, a style that only superficially resembles Gérôme-school academic realism (cat. 91). Thus Bernard renounced the possibility of pioneering a modernist Orientalism equivalent to Gauguin's in Tahiti.

That burden was largely taken up by the various students of Gustave Moreau. No doubt Moreau, a close friend of Fromentin's in his youth, transmitted a vision of the Orient as a place of inspiration to his disciples at the Ecole des Beaux-Arts in the 1890s. Moreau's primary interest was in the ancient East, in the art and myth of Assyria, Mesopotamia and Egypt, as well as India and Persia. His paintings on Greek mythological themes had an Oriental insistence on visual extravagance, while in his biblical images like the celebrated *Salome (dancing before Herod)* (fig. 13) an aesthetic is developed in which a love of syncretic eastern religion, profuse ornament and flashing colours create a highly personal conception of the East.

The young Belgian artist Henri Evenepoel was the first of several of Moreau's students to make the journey to North Africa (cat. 92). An intimate of Henri Matisse at the Ecole des Beaux-Arts, he had, around 1898, adopted a progressive style in which a decorative element and an ability to compose in broad planes of intense colour betrayed an interest in Vuillard and Gauguin. Evenepoel's important group of paintings from Algeria have a concrete grasp of the local scene, where he was drawn to black African musical performers, to the marketplace at Blida, and occasionally to the landscape and to classical ruins. A sophisticate with a mordant eye, he wrote letters containing withering denunciations of the European degradation of Algiers and the attack on traditional cultures presented by industrial modernity.[47] Yet, true to the Orientalist precedent, he avoided all reference to such matters in his pictures.

The example of Evenepoel perhaps encouraged Matisse's first visit to the Maghreb in 1906, when he took the railway south to what was now a winter tourist resort, the oasis of Biskra. He shared Evenepoel's scepticism about the effects of Europeanisation, writing of the famous Ouled-Nail dancers: 'that joke? One has seen it a hundred times better at the Exposition'.[48] Too exhausted by the unfamiliarity of the Algerian scenery to manage painting it, Matisse wrote home, echoing Fromentin, of the apparently insuperable problems this new visual order presented to the painter sensitised to the more muted European light.

Fig. 13
GUSTAVE MOREAU
Salome (dancing before Herod)
1876
oil on canvas
143.8 x 104.2 cm
The Armand Hammer Collection, UCLA at the Armand Hammer Museum of Art and Cultural Center, Los Angeles, CA
(cat. 89)

'ART COLONIAL'

Matisse remarked that a painter needed months, if not years, to adapt to North Africa. Such an opportunity was accorded a fresh group of young French artists by an Algerian government scholarship set up in 1908 and tenured at the Villa Abd-el-Tif, a restored Turkish mansion near the Algiers Jardin d'Essai. The many painters and sculptors who spent a two-year term there elaborated a kind of summary, highly coloured ethnographic painting that after 1920 was often identified as 'School of Algiers' painting.[49] Typical of them was Léon Cauvy, one of the first Abd-el-Tif scholars, who was appointed director of the Algiers Ecole des Beaux-Arts and became an influential teacher (fig. 14). A painter of official mural decorations and many posters, Cauvy's style influenced one of the early indigenous Algerian painters, Abdelhalim Hemche, in the 1920s.

Fig. 14
LEON CAUVY
Boghari markets
(*Marché de Boghari*)
n.d. (1920s)
gouache
37.5 x 45.5 cm
Private collection

Other Abd-el-Tifians struck out on a more independent path, none more so than Charles Dufresne who, along with André Suréda (q.v.), received enthusiastic reviews at the Société des Peintres Orientalistes Français before the First World War. Dufresne and Suréda are significant figures in what the French increasingly called *l'art colonial* between the two world wars – a latter-day Orientalism that has received very little attention in English-language publications.

A prolific figure painter, Suréda was resident in Algiers for much of each year, placing his virtuosic skills as a draughtsman at the service of a primarily ethnographic interest. As a 'painter of race', he drew figures from the Jewish and Islamic communities which could achieve an almost mesmeric sense of presence (cat. 104). In the early 1920s Suréda was invited by the government of the protectorate to work in Morocco, where he did powerfully cursive portraits of notables such as the 'Lord of the Atlas', the Glaoui el-Thami. Dating from that stay is his decorative, almost naive image of the Glaoui's fortress of El Télouet, *Caïds' encampment*, which exhibits Suréda's unusual gifts as a colourist (cat. 106).

Charles Dufresne, a key Abd-el-Tifian, evolved in a more progressive direction towards an application of the new cubist language to the North African scene. Alert to work in the radical Salon d'Automne and Salon des Indépendants before travelling to Africa in 1910, once established there Dufresne tried out ideas analogous to those of the early Cubists in works on paper studied before motifs of exotic vegetation and landscape. He moved from meticulous pencil topographies of Bou Saâda to a series of gouache and watercolour oases (cats 113–16). In them Dufresne constructs the image in a boldly abstracting manner, using plant and animal elements to produce an exotic décor that has resonances with Matisse's contemporary Moroccan work on the one hand, and Paul Klee's Tunisian views on the other.

AVANT-GARDISTS IN THE EAST

There is a tendency in both conventional histories of Orientalism and in books on avant-garde artists to see the North African pictures of artists such as Matisse or Klee as outside the Orientalist tradition, as self-contained adventures which transcend their historical context. This seems like a form of special pleading, the effect of which is to exempt such artists from the problems of interpreting colonial culture.[50] There is little to distinguish the tourism and work patterns of the avant-garde from those of their predecessors, or the practitioners of *art colonial*, whose work forms a stylistic bridge between mainstream Orientalism and such abstractionists.

As with the travels of Gérôme and Regnault and their cohorts, a feature of avant-garde Orientalism is that a close-knit artists' group, rather than an isolated individual, is often the social unit of production. There was, for example, the group consisting of Matisse, his wife, Amélie, and his male friends Marquet, Charles Camoin and J. W. Morrice (Tangier 1912–13); the artist couple Wassily Kandinsky and Gabrielle Münter (Tunis, 1905); and the trio from Munich – Paul Klee, Auguste Macke and Louis Moilliet (Tunis–Kairouan, 1914).

In dealing with the two German-speaking artists' groups it is important to state that the political relationship obtaining between these travellers and the Tunisian community differed from that of French artists in Morocco or Algeria.[51] It was in principle more neutral: Germany had no colonial possessions in North Africa, and it was the French who since 1883 had administered Tunisia as a protectorate under a treaty with the relatively disempowered beys. There is little evidence as to why Kandinsky and Münter chose Tunis as their destination in 1905, but Morocco (before being declared a French protectorate in 1912) was still largely closed and Algeria may have seemed too hackneyed, too much prey to the vicissitudes of colonial modernisation. Certainly Klee was alert to such issues in 1914, when the invitation to stay at the country house of a friend of Moilliet's provided a pretext to visit Tunisia. As a neutral Swiss, Klee, in his invaluable diaries, observed the 'severe tension between the French and the Italians', explaining that: 'Tunis is Arab in the first place, Italian in the second, and French only in the third. But the French act as if they own the place'.[52] In several of Macke's and Moilliet's snapshot photographs of the trip, the laughter of Macke and Klee on a donkey-ride or the smiling faces of young Tunisian guides capture the *détente* of a situation that involved amicable tourism rather than colonial constraint.[53]

Several progressive artists made use of the camera after 1900 in a way that breaks the formulaic mould of the 19th-century photographic Orient. Macke, Hilda Rix Nicholas in Tangier, and Münter in Tunis used the newly available hand-held Kodaks, portable models whose fast exposure times encouraged an informal amateur photography. Often, blurred or ill-framed views of Tunisian buildings, street crowds and people give a look of edgy modernity compared with the stills traditionally used for 'documenting' pictures (in Gérôme's sense). On the basis of these photographs, the watercolours of Macke and Moilliet and the gouaches of Münter and Kandinsky were often worked up back in the artists' hotel rooms, a procedure which circumvented the likelihood of hostile responses to the artists painting in public.

Kandinsky's little-known Tunisian works (fig. 15), rather few in number and too fragile to be on loan for this exhibition, nevertheless have an important role in the developing avant-garde encounter with the Orient. While a lecturer in political economy at Moscow University in the late 19th century, Kandinsky had done ethnographic field-work along the Volga, studying the traditions, costume and decorative arts of the peasantry. Such images drove his pre-abstract Russian subjects of 1904–07, and Kandinsky's brightly coloured Tunisian gouaches belong to the same 'ethnographic' idiom. He and Münter worked in gouaches that explored the relief of bright colours against a sombre ground. Tunisia continued to resound in Kandinsky's art: in his first abstract series of 1909 he reworked Tunisian memories in oil paintings of sonorous colour.[54]

The work of the modernist avant-garde has often been associated with the new cultural exchanges constituted by Japonism and Primitivism. Although well outside the scope of this exhibition, Japonism did provide a conceptual model for the way Europeans might modify their art by learning from other visual traditions. French promoters of Orientalist art were already mindful of this in 1893 when a large exhibition of Islamic artefacts was organised in Paris, partly in the hope of inspiring a decorative-arts movement parallel to the japonist movement.[55] Although there had been isolated instances of liberal-minded European painters learning from Persian or Mogul miniatures (Rembrandt, Delacroix and Ingres among them), it was not until the time of Matisse and Kandinsky that painters significantly modified their pictorial practice in response to visual models provided by miniature painting and arabesque decoration.[56]

Even the Tunisian work of Paul Klee has been seen in this light. Klee's cross-cultural sympathies are often asserted more on the basis of biographical than formal elements: said to have North African ancestry on his mother's side, Klee apparently considered he had an 'Oriental' cast of face, and recorded thoughts suggesting that his journey East was partly motivated by a desire to encounter his ethnic avatars. Although an associate of Kandinsky's Blaue Reiter collective that was famously open to peasant and non-western cultures (and also a resident of Munich whose 1910 retrospective of Islamic art had attracted Matisse and Marquet from Paris), there is scant direct borrowing from Islamic tradition in Klee's Tunisian work. Avant-gardist considerations (such as reworking Robert Delaunay's high-colour version of the cubist quadratic structure)

Fig. 15
WASSILY KANDINSKY
Arab town
1905

tempera on cardboard
67.3 x 99.5 cm

Musée National d'Art Moderne, Centre de création industrielle, Centre Georges Pompidou, Paris

Fig. 16
PAUL KLEE
*St Germain
near Tunis*
1914

watercolour
21.8 x 31.5 cm

Musée National
d'Art Moderne,
Centre de création
industrielle, Centre
Georges Pompidou,
Paris

influenced Klee's Tunisian experiments. As Delaunay had used steeples and suns to restructure the visual field, so Klee focused on Islamic buildings and the distinctive African vegetation (fig. 16). The forms of mosque and kasbah architecture in Kairouan helped him clarify the 'pictorial architecture' (as he put it) of his own emerging visual idiom. The same is true of Macke's and Moilliet's closely related Tunisian watercolours, although these artists were more drawn to images of Tunisian commerce and the figure than was the idiosyncratic landscapist Klee. Above all it was the place that moved Klee intensely, and he attributed a new mastery of colour in his work directly to the sensual promptings of his Tunisian sojourn.

More than Klee, whose highly abstracted landscapes bear only limited comparison to pre-existing works in the Orientalist tradition, Matisse's Moroccan paintings of 1912–13 embody the fraught relationship between modernist experimentation and the Orientalist legacy.[57] The fact that Matisse was a learned artist very well versed in the history of his national school may explain why much of his figure painting, more or less radical in technique, restates selected iconographies prevalent in 19th-century Orientalism, from Delacroix and Ingres to the Gérôme school. His series of seated Zorahs (fig. 17) evoke Delacroix's *Women of Algiers*, his *Arab café* recalls the Turkish coffee-houses of Decamps and Diaz, his Riffian warriors and Moorish menfolk reconfigure the costume portraits of Gérôme and Clairin. Lastly, Matisse's famous odalisques of the 1920s suppose a quasi-realist nostalgia for Ingres (cat. 124). This tendency to understand the exotic in terms of typologies established by his European origins is a good example of the circularity that Said detected in much of the western discourse on the East.

However, what transforms such images and stretches the limits of Matisse's 'Orientalism' as an art-historical, rather than broader cultural, category is their extreme visual modernism. To view such Matisse pictures, with their open, glowing colours stretched across the broadly brushed spaces of the modernist canvas, is experientially quite unlike inspecting the often minutiose, tangible descriptions of most 19th-century Orientalism. As with Kandinsky, costume is important to Matisse and, while it encodes an ethnographic awareness of cultural difference, costume's prime message in Matisse's paintings is a delectation of the decorative and aesthetic order. This is where Matisse's identification with Oriental art begins: more than any other western artist, Matisse in his Moroccan paintings was capable of making something new of the colour, of the flat decorative composition, and of the arabesque as conveyed in the traditional Islamic arts he studied so well.

INDIGENOUS ARTISTS

It is at such a point that the dichotomous, oppositional model of Orientalism as defined by the early Said falters again: empowered though he undoubtedly was by the French colonial presence, Matisse's insistent longing for the cultural expression of the Other opens a different cultural space, already hinted at by Orientalists such as J. F. Lewis and Owen Jones. Matisse is famous for having said, 'My revelation came from the Orient'.[58] Some Orientalists went much further than Matisse in crossing the borders of cultural identification: Etienne Dinet for instance, not so much in his mode of painting (which followed a ruggedly descriptive naturalism up to his death in 1929), as in subjects drawn from the inside of Arab life and by the lesson of how he shaped his own life. As a fluent speaker of Arabic and a convert to Islam, Dinet maintained a house at the oasis town of Bou Saâda for thirty years, and in his art and public life worked to promote French understanding of the Algerian people. As a result Dinet, or Nasreddine Dinet as they called him, came to enjoy great prestige in post-colonial, independent Algeria.[59]

Fig. 17
HENRI MATISSE
Zorah on the terrace
1912–13
oil on canvas
115 x 100 cm
State Museum of Fine Arts, Moscow

Rare figures such as Dinet helped facilitate cultural exchange from the other side of the porous Orientalist divide by encouraging 'indigenous' artists who wished to adapt the European technologies of visual art to their own purposes. This exhibition means to reinsert such figures into the mainstream: the Turkish painter Osman Hamdy Bey has been mentioned, and this essay will close with the spotlight firmly on two very different artists of Algerian descent – Azouaou Mammeri and Mohammed Racim.

If certain western painters aspired to the condition of the Islamic arts, Mammeri can be remembered as 'the first Muslim painter to master the European art of painting'.[60] Born into a privileged family of hereditary caids in the temperate Kabylian mountains of Algeria, Mammeri trained as a schoolteacher in the French system. Bilingual and of intellectual bent, around 1910 he received painting lessons from the French artist Léon Carré, and in 1914 moved to Fez where a cousin, Mohammed Mammeri, was the discreet but influential tutor to the children of the Sultan of Morocco. From 1917, with encouragement from the administration of Lyautey (the French Resident-General and author of a revisionist colonial policy which stressed the value of traditional Moroccan arts), Mammeri successfully exhibited his quasi-modernist landscapes of an angular graphic style in Rabat, Paris and Algiers. With his mastery of perspective and tonal realism, Mammeri could lay claim to having proved his equality with the colonist, on the colonist's own cultural terms.[61] Yet his subjects show a sensitivity to his Islamic co-religionists, concentrating as he did on landscape, and when painting the figure (later in his career) avoiding stereotypical or licentious subject matter.

A quite different trajectory was chosen by Mohammed Racim, the 'father of the Algerian miniature'.[62] Born into an old Turkish family of decorative artists in Algiers, Racim was a precocious student of drawing who in 1910 was invited to work for a French arts administrator, Prosper Ricard, who was documenting traditional arts with a view to their revival. Initially an exponent of the art of illuminating sacred Koranic texts (fig. 18), Racim became interested in the art of the miniature as practised by 16th- and 17th-century painters to the Persian and Mogul Indian courts. In trying to adapt such traditions for the representation of a more specifically Maghrebian experience, the young Racim was encouraged by Dinet, who helped him devise perspectivally correct figurative scenes which Racim inserted into his elaborate arabesque borders.

Fig. 18
MOHAMMED RACIM
Illumination
1916–17

gouache and gold leaf
24.5 x 19 cm

(design for pl.172 of Etienne Dinet & Sliman ben Ibrahim, *La Vie de Mohammed*, 1918)

This was a new, hybrid art form that combined the virtues of several traditions, eastern and western. It expresses very exactly the status of a figure such as Racim at a crossroad between cultures, taking from Europe where the modern had its advantages, but above all promoting Islamic tradition. Racim's imagery in a subtle way resists the coloniser, as his preferred theme was the golden age of Western Islam's political and cultural might: scenes from the caliphate of Moorish Andalusia, and of Algiers under the regency of the corsair bey Barbarossa (1480–1543) and his lieutenants the Rais, whose fleet of galleys was the scourge of Christian shipping in the Mediterranean (cat. 111).

Yet Racim's French admirers were so confident of their hold on historical destiny (1930 marked the centenary of French Algeria and is a fitting terminus for this exhibition) that they saw no threatening nationalist sentiment in these remarkable miniatures. On the contrary, Racim was decorated by the Parisian Société des Peintres Orientalistes Français: this 'Oriental' was claimed by them as a consummate 'Orientalist'. It is appropriate that the exhibition close with an artist who transcends the stereotype, who offers an affirmation of the value of an art forged *between* cultures, and yet simultaneously looks back to a time before colonial subjection, and forward to the renewal of Algerian sovereignty in the post-colonial era. ♦♦

1 The research for this essay and catalogue form part of a larger project which has been generously supported by the following organisations: the Australian Research Council, the J. Paul Getty Postdoctoral Fellowships Program, and the University of Melbourne. I would like to acknowledge the contribution of so many colleagues; of my former research assistants, Peter Rudd and Lara Smith, and to thank my wife, Kate Sands, for her academic and emotional support. All translations are my own unless otherwise indicated.

2 In contrast to current English-speaking usage, in which 'the Orient' (from the Latin for 'rising sun') would usually suggest Far Eastern countries like China and Japan.

3 *Oxford English Dictionary* (*O.E.D.*), 1933, vol. 6, p. 487, quoting W. H. Wollaston in *Philosophical Transactions*, vol. 93, no. 1, 1803; the word is derived from the French *mirer* or *se mirer*, to look at oneself in a mirror, or to be reflected.

4 For a discussion of these issues see James Clifford, 'Ethnographic authority', in his *The Predicament of Culture*, Harvard University Press, Cambridge, Mass., 1988, pp. 21–55.

5 *O.E.D.*, quoting *Court Life at Naples*, 1861, vol. 2, p. 106.

6 For an account frankly cataloguing the diverse sexual opportunities available to wealthy male Europeans travelling in the East, see Flaubert's 'Voyage en Orient, 1849–1851', in *The Letters of Gustave Flaubert, 1830–1857*, ed. and trans. Francis Steegmuller, Belknap, Cambridge, Mass., 1980, pp. 99–139.

7 The Mirage Resort, Port Douglas, North Queensland, the destination of President Clinton on his 1996 visit to Australia. Names connected with the Orient have been prominent in 20th-century western ideas of leisure, be they cinemas called 'The Alhambra', or bars named 'The Oasis'.

8 Letter of 2 April 1832, in Eugène Delacroix, *Selected Letters, 1813–1863*, ed. and trans. Jean Stewart, Eyre & Spottiswoode, London, 1971, p. 192.

9 See Claire Constans (ed.), *La Grèce en révolte: Delacroix et les peintres français (1815–1848)*, exh. cat., Réunion des Musées Nationaux, Paris, 1996.

10 In this Delacroix was following the example of the earlier chroniclers of the Napoleonic wars in Egypt and Palestine around 1800, in particular Baron Antoine Gros, arguably the first Orientalist in the modern tradition.

11 See Edward W. Said, *Orientalism*, Routledge & Kegan Paul, London, 1978; repr. with an afterword, Penguin, Harmondsworth, 1995.

12 The French term *odalisque* is derived from the Turkish word *odalik*, denoting the room-servant of the *cadine* or lady of the house.

13 Denoting the setting sun (or West), 'Maghreb' is the Arabic term for the North African Mediterranean States, in particular Tunisia, Algeria and Morocco.

14 On 19th-century practice see Lynne Thornton, *The Orientalists: Painter–Travellers 1828–1908*, Les Orientalistes, vol. 1, ACR, Paris, 1983, and Christine Peltre's *L'Atelier du voyage: les peintres en Orient au XIXe siècle*, Gallimard, Paris, 1995.

15 The evidence is that Delacroix was invited to visit the family of a port official, a former Christian who had converted to Islam, i.e. a 'renegade' of dubious religiosity; see Lee Johnson, *The Paintings of Eugène Delacroix: A Critical Catalogue*, Clarendon Press, Oxford, 1986, vol. 3, p. 166.

16 See Gustave Planche, 'The French School at the Salon of 1834', quoted in *The Triumph of Art for the Public*, ed. Elisabeth Holt, Doubleday, New York, 1979, p. 337.

17 See François Pouillon, 'Simplification ethnique en Afrique du Nord: Maures, Arabes, Berbères (XVIIIe-Xxe siècles)', *Cahiers d'études africaines*, vol. 33, no. 129, 1993, pp. 37–49.

18 On this question see the essay 'Post-Colonial Taste: Non-Western Markets for Orientalist Art', n. 9.

19 See for example Jérôme Tharaud & Jean Tharaud, *Marrakech, ou les seigneurs de l'Atlas*, Plon, Paris, 1920.

20 Jules-Antoine Castagnary, 'Année 1876', in his *Salons*, vol. 2, *1872–1879*, Charpentier & Fasquelle, Paris, 1892, p. 248.

21 Eugène Fromentin, *Une Année dans le Sahel*, ed. Elisabeth Cardonne, Flammarion, Paris, 1991 (1859), pp. 184–5.

22 ibid., p. 186.

23 ibid., pp. 186–7.

24 Théophile Gautier, 'Exposition de 1859', *Le Moniteur Universel*, 28 May 1859, cited in Gautier, *Voyage en Algérie*, ed. Denise Brahimi, La Boîte à Documents, Paris, 1989, p. 193.

25 Théophile Gautier, *Abédécaire du Salon de 1861*, Dentu, Paris, 1861, p. 51.

26 ibid., p. 253.

27 ibid., p. 54.

28 ibid., pp. 73–4; on Browne see Reina Lewis, *Gendering Orientalism: Race, Femininity and Representation*, Routledge, London & New York, 1996.

29 John Sweetman, *The Oriental Obsession: Islamic Inspiration in British and American Art and Architecture 1500–1920*, Cambridge University Press, Cambridge, 1987, p. 144; unfortunately the scope of this introduction precludes a proper discussion of British Orientalism; see also Gerald M. Ackerman, *Les Orientalistes de l'école britannique*, Les Orientalistes, vol. 9, ACR, Paris, 1991.

30 ibid., p. 135.

31 The definitive study of his practice is Gerald M. Ackerman, *The Life and Work of Jean-Léon Gérôme*, Sotheby's, London & New York, 1986.

32 The homoerotic subject of this picture finds confirmation in a letter of Flaubert on the *bardache* or male performer-prostitutes of Cairo; see *The Letters of Gustave Flaubert*, op. cit., pp. 110–12.

33 Jules-Antoine Castagnary, 'Année 1864', in his *Salons*, vol. 1, *1857–1870*, Charpentier & Fasquelles, Paris, 1892, p. 211.

34 Linda Nochlin, 'The imaginary Orient', *Art in America*, May 1983, repr. in her *The Politics of Vision*, Harper & Row, New York, 1989, pp. 33–59.

35 See Charles-Robert Ageron, *L'Anticolonialisme en France de 1871 à 1914*, Presses Universitaires de France, Paris, 1973.

36 Castagnary, 'Année 1857', in *Salons*, vol. 1, pp. 31–2.

37 See Patrick Conner, '"Wedding archaeology to art": Poynter's *Israel in Egypt*', in *Influences in Victorian Art and Architecture*, eds S. Macready & F.H. Thompson, Society of Antiquaries, London, 1985, pp. 112–20.

38 Castagnary, 'Année 1873', in *Salons*, vol. 2, pp. 80–1.

39 Castagnary, 'Année 1876', in *Salons*, vol. 2, p. 249.

40 ibid., p. 250.

41 Léonce Bénédite, 'Gustave Guillaumet', in *Société des Peintres Orientalistes Français*, 6th exh. cat., Galeries Durand-Ruel, Paris, 15 February–4 March 1899, p. 16.

42 Léonce Bénédite, 'La peinture orientaliste au salons de 1890', *L'Artiste*, vol. 60, no. 2, August 1890, pp. 84–5.

43 Renoir to his son, quoted in MaryAnne Stevens (ed.), *The Orientalists: Delacroix to Matisse*, exh. cat., Royal Academy of Arts, London, 1984, p. 222.

44 See Jean Alazard, *L'Orient et la peinture française au XIXe siècle*, Plon, Paris, 1930, pp. 186–92.

45 The work in question was *Madame Roger Jourdain*; see *Paris in the Late 19th Century*, exh. cat., National Gallery of Australia, Canberra, 1996, p. 76.

46 See Tapati Guha-Thakurta, *The Making of a New 'Indian' Art: Artists, Aesthetics and Nationalism in Bengal, c. 1850–1920*, Cambridge University Press, Cambridge, 1992.

47 See *Henri Evenepoel à Paris, lettres choisies, 1892–1899*, ed. Francis E. Hyslop, La Renaissance du livre, Brussels, 1972, pp. 161–2.

48 Letter to Henri Manguin, quoted in 'Orientalist excursions: Matisse in North Africa', in *Matisse*, exh. cat., eds Caroline Turner & Roger Benjamin, Queensland Art Gallery & Art Exhibitions Australia, Brisbane, 1995, p. 73.

49 See Victor Barrucand, *L'Algérie et les Peintres Orientalistes*, Artaud, Grenoble, 1930.

50 An example is Pierre Schneider's 'The Moroccan hinge', in Jack Cowart et al., *Matisse in Morocco: The Paintings and Drawings 1912–1913*, exh. cat., National Gallery of Art, Washington, 1990, pp. 25, 29.

51 This echoes the argument made against Edward Said, that in neglecting the rich tradition of Orientalist scholarship by the Germans (who had few colonial possessions), he could assert an oppositional political model based on the fraught Franco-British colonial histories; see James Clifford, 'On Orientalism' (1980), in *The Predicament of Culture*, Harvard University Press, Cambridge, Mass., 1988, p. 267.

52 *The Diaries of Paul Klee*, ed. and intro. Felix Klee, University of California Press, Berkeley, 1964, p. 292.

53 See *Die Tunisreise: Klee, Macke, Moilliet*, exh. cat., ed. Ernst Gerhard Güse (Westfälisches Landesmuseum für Kunst und Kulturgeschichte, Münster), Hatje, Stuttgart, 1982, pp. 49, 113ff.

54 The topic of Kandinsky's Tunisian work is ripe for serious research; the main compendium is Vivian Endicott Barnett, *Kandinsky Watercolours: Catalogue Raisonné*, 2 vols, Cornell University Press, Ithaca, NY, 1992–94; see also Magdalena M. Moeller (ed.), *Der frühe Kandinsky, 1900–1910*, Hirmer, Munich, 1994.

55 Georges Marye, preface to *Première Exposition d'art musulman*, exh. cat., Palais de l'industrie, Paris, 1893, p. 9.

56 See Fereshteh Daftari, *The Influence of Persian Art on Gauguin, Matisse, and Kandinsky*, Garland, New York, 1991.

57 On these works see Cowart et al. and my critique of the exhibition, 'Matisse in Morocco: a colonizing esthetic?', *Art in America*, vol. 78, no. 11, November 1990, pp. 157–64, 211–13.

58 Henri Matisse, 'The path of colour' (1947), in *Matisse on Art*, ed. Jack D. Flam, Phaidon, Oxford, 1973, p. 116.

59 See François Pouillon, 'Legs colonial, patrimoine national: Nasreddine Dinet, peintre de l'indigène algérien', *Cahiers d'études africaines*, vol. 30, no. 3, 1990, pp. 329–63.

60 'Le premier peintre musulman', *L'Illustration*, no. 4094, 20 August 1921, pp. 162–3; thanks to Brahim Alaoui for bringing this article to my attention.

61 In this sense Mammeri's venture is reminiscent of that of Albert Namatjira, the initiated Aboriginal man who adapted a western landscape idiom to paint his own country, and became one of the best-known Australian artists of his era; see Jane Hardy, J. V. S. Megaw & Ruth Megaw (eds), *The Heritage of Namatjira*, Heinemann, Melbourne, 1992.

62 See *Mohammed Racim: miniaturiste algérien*, exh. cat., Musée de l'Institut du Monde Arabe, Paris, 1992.

CREDITS

Post-Colonial Taste
Non-Western Markets for Orientalist Art[1]

Roger Benjamin

If Islam did not forbid them painting, the Arabs would represent themselves in just such a way. Théophile Gautier, Salon of 1861[2]

THE CRITIC GAUTIER'S CONCEIT, DEVISED TO PAY TRIBUTE TO THE PROMINENT ORIENTALIST PAINTER EUGENE FROMENTIN, HARBOURED A TRUTH THAT HAS BECOME APPARENT IN RECENT DECADES: THE DESIRABILITY OF PAINTING AS A MIRROR OF THE SELF APPLIES IRRESPECTIVE OF WHO MAKES THE PICTURE. GAUTIER EFFECTIVELY PREDICTS A SITUATION THAT HAS COME TO OBTAIN – A CENTURY AFTER HE WROTE – IN WHICH COLLECTORS OF NORTH AFRICAN, NEAR AND MIDDLE EASTERN DESCENT DOMINATE THE MARKET FOR ORIENTALIST ART. THE PURPOSE OF THIS ESSAY IS TO INVESTIGATE THIS PHENOMENON, BOTH TO SKETCH ITS HISTORICAL FORMS, AND TO CONSIDER ITS RAMIFICATIONS FOR ORIENTALISM IN ART.

For students of Orientalism raised in the tradition of Edward Said, the Arab taste for Orientalist art seems paradoxical. Said had proposed that Orientalism be properly understood as a set of western cultural projections concerning the East that were strongly tied to the historical fact of European colonial expansion.[3] The Orientalist mind-set, he argued, might be genuinely open in its desire to investigate the culture of the Other (for example in ethnographic studies), but finally it was always circumscribed by preconceptions and prejudices due to the fact that such representations were controlled by western interests. Said's study (which had the salutary effect of exposing the roots of current western prejudice against the Arabo-Muslim world) revealed a one-sided Orientalism, in which authority and activity flowed from the West, and the Arab voice was silent. When applied to painting by art historians such as Linda Nochlin or Olivier Richon, this model resulted in interpretations that classed the imagery of 19th-century Orientalism as subtly demeaning: the pictures were said to impute a 'decadence' to Islam in its treatment of women, in its administration of justice, and in the neglect of its architectural heritage.[4]

The paradox becomes clear: if the Saidian critique of Orientalism rang true, why would collectors of Arab, Turkish or other non-western ethnicities favour such a demeaning imagery of their cultures today?[5] And why would Maghrebian collectors in particular patronise the art of those foreigners who had long ruled their countries before (in the case of Algeria) bloody wars of liberation?

The first point to make is of a theoretical nature: as Said himself has partly acknowledged,[6] his early model of Orientalism suffered from neglecting the element of exchange in the cross-cultural, colonial relationship. It has been pointed out that power in the colonial situation is not exclusively one-sided, favouring the coloniser alone. The colonised (and this black-and-white terminology has itself been questioned) have a distinctive agency or ability to effect outcomes, be it in military situations, or cultural ones, or matters of everyday life. The stereotype of the benighted, coerced, or simply absent colonial 'victim' has in recent post-colonial writing been rejected in favour of investigating the modes of agency open to non-western subjects in their interaction with colonial authorities and their representatives.[7]

The decision in this exhibition to study the painting of 'indigenous' artists is one result of this new approach: how did artists like Hamdy Bey, Mammeri or Racim take up the language of western pictorial art (much as the colonised intelligentsia took to writing in French or English) and turn it to their own purposes? It was surely a way of asserting their own identities, of mirroring the complexity of their own hybrid cultural situations, and can be understood as revising (if not resisting) the imagery foisted on them by the European school.

The activity of art collecting can be understood in an analogous way: as an assertion of selfhood, and as redressing historical imbalances. Responding to the title 'The Oriental Mirage', Moroccan curator Brahim Alaoui remarked that painting is indeed a 'game of mirrors':

That image of the Orient which set the Occident dreaming in the 19th century returns something to those Orientals [sic] who also seek an image of their past. They find in this painting a world on its way to disappearing: this Orient that is highly coloured, shimmering, this Orient of arabesques, of costumes and the richness of forms is in the process of being eclipsed by a much more modern world. The image that was fixed by the Occident in the 19th century – the Orientals are now attempting to recover it.[8]

The fact that it was western artisans who had the means to record such images is almost incidental from this perspective; the act of collecting such paintings becomes a means by which privileged non-westerners have exerted control over the image of their past and of their heritage – an act of repossession.

PRECURSORS

Neither the ownership nor the practice of painting in the Islamic world is the recent phenomenon it seems, as the religious ban on the human image has never been totally effective. According to Alaoui:

Although theologically the image has been banned by certain dogmas,[9] the image has always co-existed, has always transgressed that interdiction, through the miniature, through certain kinds of popular imagery such as painting on glass, mural painting, the metalwork of the Mamelukes, and even before…The image has always existed amongst the aristocracy and amongst ordinary people, while the interdiction has been much more manifest amongst the middle classes.[10]

Thus in the great age of Islamic miniature painting (16th–17th centuries) it was the Savafid princes of Persia and the Mogul rulers of Northern India – courtly aristocracies both – who overlooked the tradition of the *Hadith* and commissioned illuminated books for private use. The Ottoman court adopted similar practices and, by the 19th century, oil portraits of prominent figures were being commissioned in Istanbul from Turkish or European painters – a practice also adopted in the Maghreb by the beys of Tunis.

If the commissioning of such painting implies its collection, housing and display in palace treasuries and buildings, there have also been early modern instances of personalities from the Near East forming collections of European painting, most notably Khalil Bey in the 1860s and Mahmoud Khalil in the 1920s. In Second Empire Paris one of the best collections of contemporary French art was formed by Khalil Bey (Halil Serif Pasha), an Ottoman diplomat and reformist politician who was heir to the fortune his Turkish father had accumulated in Egypt. Well known in Parisian high society as a gentleman of culture (and heavy gambler), Khalil Bey's taste for Delacroix, Ingres and Gérôme, as well as for Rousseau, Corot and his friend Courbet meant, for Francis Haskell, that 'his picture gallery could not in essence be distinguished from that of any other rich man living in Paris' – and therein lay the lesson of equality that this 'child of Islam' gave to the French.[11]

Yet in all collecting certain emphases emerge, and Khalil Bey's background gives specific resonance to two features of his collection. First, his famous erotic pictures: Courbet's notorious *Origin of the world* and his nudes with lesbian themes, *The jealous Venus pursuing Psyche* and *The sleepers*, as well as Ingres's *Turkish bath* (reputedly returned by the wife of its first owner, the Prince Napoleon, for indecency). Khalil Bey's collecting of these works casts him as more libertarian in sexual matters than his French bourgeois peers (as well as feeding the western cliché of the 'lustful Turk'). As a measure of his faint religiosity, however, it should be noted that the female nude is the only major Orientalist genre that is regularly shunned by today's Muslim collectors.[12]

Secondly, Khalil Bey owned a number of French paintings on Orientalist themes (Chassériau battle scenes like cat. 16, scenes of Arab life by Fromentin as in cat. 20, Marilhat's *A Cairo street* and the *Turkish bath*, fig. 9). These surely opened up pathways of nostalgia and positive cultural identification for their owner in ways that prefigure current patterns. Such collecting must have differed in kind from, for example, the Duc d'Aumale purchasing Orientalist paintings in memory of his campaigns as a victorious general in Algeria.[13]

Closer to the present day, in the Francophile élite circles of Cairo after the First World War, a number of wealthy Egyptians, in particular the politician Mahmoud Khalil, became collectors in the buoyant 1920s Parisian art market that also witnessed energetic collecting by figures such as the Japanese industrialist Kojiro Matsukata (who acquired Orientalist pictures by Renoir, Dinet, Cottet and Lewis, cat. 24). Mahmoud Khalil, a product of Cairo's French Lycée and married to a Frenchwoman, was by 1928 able to lend over fifty works to a major exhibition of French art in Cairo. His taste for progressive impressionist art of the later 19th century encompassed French landscapes and figure scenes by Corot, Monet, Pissarro and Gauguin (in works virtually unknown before the 1995 exhibition 'Les Oubliés du Caire').[14] Mahmoud Khalil's Francophilic brief is still clearer in his collection of small bronzes by Barye and Rodin; if sculpture was the figural art most proscribed by Islam,[15] it was also part of the ancient Egyptian heritage.

Like the Turk Khalil Bey, Mahmoud Khalil and certain compatriots also had a taste for Orientalism. A group of their paintings by Marilhat, Gérôme (including a version of *Bonaparte before the Sphinx*, cat. 45), Belly, Frère, Fromentin, Dauzats and even Albert Marquet displayed a marked preference for the Egyptian scene, and specifically the monuments of Cairo and its surrounding hinterland. Yet local topographical memory and nostalgia for scenes already a half-century old was not the only motivation for these Egyptians, as Khalil Bey's Ingres (a replica of his *Grand odalisque*) or Prince Tewfik's Regnault (an astonishing *Execution of a janizary*) show. Nevertheless, Geneviève Lacambre suggests that Mahmoud Khalil's 'acute sense of hierarchy in western art' meant he 'considered that Orientalist pictures had first and foremost a decorative value', and thus gifted most such works to the Egyptian Diplomats' Club in Cairo rather than the museum founded in his name.[16]

This pattern of collecting by wealthy Easterners in the colonial era reveals both an ambition to equal (if not emulate) Europeans in their passion for European art, and a stake, perhaps more cautiously expressed, in affirmations of their indigenous identities through images of the pre-colonial past. The Egyptian pattern of implanting European paintings (some of which were Orientalist) in local museums was mirrored in various North African countries under French influence or direct rule (particularly at the Musée National des Beaux-Arts in Algiers and the Musée Demaeght in Oran, which opened their doors in 1930). But, increasingly, oil painting in such countries was generated and sold locally: on the one hand by immigrant or visiting Europeans, and on the other by artists of the indigenous intelligentsias inspired by modernism or local art traditions (in the Lebanon, for example, ancient Christian traditions had favoured the art of painting even under Ottoman rule).[17]

PAINTING AND PETRODOLLARS

It seems proper to term the recent non-western market for Orientalism[18] *post-colonial* – firstly because in the literal sense it postdates many of the mid-century struggles of decolonisation and independence in North Africa and the Middle East, and secondly because it involves a new sense of positive empowerment expressed through the acquisition and thus redefinition of western cultural documents.

The most surprising new players in this market for Orientalist art have been wealthy individuals from Arab countries, in particular the Gulf States of Bahrain, Oman and Qatar, as well as Saudi Arabia itself. It is important to note that their countries were never European colonies as such. Enabled primarily by oil revenues, their patronage of art reflects a revolution in traditional attitudes towards the image. As Brahim Alaoui notes of the Middle Eastern region: 'these days the image has compelled recognition like other forms of modernity, via the mass-media, via photography, via television and so on. Little by little the image has been completely accepted and integrated by official as well as popular culture'.[19]

However, Arab collectors by no means initiated the revival of the market for Orientalist art after almost a half-century of art world indifference. According to the art historian and saleroom expert Lynne Thornton, the recognition of the genre as a sector of the market dates to the early 1970s, and reflects a 'subtle conditioning' brought about by exhibitions, specialist publications and 'the enthusiasm of a small number of pioneer collectors' in Paris and London.[20] The revaluation of 19th-century academic painting, which was proceeding on the twin fronts of revisionist scholarly research and dealer-driven exhibitions and sales, lent a new popularity to the many meticulous paintings of the East from that era.

In the nascent market for Orientalist pictures in Paris from 1974, the initial trade was in images of North Africa, selling largely to French inhabitants of colonial Algeria who had fled after the War of Independence nearly two decades before; a market premised on memories and indeed a sense of dispossession. Soon a broader public developed: the 1975 exhibition 'Mahmals et Attatichs', a scholarly presentation of quality works mounted by Thornton and the Islamic art expert Jean Soustiel, was a great commercial success:

> *We sold mostly to museums, to people like Yves Saint-Laurent or Edmonde Charles-Roux, the writer who comes from a family which was involved in Egypt since the 19th century, and to the dealer Alain Lesieutre, who was one of the first to really get into Orientalists...As always, a market is started when there are museum exhibitions and books. Philippe Jullian [wrote] his book...the Musée Cantini (Marseilles) did an exhibition in 1974, 'Vers l'Orient'...people have more confidence in the market when there is this media support.[21]*

At the same time the major salerooms began to focus on Orientalism: Drouot in Paris (followed by Christie's and Sotheby's in London and New York) began organising dedicated sales. Turkish private collectors and museum curators began entering the market, as did North Africans; both still constitute a significant force. The focus of the major Orientalist dealership in London was, however, more towards the Arab world, as the director of the Mathaf Gallery, Brian MacDermot, recounts:

> *I'd had a lot of dealings in the Arab world over the years as an investment banker and broker. But it wasn't until 1975 that I started this gallery, and called it*

Al Mathaf, which means 'museum' or 'old things'...The timing was very fortuitous because Britain at that time was involved in the World of Islam Festival and all London was putting on Islamic shows in 1975...I co-operated with the various Arab embassies to show paintings, initially by their contemporary artists. It was from that base that we discovered that there was an interest in the 19th-century paintings of the Arab world.[22]

Coinciding as it did with the growing influence of the Arab world in the economic sphere, interest in the Orientalist market developed so rapidly that by 1978 the organisers of the exhibition 'Eastern Encounters' in London sold 40 per cent of works to Arab clients.[23] Many of these clients lived in Europe and were already collectors of European paintings (rather after the pattern of Khalil Bey) but, in the next phase, new clients appeared who preferred not to leave the Gulf or Saudi Arabia but rather to bid via intermediaries in Paris and London. According to Thornton, these clients were uncomfortable with French saleroom practice and the auction system 'where, by definition, the prices mount; a system opposed to the traditional Arab method of transaction, in which the price is asked after discussion'.[24]

Professional decorators began buying to adorn palaces in the Gulf, a fact linked to a distinctive feature of the Arab market: once purchased to hang on the wall, works are rarely sold again; 'the idea of selling things to buy other paintings is very much a western concept of a market'.[25] This idea of permanent acquisition means that Middle Eastern buyers have seldom been art market speculators. It is important to note that private collectors rather than public museums dominate the Arabo-Muslim market for Orientalism. Although rare figures such as the Sultan of Oman have collections of Orientalist art that are to an extent accessible (and at least one other private museum is being formed), the few official museums in Bahrain, Kuwait and Qatar concentrate on masterpieces of traditional Islamic art.[26]

HERITAGE

The notion of heritage values is a useful tool in explaining the still-expanding market for Orientalist art. 'Heritage', however, admits of many dimensions, which vary according to differing national or ethnic interest groups. The pluralism of the art market in this regard is striking. An important principle appears to be buying along national lines. Americans have been the strongest collectors of the painter Bridgman, the British of Lewis, the French of Regnault and so on – Orientalists as representing the exoticist moments of established national schools. Non-western collectors, however, alter this criterion: the principle of identification is, rather, in terms of the site or culture depicted.

Thus there has been a steady flow of pictures representing Turkish sites and peoples back to Turkey,[27] or Moroccan sites and people back to Morocco. Brahim Alaoui cites two prominent Moroccan collections: that of the Benjellouns, which has been published and is to be housed in a museum under construction, and a Moroccan bank which collects both western painters who lived in Morocco, and Moroccan artists. According to Alaoui the admiration is not just for the 'nostalgic image of a Morocco which threatens to disappear', but also for the picture as work of art.[28] The most favoured artists have been '*valeurs sûrs*', talented artists who were attached to these countries and may have spent decades living there: Jacques Majorelle for Morocco, or the market leader Etienne Dinet for Algeria. The collecting by Algerian, Tunisian, Egyptian and, latterly, Greek nationals in the European salerooms has usually been along such lines of identification.

The case is more complicated where an artist like Mohammed Racim was of indigenous identity (an Algerian of Turkish descent), and incorporated a quasi-nationalist nostalgia

FROM EMPIRE'S END

AUSTRALIANS AS ORIENTALISTS, 1880–1920

Ursula Prunster

EUROPEAN PAINTERS WHO DECIDED TO SETTLE IN COUNTRIES UNDER COLONIAL INFLUENCE – WHETHER MOROCCO, ALGERIA, OR EGYPT – MADE A RICH CONTRIBUTION TO ORIENTALIST TRADITION. THOSE IN MORE DISTANT REGIONS – BRITISH PAINTERS WORKING IN INDIA OR AUSTRALIA, OR FRENCH ARTISTS IN INDOCHINA OR TAHITI – HAVE FOR REASONS OF GEOGRAPHY SELDOM BEEN CALLED ORIENTALISTS. RATHER, THEIR WORK HAS USUALLY BEEN LINKED TO FLEDGLING NATIONAL SCHOOLS OF PAINTING IN THE COLONY CONCERNED OR, IN THE CASE OF GAUGUIN, TO THE HISTORY OF EUROPEAN EXOTICISM.

This exhibition nevertheless demonstrates an unexpected and indeed little-known twist in the history of colonial art: how certain Australian artists, momentarily forsaking their homeland, rejoined their European counterparts and went to paint in the desert countries of North Africa as Orientalists.[1]

Before Federation in 1901 the group of six colonies that constituted Australia were under the direct rule of Great Britain, and 'Australians' were British subjects at the farthest end of the world's largest empire.[2] Until the later 19th century most white artists working in Australia had been born and trained in Europe. However, during the 1880s and 1890s a growing number of Australian-born, or raised, painters emerged whose affection for landscape enabled the rise of the Heidelberg School. The artists who are the subject of this essay all have connections with this Australian 'impressionist' school. Trained by European emigré artists such as G. W. Folingsby and Louis Buvelot, the height of their professional expectations was, to a man and, increasingly woman, success on the stage of the European art capitals of London and Paris.

From the turn of the 19th century, European aesthetic fashions had dominated the colonial art scene. In Melbourne and Sydney, artists who made the new commitment to painting out-of-doors emulated the international *plein air* and Impressionist movements; similarly, their studio décor followed the craze for Whistlerian aestheticism. Numbers of Australian artists, male and female, travelled in the period under consideration and were entitled to the status and protections accorded to citizens of the British Empire. For the colonial-born, such as Arthur Streeton, London beckoned like Mecca, but for others, such as Emanuel Phillips Fox, Rupert Bunny and Hilda Rix Nicholas, the pilgrimage was to Paris.

Australian awareness of Orientalism followed this pattern of reference back to European knowledge, to the dissemination of cultural concepts through the Empire's channels of communication. Itself an aspect of the culture of imperialism or colony-building, Orientalist art takes on, in the Australian context, an intriguing ambivalence. Australian Orientalist practice dictated the terms of the artists' self-awareness according to a European ideology of dominance, against which they can also be seen as colonials – 'not quite' possessing mastery (to use Homi Bhabha's phrase).

Certain major Orientalist artworks imported to Australia in the late 19th century demonstrate the way colonials embraced exotic subject matter as a reflection of their cosmopolitan aesthetic aspirations. Two works, then as now prized possessions of the Art Gallery of New South Wales, form cornerstones of this exhibition and in a sense prompted the reconstruction of their art-historical context from a post-colonial vantage point. In 1890 the Gallery's overseas advisers in Paris purchased Etienne Dinet's

Fig. 19
THOMAS SHEARD
The Arab blacksmith
c. 1900
oil on canvas
115 x 163 cm
Bendigo Art Gallery

Algerian picture *The snake charmer* (fig. 21, cat. 69), which was painted at Laghouat in 1889. It was to prove an important model for the first wave of Australian Orientalists – artists who felt it was essential to travel abroad and paint on the spot. Throughout the 20th century *The snake charmer* has remained popular with the Art Gallery's public, a fact suggesting that the lure of Europe's Near East has diminished little with time. *The Arab blacksmith* (fig. 19), a painting acquired for the Bendigo Art Gallery in 1903, remains similarly popular. By Thomas Sheard, a British academician following in Dinet's footsteps, this painting too focuses on the ancestral custom of North African desert nomads.

However, the most expensive example of Orientalist art to enter Sydney's early collection was Edward Poynter's vast studio picture, *The visit of the Queen of Sheba to King Solomon* (cat. 34). It was purchased in London in 1892, the following cablegram being forwarded to the Sydney Gallery Trustees: 'The Earl of Carlisle and Mr. Chevalier have secured Mr. Poynter's important Gallery picture, *The Queen of Sheba visiting King Solomon* for 2,900 pounds...I am asked to telegraph if it is possible to increase the remittance as both the London and Paris votes are exhausted'.[3] Ten years earlier the Trustees had been disappointed by their failure to acquire Edwin Long's famous *Babylonian marriage market* (fig. 20) for the Sydney collection. Long's large-scale depiction set exotic Babylonian beauties among the reconstructed splendours of the ancient world. Poynter's painting was in the same vein of archaeological costume drama and, as far as the Trustees were concerned, its high price was justified because it would be a direct means of 'attracting throngs of persons to the Art Gallery'.[4]

Reporting the new purchase, the *Sydney Morning Herald* announced that Poynter's picture 'was shown throughout the United Kingdom by Mr. Thomas McLean of the Haymarket Gallery, who paid six thousand pounds for it and realised great sums by its exhibition'.[5]

Some Australians were impressed by Poynter's 'scene of oriental splendour' and praised its 'marvellous impression of luxury, magnificence and space' and 'the unparalleled industry and talent on the part of the painter'.[6] Six months after its arrival it was recorded with some satisfaction that 'the attendance since its appearance has increased very largely'.[7] But the picture also aroused lively debates on its aesthetic merit, method of display, and cost. A year later the debate was capped with this tersely worded judgement: 'Mr Poynter will probably live in history as a disap-Poynter'.[8] The change in public mood was also signalled when Edwin Long's *Queen Esther* was exhibited in Sydney in 1894 and a local critic spoke up on behalf of those who 'feel compelled to regard it as rather the highest type of artifice than Art, and to class it among an order of paintings which is gradually losing its hold upon cultivated connoisseurs'.[9]

The shift away from studio history paintings towards directly observed, spontaneously recorded scenes from everyday life was championed by Australian painters who developed a local form of Impressionism in the closing years of the 19th century. A key figure in the development of this new aesthetic was Tom Roberts. When he described a tour of the then National Art Gallery of New South Wales for Melbourne readers of

Fig. 20
EDWIN LONG
Babylonian marriage market
1875
oil on canvas
Royal Holloway and Bedford New College, University of London

the *Argus* in 1891, Roberts began his account appreciatively: 'Spring in Sydney, a clear sky and hot sun…an avenue of Moreton Bay figs…A glimpse of sea of a colour that cannot be told, the hills beyond glowing ruddily in the brilliant light'. With the same sensitivity to light and atmosphere he discussed the Gallery's collections inside, writing of Dinet's *The snake charmer*.

Fig. 21
ETIENNE DINET
The snake charmer
1889

oil on canvas
175.6 x 180.4 cm

The Art Gallery
of New South Wales,
Sydney
Purchased 1890
(cat. 69)

it is a peep into the East itself – and every figure and head impresses with its truth and character. There is a certain apparently haphazard arrangement, which at first strikes one as a defect, but looking from it to a lot of neighbouring works in which there is certainly 'composition', it is curious how trite they look, and we come back to this Eastern piece, as from a dull common room to a brilliant open air, with a sense of freshness and healthfulness.[10]

Roberts was the first artist from the Australian generation of the 1880s to paint Orientalist themes on the basis of travel. However, he was by no means the first artist from the Australian colonies to paint in the East. Robert Dowling, whose academic *magnum opus, A sheikh and his son entering Cairo on their return from a pilgrimage to Mecca,* was celebrated at the time it was acquired by the National Gallery of Victoria in 1878, had lived and worked in Cairo between 1872 and 1873. Dowling's career established a pattern of repatriation for successful Australian artists: study overseas, exhibiting at the London Royal Academy or Paris Salon, demonstrated accomplishment in fashionable genres (including Orientalism), and sales bolstered by the practice of exhibiting works painted overseas back in Australia, expanding the colonial market.

Roberts's insertion into the European culture of Orientalist art is evident in his contact, on his first trip 'home' to London, with two masters of the contemporary Orientalist picture: Edwin Long and Jean-Léon Gérôme. In 1883 he took a break from his studies at the Royal Academy Schools to follow in the footsteps of his mentor, Long, and went on a sketching tour through Spain. From the 1830s onwards, Andalusia had become a popular destination for French and English painters not only interested in intense light and images of Gypsy culture, but also in a vanished exotic history. The Moorish architecture of the Alhambra palace at Granada had been sketched by generations of British watercolourists like David Roberts and J. F. Lewis, and had been the backdrop to Orientalist subject pictures by Regnault, Clairin, Benjamin-Constant and Moreau (qq.v.). Roberts's *Moorish doorway* (cat. 73), inscribed 'Granada, October 1883', acknowledges that exoticist tradition. At the same time it is his first attempt to capture the 'glare' effect of strong sunlight in a landscape. He rendered his Moorish 'postcard' motif in high-key russets and creams, against the summer-blue of the sky and hot, dusty hillside behind. Roberts's chance meeting in Granada with the leading young Spanish painters Ramon Casas and Laureano Barrau (a student of Jean-Léon Gérôme') had a lasting impact on his art. In the first place he was encouraged to visit Paris the following winter, where he sought out Gérôme's class at the Académie Julian. It was surely there that he produced his most obviously Gérômesque work, the *Untitled (Seated Arab)* (cat. 74). This typical Orientalist depiction of a costumed male figure, meditatively posed smoking a hookah, has strong thematic affinities with the more finished works of Bonnat and Deutsch (qq.v.). The striking green of the Arab's dress and the Orientalist props help establish the exotic subject, while the décor of an alleyway with *mashrabiyyas*, as if from an Algiers kasbah he had never visited, provide sketchy atmospherics of place.

In fact, for the history of Australian Orientalism, the lesson of Gérôme lay less in such subjects than in the attitude to *plein air* painting that the veteran traveller to Egypt and Sinai had promoted. As William Moore later declared, 'the story of how Tom Roberts introduced impressionism in Australia begins in Granada, in Spain, in 1883'.[11] Barrau had told Roberts that his master encouraged pupils to paint a direct sketch every day and just go for the 'effect of colour'.[12] It was the sketches Roberts brought back to Australia in 1885 that put Arthur Streeton and Charles Conder in touch with the new method; according to Streeton, 'the fresh air–true tone in values idea, which conflicted with the academic training under Folingsby'.[13] In 1889 Roberts used a dictum by Gérôme to launch the landmark '9 x 5 Impressions' exhibition which featured work by Roberts, Streeton and Conder: 'When you draw, form is the most important thing; but in painting the first thing to look for is the general impression of colour'.[14]

The application of this program to the landscapes around Heidelberg (to Melbourne's north) is one of the defining moments of Australian art history. The suggestion here is that an aesthetic of landscape painting, developed partly in response to the hot climates of the Orient (beginning in southern Spain), helped the *plein-airists* in Roberts's group interpret the shimmer and glare of the Australian summer. As with Dinet's *The snake charmer*, the sketching methods of the painter–traveller Gérôme acted as a catalyst in confronting visual conditions in a dry country with a desert heart.

Even as they worked in the Antipodes, a conception of the East modified the decorative sense of Roberts, Streeton and Conder. Whistlerian aestheticism determined their preferred studio décors, and Oriental touches provided a sympathetic environment for the '9 x 5 Impressions' exhibition. The artists looped and knotted 'Whistler draperies' in Liberty silk around Buxton's Gallery, arranging 'art' furniture and Japanese umbrellas, screens and fans in the rooms.[15] Conder's studio, whether in Collins Street, Melbourne or the rue Ravignan, Paris, was decorated with primrose Madras muslins his uncle had brought as a gift from India.

Conder left Australia for Europe in 1890, and within a year found himself in the North African city of Algiers. He had rapidly become a personality in the artists' quarter of Montmartre: the long fair hair, dandyish dress and sleepy manner of the 'eccentric Englishman' blended easily with the raffish café society frequenting the Rat Mort or the Cabaret Aristide Bruant. By the end of 1891 the destructive combination of a dissipated night-life, and venereal disease contracted in Australia, forced him to leave Paris for a time to recover his health. A wealthy French friend, Henri de Vallombreuse, offered him the use of his villa near Mustapha, Algiers – the very location where Fromentin had lived and painted in 1846, and from which Renoir had written to a patron in 1881: 'I will find you a house in Paradise, at Mustapha inférieur'.[16] Conder spent the next few months convalescing in de Vallombreuse's beautiful garden with its rows of almond trees and white bengal roses, overlooking the blue sea of the bay of Algiers. He wrote from Mustapha to his friend William Rothenstein, 'Here one feels quite in Australia again'.[17]

Fig. 23
ARTHUR STREETON
Egyptian drink vendor
1897
oil on canvas on paperboard
33.2 x 18.3 cm
Collection National Gallery of Australia, Canberra. Bequest of Henriette von Dallwitz and of Richard Paul in honour of his father, Dr Oscar Paul 1965
(cat. 76)

Fig. 22
CHARLES CONDER
Flowers in a vase against a background of the coastline of Mustapha, Algiers
1891
oil on canvas
46 x 55.3 cm
The Art Gallery of New South Wales, Sydney. Purchased with assistance from Katies 1982
(cat. 93)

Conder's few Algerian pictures, among his most beautiful, have the poignant, attenuated air of the convalescent about them. *Flowers in a vase against a background of the coastline of Mustapha, Algiers* (fig. 22, cat. 93), dated December 1891, with its japonist high horizon and blossom-scented sunshine, incorporated what Barry Pearce describes as 'a splendid strip of seascape which could pass as a Streeton panel painted in Sydney at that time'.[18] However, a faintly melancholy symbolism of faded rose petals also perfumes the work. In soulful colours of blue and mauve, Conder carries a nostalgia for the days of his youth in 'the Sunny South' (and a new awareness of his own mortality) into the Orientalist setting of a pasha's house from the *Arabian Nights*. It is the beginning of his flight from reality into reverie and fantasy, from Impressionism to Symbolism, from landscape into decoration.

Early in 1897, Arthur Streeton, then in his thirtieth year, also sailed for Europe. He stopped in Cairo to paint a series of pictures. Like Roberts and Conder before him, these Orientalist works mark a watershed in his art. In Streeton's case the five or six weeks he spent in Cairo resulted not only in the first pictures he ever painted outside Australia, but also ended the first stage of his career as a young painter of poetic, instinctively bright, lyrical landscape 'impressions'. In England he would struggle to consolidate his art, becoming more self-conscious about composition and muted in his choice of colour. But in Cairo he felt himself paradoxically at home: 'revelling in the white hot

glare of the African sunshine, and in the tawny hills and plains, accented with dashes of barbaric colour'.[19] Still optimistic about his chances for success in London, Streeton immersed himself in the atmosphere of the city, making rapid oil sketches, watercolours and drawings, and taking and collecting photographs.

In a letter posted from 9 Waghe-el birghet in Cairo and later published in the *Bulletin*, Streeton wrote:

> *T'is a wonderful land this Egypt; I've been time after time through the slipper, brass and bronze, jewellery, perfume, silks, ring, curio bazaars – and yesterday with another artist I did a quick sketch of a spice bazaar; and the alley was choc-a-block all the time…All are orientals here – Arabs and Copts with many a grand old face. Princely looking chaps a few of them…Little by little the French official markings about the city are being taken down, and the notices, directions etc. printed in plain English and Arabic…It must annoy the French very much, to see the place held by a few English troops – who, by the way, are all waiting ready.*[20]

Although proud to be counted an Englishman, Australian-born Streeton did not depict the British presence in his Cairo pictures, preferring, like most of his predecessors, to seek out picturesque local types and buildings untouched by the modern realities of colonialism (fig. 23).

Depicting famous mosques and bazaars, street vendors and veiled women, Streeton's repertoire of subjects would set the pattern for other Australians working in the impressionist tradition who were to follow him to North Africa in the early years of the 20th century. Prepared for painting in strong sunlight by his experience of working outdoors in the Australian summer, Streeton delighted in the high-key intensity of Egyptian light and adapted a palette of creamy beiges, scarlet and cobalt blue to render the exotic atmosphere of his new surroundings (cats 75–8). Like Emanuel Phillips Fox, his wife, Ethel Carrick, and their young friend Hilda Rix (as she was known before her marriage to Captain Nicholas), Streeton found his subjects among the public life of the street and marketplace, quickly sketching on the spot and elaborating in his hotel. The figures he depicted were exotic 'types' – symbols for the eastern milieu in which he encountered them – rather than portraits of individuals. He did not know the language and was little concerned to learn more about the religious beliefs and customs of a people whose colourful appearance enchanted his eye.

By the early 1900s there were a number of Australian artists working in Paris, among them Emanuel Phillips Fox and his friend Rupert Bunny. In 1889 Fox had gained entry to the Ecole des Beaux-Arts, enrolled at Gérôme's atelier, and was awarded the *premier prix*. Once again Gérôme exerted an unexpected influence on the development of Australia's Impressionists. Although his own work was academically finished and tight in its drawing, his students found the master's attitude towards colour much more permissive. Even Renoir, according to Ackerman, 'always spoke well of him'.[21] Like Renoir, Roberts and Fox did not regard Gérôme as the enemy of original expression in painting: his emphasis on the general impression of colour as the key to feeling and the value of the small-scale oil sketch has been noted. Where Roberts and Fox departed from their teacher was in believing, like the Impressionists proper, that the study–sketch could also be an independent artwork, not simply a stage in the development of a studio picture.

After Fox's marriage to the English-born artist Ethel Carrick in 1905, the couple established themselves in Paris, taking an apartment on the Boulevard Arago. Both were keen painter–travellers, working at a number of popular European outdoor painting sites. In February 1911, accompanied by his wife and one of his male students,

Fig. 24
ETHEL CARRICK
The mosque at Tangier
c. 1911

oil on canvas
on board
46 x 35.5cm

Collection Philip
Bacon, Brisbane
(cat. 84)

Fox set out on a six-week painting tour to Algeria and Morocco, where some of his most delightfully extemporaneous landscape and figure studies were painted. He went there, he said, 'determined to get some settled sunlight', adding, 'I depend so much on sunlight effects'.[22] As Ruth Zubans has pointed out, 'by 1911 a trip to the Near East was no longer an exotic event'.[23] Fox was following in the footsteps of many earlier artists: his teacher Gérôme, Renoir, Dinet, Conder and his American friend Henry Ossawa Tanner (qq.v.), to name a few. However, his North African series stands out from his other work as an exceptional moment of painterly freedom and concentrated intensity. Spontaneous, sun-drenched, fluently painted in liquid, curling strokes, *Moslems in procession* (cat. 83) epitomises the vibrant series of small pictures he painted outside Algiers and at Bou Saâda, the home of Dinet (q.v.), where Fox and his wife spent several weeks. Fox was not interested in going beyond the tenets of Impressionism in his work. In a 1913 interview published in his home town of Melbourne, he was quoted as saying he disliked the Post-Impressionists because they did not 'go to nature to learn', concluding acerbically, 'I think one might just describe them as posts'.[24]

Ethel Carrick's view differed from her husband's: in 1911, when she decided to exhibit the first of her Orientalist pictures at the Salon d'Automne, she deliberately chose a venue associated with advanced forms of painting in Paris. Emanuel Phillips Fox informed Hans Heysen: 'my wife is doing some very interesting and personal stuff – she is Sociétaire of the Autumn Salon and is very keen on modern outlook'.[25] The critic for *L'Art et les Artistes* reviewing the 1911 exhibition was struck by her work, stopping to admire 'a small but perfect painting', a colourful depiction of an Arab woman. He declared himself to be 'charmed by the extraordinary boldness, verve, and assurance' of Carrick's painting, 'with its breadth of atmosphere...and extremely seductive colouring'.[26] This work was apparently sold from the exhibition, but its companion piece, painted at Bou Saâda and titled *Arab women washing clothes in a stream* (cat. 85), was shown in Australia in 1913. Local critics were no less struck by Carrick's dazzlingly summary brushwork, praising its 'gorgeous colour' and pronouncing the whole effect 'daringly modern'.[27]

Fig. 25
HILDA RIX NICHOLAS
Negro Boy
1914
coloured pastel
53 x 36.5 cm
Rix Wright Collection
(cat. 81)

In certain Orientalist works like *The mosque at Tangier* (fig. 24, cat. 84), Carrick employs a modernist approach of simplifying the architectural motif and drawing attention to the picture surface with openly worked brushstrokes. This small canvas is directly comparable to the paintings Albert Marquet did in Tangier around the same time: it profits from a similar pervasive blue tonality and a broad generalisation of form. Indeed *The mosque at Tangier* almost certainly shows the tomb of the marabout, Sidi Berraisoul on the rue Ben Abbou which is the subject of Matisse's sumptuous (if for him rather unadventurous) canvas of 1912–13, *The marabout*.[28]

After her husband's death in 1915, Ethel Carrick continued to travel extensively, moving between Paris and Australia. She joined the Theosophist movement in Sydney, taking advantage of her contacts to tour India, and lived for a time in the mid-1930s on a houseboat in Kashmir. She also returned to work in North Africa, and painted in the desert around Tunis and Kairouan (cats 86, 87). If in the conservative environment of Australia in the later 1920s she might denounce 'ultra-modern' art, her pre-war Orientalist works are the equal of many an itinerant French progressive's. In claiming that 'the light in Australia reminds me of North Africa more than any other country I have ever visited',[29] the Englishwoman reversed the equation usually made by her Antipodean colleagues on visiting the Orient.

Fig. 26
RUPERT BUNNY
The harem
c. 1913
oil on canvas
51.8 x 79.5 cm
Lionel Lindsay
Collection,
Toowoomba
Regional Art Gallery,
courtesy of the
Lionel Lindsay Art
Gallery and Library
Trust
(cat. 102)

Even more than Ethel Carrick, her friend Hilda Rix Nicholas made her reputation as a successful artist in Paris by means of Orientalist work. As John Pigot has argued, both women evidenced a greater sense of freedom and possibility – personal and artistic – when working in the East. A female artist in England or France was hemmed in by social constraints, especially when attempting to work in public spaces. In Morocco, the colonial situation gave Rix and Carrick a perceived superiority of status vis-à-vis the locals that emboldened them in an unorthodox way. Rix's many letters home in 1912 and 1914 explain how she moved with relative freedom about the Tangier marketplace, often without a chaperone, drawing and working in pastels. European gentlemen or colleagues like her American friend Henry Ossawa Tanner no doubt kept an obliging if distant eye on the proceedings. A consummate draughtswoman who surely worked up her sketches back in her room (at the Hotel Villa de France, where Henri and Amélie Matisse also stayed), Rix sometimes sketched furtively among the crowds, because those she called her 'game' were usually moving about, either uncomprehending of her purpose or unwilling to be 'captured' by her pencil or brush.

When able to coax locals into sitting, however, Rix tried to portray her subjects sympathetically. Her pastel drawing of a young *Negro boy* (fig. 25, cat. 81) is a sensitive portrait of an individual, as well as a costume piece in the ethnographic tradition. But, with true Edwardian bathos, her letters also spoke of Tangier as a beautiful dream, its people as figures from the Bible or characters out of the *Arabian Nights*. Rix was so captivated by their costume that she collected examples and sometimes wore them – as a combination of fancy dress and camouflage – to allow her to move more freely among 'her' crowds of 'glorious…wonderful people'.[30]

Hilda Rix's Moroccan work made an impact not only in Paris (where one critic called her 'an Orientalist and an impressionist by natural vocation and by love of light'),[31] but

EUGENE DELACROIX

6 ROYAL TIGER (Tigre royal) 1829

Lithograph on chine appliqué (third state of four) 32.5 x 46 cm
The Art Gallery of New South Wales, Sydney. Purchased 1993

Often considered Delacroix's finest achievement in lithography, *Royal tiger* is contemporary with the artist's set of seventeen plates for Goethe's *Faust*, and it has a strange kinship with his famous image of a betaloned Satan flying over Faust's home town: this tiger has a similarly sulphuric and wildly unpredictable look in its eyes. Both are key images from the Romantic movement of 1830.

Although Orientalist in theme, the *Royal tiger* (with its lesser companion, *Lion of the Atlas*) prefigures Delacroix's actual journey to the East. Sometimes in the company of the animal sculptor Antoine-Louis Barye (who made his Salon début in 1831 with *Tiger devouring a gavial*), Delacroix would dissect cats to learn their anatomy, and study the animals in the Paris zoo at the Jardin des Plantes. At the big cats' feeding-time he declared himself 'penetrated by happiness' – a sentiment that presages the fascination with blood and the violent combat between men and animals evident in his post-Moroccan canvases of the hunt. The *Royal tiger* is more easeful than these: recumbent in a sketchy Eastern plain, the tiger's relaxed hindquarters are belied by the tense head and shoulders of this beautifully powerful beast seen awaiting its prey.   RB

EUGENE DELACROIX

7 JEWESS OF ALGIERS (Juive d'Alger) 1833

Etching on cream vergé paper (third of four states) 21.4 x 17.4 cm
The Art Gallery of New South Wales, Sydney. Purchased 1990

Delacroix's first attempts at etching, made as a youth in 1814, were rapidly superseded by his interest in the new print-making technology of lithography which resulted in works such as *Royal tiger* (cat. 6). The year after his return from Morocco in 1832 the artist resumed etching, making ten plates in that year. *Jewess of Algiers* and *Arabs of Oran* are among the most significant of these.

While in Tangier, his diplomatic status helped give Delacroix an entrée into several Jewish households. The imagery of this print relates to the series of detailed watercolours Delacroix made of Jewish women (the 'Algiers' of the title is thus a misnomer).[1] While some of these show women in bridal costume, others, like his portrait of the wife and daughter of Abraham Benchimol (interpreter to the French Consul) show mature women in formal costume.[2] Delacroix wrote home to a friend: 'The Jewish women here are also very handsome and their dress is most picturesque. I have witnessed a number of their ceremonies…'.[3] In this print, a woman of means is seated indoors with her servant; the informality of her bare feet on the rug, so evocative of the Oriental interior, contrasts with her heavy costume and dignified, pensive carriage.   RB

1 All the more so since in 1852 Delacroix exhibited a painting of the same motif, described as 'A Jewess at home with a Moorish woman (Moroccan dress)'; see *Delacroix in Morocco*, exh. cat. (Institut du Monde Arabe), Flammarion, Paris, 1994, cat. no. 61, p. 192.

2 Illustrated in *Delacroix in Morocco*, p. 179.

3 Letter of 23 February 1832, in *Eugène Delacroix: Selected Letters 1813–1863*, trans. Jean Stewart, Eyre & Spottiswoode, London, 1971, p. 185.

EUGENE DELACROIX

8 ARABS OF ORAN (Arabes d'Oran) c. 1833

Etching on cream vergé paper (fourth of six states) 17.2 x 21.3 cm
The Art Gallery of New South Wales, Sydney. Purchased 1990

[1] See Lee Johnson,
*The Paintings of Eugène
Delacroix: A Critical
Catalogue*, Clarendon
Press, Oxford, 1986,
vol. 3, p. 170, and
Delacroix in Morocco,
exh. cat. (Institut du
Monde Arabe)
Flammarion, Paris,
1994, cat. nos 55, 60, 70.

[2] 'Arabes sur un marché';
see *Delacroix in
Morocco*, pp. 180, 185.

Arabs of Oran recalls Delacroix's brief visit to the west Algerian port of Oran on 20 June 1832, before he finished his North African journey in Algiers. It was based on a wash drawing the artist made outside Oran's city walls, traces of which were dropped from the etching as well as from the watercolour version that Delacroix presented to the Comte de Mornay after the journey's completion. This print refines the watercolour's composition by the addition of a horseman to the background and a rifle to the foreground.[1]

If considered as a pendant to the cloistered *Jewess of Algiers* (cat. 7), *Arabs of Oran* seems to emphasise the place of North African men out in the open, in public space. Yet these two figures seated on a sketchy bank, with a minaret visible far off, seem idle and more bored than the women – the lassitude of Oriental life being a constant theme in the Orientalist arts and letters of Europeans, who considered themselves paragons of energy. The presence of paniers, of a kind used to contain grain, seems to support a 19th-century title of the composition indicating 'Arabs at a market'.[2] Delacroix's etched title serves to localise an image that otherwise seems generic in intent.   RB

EUGENE DELACROIX

9 ARAB SOLDIER BY A GRAVE 1838

Oil on canvas 47.3 x 56.2 cm
Hiroshima Museum of Art*

This modestly scaled canvas was one of the highlights of the 1994 exhibition 'Delacroix in Morocco'. Refused at the Salon of 1839 (to the chagrin of more than one critic), it belonged to the Duc d'Orleans, the son of the king, Louis-Philippe, who, like his older brother, the Duc d'Aumale, was prominent in the ongoing French colonial wars in Algeria. Both soldiers collected Orientalist paintings.

The ennobling sentiment of the image may have appealed to such a collector. Delacroix identified the kneeling soldier as the Moroccan commander Mohammed ben Abou (thought to be portrayed in cat. 1).[1] His painting is a rare European expression of reflective Arab religiosity. As if on a deliberate detour to visit the grave of a fallen friend, the dismounted ben Abou gently bends his knee before a simple grave set with stones (such as may still be found in the Moroccan countryside today) among the wild aloe plants.[2] With his open cape revealing his exquisite military harness, the 'calm, religious, touching expression of this man' is matched only by the almost human solicitude of his superbly caparisoned horse, 'which lowers its head as if to kiss the hand that his master offers him'.[3]

Delacroix's virtuoso control of the brush is fully evident in his rendering of horse and rider, while an impeccable compositional sense means that the weight of the image falls on the cream-clad figure of ben Abou, offset to the right. The yellow light of the stormy sky visually balances the man, and metaphorically evokes a sense of portent and the after-life fitted to his meditations.   RB

[1] See *Delacroix in Morocco*, exh. cat. (Institut du Monde Arabe), Flammarion, Paris, 1994, p. 201.

[2] See Lee Johnson, *The Paintings of Eugène Delacroix: A Critical Catalogue*, Clarendon Press, Oxford, 1986, vol. 3, p. 174.

[3] The critic Eugène Bareste (1839), quoted in *Delacroix in Morocco*, p. 201.

EUGENE DELACROIX

10 COLLISION OF ARAB HORSEMEN 1843–44

Oil on canvas 81.3 x 99.1 cm
The Walters Art Gallery, Baltimore, Maryland, no. 37.6

This important canvas records an incident witnessed by Delacroix soon after the outset of the journey from Tangier to Meknès: a collision of horses in the course of a *fantasia* (from the Arabic *fantaziya*, or 'ostentation'), defined as an 'eques- trian entertainment by Arab horse- men who execute various manoeuvres at the gallop, while firing off their arms and shouting out loud'.[1] Delacroix witnessed many ceremonial fantasias as the Comte de Mornay's en- tourage was met by succes- sive tribes on the way to Meknès. The painter noted in his diary for 6 March 1832: 'Powder-play in the

plain facing the river – the riders who collided: the one whose horse's rump touched the ground'. This became the subject of a painting, refused at the Salon of 1834, which Delacroix thought important enough to reproduce in an etching the same year, and paint again a decade later (the present version).

Delacroix's obsession with feats of horsemanship and the splendour of the Arab breed was something he shared with French romantic painters from Géricault to Fromentin. In the new industrial age the horse remained a vivid index of social status and primarily masculine values. Yet in their love of horses the Europeans were outdone by the Arabs. According to the great Algerian soldier and theologian, Abd-el-Kader:

We believe that God created the horse out of the wind, as he created Adam out of clay. This is irrefutable. Several prophets – a blessing on their souls! – proclaimed: 'When God wanted to create the horse, he said to the South Wind: Out of you I wish to bring forth a creature, condense yourself. *And the wind condensed itself. Then the angel Gabriel took a handful of this substance and presented it to God who fashioned it into a burnt chestnut horse and cried I name you* horse, *I create you* Arabian...'.[2]   RB

1 *Le Petit Robert 1: Dictionnaire... de la langue française*, Le Robert, Paris, 1977.

2 Letter to General Daumas of 1857, quoted in Edmonde Charles-Roux, 'Delacroix and the Arabian horse: a tribute to the Son of the Wind', in *Delacroix in Morocco*, exh. cat. (Institut du Monde Arabe), Flammarion, Paris, 1994, p. 18.

EUGENE DELACROIX

11 A MOROCCAN OF THE EMPEROR'S GUARD (Un marocain de la garde de l'Empereur) 1845

Oil on canvas 32 x 41 cm
Musée des Beaux-Arts de Bordeaux

Painted in the same year as Delacroix's enormous *Sultan of Morocco and his entourage* (Musée des Augustins, Toulouse), where all is the grandeur of a ceremonial occasion, this small oil has the relaxed informality of a genre scene. One of several images of North African men taking their ease in the open countryside (cf. *Arabs of Oran*, cat. 8), *A Moroccoan of the emperor's guard* was based on a watercolour painted in 1833 shortly after Delacroix's return from Morocco.[1]

Rather than Delacroix tiring of his Moroccan memories, by 1845 the tempo of his painted evocations of the East was actually increasing. Here the darkened canvas gives less the idea of a luminous desert climate than a moody milieu suited to the recreation of memories. In the opulent yet masculine figure (once again plausibly identified with Delacroix's favourite subject, Mohammed ben Abou),[2] the soldier's powerful limbs, held akimbo, describe a star-shaped, twisting posture – an arabesque centred on the red blazon at his belt. The carbine's slender shaft, the eccentric peak of the soldier's burnous, and the alert head of the barb pony harkening to a distant sound cut the horizon with the imprint of the exotic.   RB

1 See Lee Johnson, *The Paintings of Eugène Delacroix: A Critical Catalogue*, Clarendon Press, Oxford, 1986, vol. 3, p. 184.

2 ibid.

JEAN-AUGUSTE-DOMINIQUE INGRES

12 HEAD OF THE GRAND ODALISQUE (Tête de la Grande odalisque) c. 1814–18

Oil on canvas 44 cm diam.
Musée de Cambrai

This exquisite bust of a young woman in a turban is based on the head of Ingres's 1814 masterpiece the *Grand odalisque* (fig. 3, cf. cat. 13). Ingres has made of it an entirely satisfying painting in its own right by carefully matching its proportions to the circular canvas (or 'tondo') which sympathetically encloses its many rounded forms: from the odalisque's shoulder and chin to the arc of her eyebrow, her undulating fringe, the gold fillet of her headband, and finally her embroidered turban. Every curved line is related to the frame in this composition of gentle arabesques.

Ingres was faithful to the detail of the larger painting,[1] suppressing only a cushion on the left and deepening the shadow over the fringed tail of the turban below the woman's chin – small refinements that allow her pristine, almost virginal head to emerge untrammelled from the soft darkness.

The eastern character of this picture is more tenuous than that of the *Grand odalisque* itself, for which Ingres claimed to have used as a model a 10-year-old girl in Rome.[2] Both works have a relationship to Renaissance precedents: this turbaned head, seen in three-quarter profile calmly surveying the viewer, was inspired by Raphael's tondo *The Madonna of the chair* (Pitti Palace, Florence). Ingres was obsessed by this picture, for which Raphael's mistress 'La Fornarina' was said to have posed. In 1814 he painted the first of several imaginary reconstructions of La Fornarina sitting on Raphael's knee; the turbaned head of Raphael's mistress closely resembles that of the exactly contemporary *Grand odalisque*.

Ingres was the quintessential 'armchair Orientalist' who never travelled East, yet the influence exerted by his odalisques was in no way lessened by the doubtful Oriental pedigree such a genealogy reveals. RB

1 Wildenstein implies that the Cambrai head may be a study for the *Grande odalisque*, describing it as 'Probably the sketch which Ingres reproduced in his drawing of the Stamaty family' (in 1818); see Georges Wildenstein, *The Paintings of J.A.D. Ingres*, Phaidon, London, 1954, cat. 97, p. 179; this is one of three known tondo versions of the head.

2 See Carol Ockman, *Ingres's Eroticized Bodies: Retracing the Serpentine Line*, Yale University Press, New Haven & London, 1995, p. 36.

JEAN-AUGUSTE-DOMINIQUE INGRES

13 THE GRAND ODALISQUE (La Grande odalisque) 1826

Lithograph on paper 16.3 x 22.6 cm
Musée Ingres, Montauban

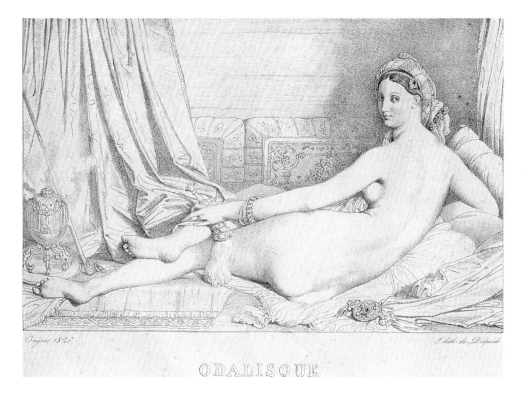

One of the rare prints for which he himself made the drawing, Ingres's lithograph was instrumental in popularising his canvas of 1814 after his triumphant return from two decades of living in Italy.[1] The *Grand odalisque* is today considered one of the greatest of 19th-century figure paintings, a rival to the reclining female nudes of Giorgione and Titian, or Goya and Manet.

Breaking with such traditions, Ingres's painting proposes an imagined East, rather than classical myth or modern life, as the preferred location for studying the female form. His cloistered, cosseted *Grand odalisque* gazes out at the viewer with an impassive, almost haughty air. The coquetry of her turban, bangles and fan is belied by her highly decorous posture – perhaps understandable given that the impeccably finished nude was commissioned by a woman, Napoleon's sister, Caroline Murat, the Queen of Naples.[2]

From its first exhibition in the Salon of 1819 the anatomy of Ingres's *Grand odalisque* excited controversy: Kératy found she had three vertebrae too many, while in 1846 Mantz found it impossible to say how the left thigh would rejoin her torso.[3] But many felt such artistic licence only promoted the sinuous arabesque line which stamped this figure with extraordinary beauty. The *Grand odalisque* is the archetype for innumerable variations on this Orientalist theme, be they (like her) painted from studio models and props, or (in rare cases) inspired by the sight of non-western women (see Gérôme, Débat-Ponsan, Trouillebert and Matisse in this catalogue).

Ingres's small lithograph reverses the image; the artist has changed the form of the incense-burner and converted the peacock-feather fan to a fly-whisk. By summarising the embroidered fabrics and making the play of lines more evident, Ingres gave the work the character of a drawing; Sudré's lithograph, in contrast, successfully imitates the meticulous rendering of the oil painting.   RB

1 Published in Delpech's *Album Lithographique* of 1826, the *Grand odalisque* was also reproduced in lithographs by Sudré and an anonymous artist; see L. Delteil, *Le Peintre-graveur illustré*, vol. 3, *Ingres, Delacroix*, Paris, 1908, repr. Collectors Edition Ltd, Da Capo Press, New York, 1969, cat. no. 9.

2 See Carol Ockman, 'A woman's pleasure: the *Grande odalisque*', in her *Ingres's Eroticized Bodies: Retracing the Serpentine Line*, Yale University Press, New Haven & London, 1995, pp. 33–66.

3 See Ockman, *Ingres's Eroticized Bodies*, pp. 85ff, on the critical reception of the painting.

Jean-Auguste-Dominique Ingres

14 ODALISQUE WITH SLAVE (Odalisque et son esclave) 1858

Graphite, white gouache, grey wash, pen and brown ink on tracing paper 34.5 x 47.5 cm
Département des Arts Graphiques, Musée du Louvre, Paris

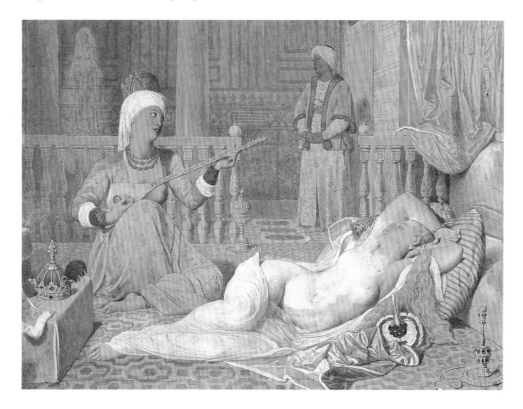

This remarkable drawing is an exact, half-size copy of a masterpiece from Ingres's middle career, *Odalisque with slave* of 1839 (The Fogg Art Museum, Cambridge). In 1842 Ingres had painted a second *Odalisque with slave* with numerous minor variations, yet in this late drawing he returned to the original version. The artist explained this obsessive will to repeat thus: 'Most of these works, which I love…seem to me worth the trouble to make them better, in repeating or retouching them…Should an artist hope to leave his name to posterity, then he could never do enough to render his works more beautiful or less imperfect'.[1]

Odalisque with slave features the most completely beautiful female nude painted in Ingres's long career. The canvas was finished in Rome, the inspiration coming (as with the later *Turkish bath*) from the *Turkish Letters* of Lady Mary Wortley Montagu:

> *One entered into a vestibule paved with marble…From there, one proceeded to a room surrounded by sofas…Around this bed there burned, in golden censers, the most agreeable aromatics of the East, and here several women devoted to this purpose awaited the sultana's exit from the bath to dry her beautiful body and rub it with the sweetest oils; and it was here that she subsequently took voluptuous relaxation.[2]*

For the women-servants Ingres has substituted the figure of a singing musician who plays the *tar* or Oriental lute. The heavy-set African eunuch was inspired by a figure Ingres traced from an Oriental miniature.[3] This image perfectly translates the hierarchy of the harem as western men conceived it: a pale-skinned beauty served by a coffee-coloured female, both confined by a black man who was nevertheless emasculated. The all-powerful sultan being absent from the scene, the European viewer was free to occupy his spectatorial position, with its visual mastery and sexual promise. RB

[1] Ingres to Delaborde, quoted in Marjorie B. Cohn, 'Introduction: in pursuit of perfection', in *In Pursuit of Perfection: The Art of J.-A.-D. Ingres*, exh. cat., The J. B. Speed Art Museum, Louisville, Kentucky, 1983, p. 11.

[2] Passage from Lady Montagu's *Letters* copied into Ingres's *Notebook IX*, quoted by Georges Vigne, *Ingres*, trans. John Goodman, Abbeville Press, New York, London & Paris, 1995, p. 222.

[3] Illustrated in Vigne, p. 219.

JEAN-AUGUSTE-DOMINIQUE INGRES

(JEAN CORABOEUF, AFTER INGRES)

15 THE TURKISH BATH (Le Bain turc) 1906

Colour etching on paper 65 x 50 cm (framed)
Département des Estampes, Bibliothèque Nationale de France, Paris

This little-known but fine etching by Coraboeuf is the only reproductive print after Ingres's great *Turkish bath* of 1862. The etching was commissioned by the then owner of the Ingres, Prince Amadée de Broglie, to celebrate its first public exhibition at the 1905 Salon d'Automne.[1] In 1905 the *Turkish bath* 'excited interminable aesthetic controversies',[2] and had a profound impact on the young artists Picasso and Matisse, whose *Demoiselles d'Avignon* and *Bonheur de vivre* applied this eroticism inspired by the East to modernist experiment with the figure.

Ingres had never travelled beyond Italy, but composed the *Turkish bath* in his Paris studio using an imagined eastern décor. His sources for specific figures included old prints imaging the lives of Ottoman women, while the general inspiration is due to the *Letters* of Lady Mary Wortley Montagu, the early 18th-century visitor to the hammams or women's baths of Turkey.[3] The *Turkish bath* was considered indecent by the wife of its first owner, Prince Napoléon, who returned it to Ingres; shortly thereafter it was bought by Khalil Bey, former Turkish Ambassador to Russia. The sale of his collection in the year of Ingres's death made the work notorious. Théophile Gautier, in a little- known text, described the *Turkish bath* as:

> *a marvellous pretext for grouping unveiled, in a circular frame, all the variety of types that the harem sends to such a rendezvous of Oriental coquetry. The great artist has drawn these beautiful bodies in postures that favour their charms: from the back, the front, in profile, foreshortened, standing, lying down, or with hips raised in a way that emphasises an opulent line; showing the neck where a fine turban is coiled above shoulders moist from the bath; mixing the marble of an antique goddess with the flesh of the Sultana...What an admirable figure is that of the young Greek girl with blond hair who, against the wall and with arms crossed under her breast, pursues through the langour of half-sleep some melancholy dream of the time when she was free...It is an important and singular moment in the work of Ingres, a canvas lovingly caressed with his suavest brush, twenty times left and taken up, like a woman with whom one cannot decide to break, a sort of harem that he only ever dismissed at the end of his life and into which he came from time to time to take an odalisque or a nymph.*[4]   RB

[1] The print was published in Jules Mommeja, 'Le "Bain turc" d'Ingres', *Gazette des Beaux-Arts*, vol. 36, no. 591, 1 September 1906, opp. p. 194.

[2] Louis Vauxcelles, 'Impressions de vernissage', *Gil Blas*, 18 October 1905.

[3] For an excellent guide see Marilyn R. Brown, 'The harem dehistoricized: Ingres' *Turkish bath*', *Arts Magazine*, vol. 61, no. 10, Summer 1987, pp. 58–68.

[4] Théophile Gautier, 'Beaux-Arts: collection Khalil-Bey', *Le Moniteur universel*, 14 December 1867.

THEODORE CHASSERIAU

16 COMBAT OF ARAB HORSEMEN (Combat de cavaliers arabes) 1856

Oil on canvas 65 x 54 cm
Département des Peintures, Musée du Louvre, Paris

Following his visit to Constantine in Algeria in 1846 as a guest of the local pasha, Chassériau frequently included North African scenes in his diverse repertoire. The success of his *Tribal chiefs defying one another to single combat* (Salon of 1852) led to a series of four small canvases, one per year, of fighting Arabs,[1] each of which seems to mount in ferocity and the level of detail packed into the whirling, highly coloured compositions. The last in the series, this *Combat* achieves a crescendo of interlocking bodies, forming a veritable arch of men and horses suspended over a shattered corpse and an unseated rider who vainly tries to protect his upturned face from the pounding hooves.

Fig. 27
THEODORE
CHASSERIAU
Moorish woman leaving the harem bath (Femme mauresque sortant du bain du sérail)
1854
oil on canvas
67 x 54 cm
Musée des Beaux-Arts de Strasbourg

The main action is a duel between two white-cloaked riders for the body of the wounded, fainting warrior on the white horse. More than Delacroix in Morocco, Chassériau was able to appreciate the bloody strife that attended the French conquest of Algeria. Fighting between Arab groups (some in league with, some against, the French) was not something Chassériau was likely to have witnessed during his visit to Constantine. But his

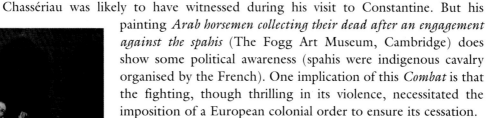

painting *Arab horsemen collecting their dead after an engagement against the spahis* (The Fogg Art Museum, Cambridge) does show some political awareness (spahis were indigenous cavalry organised by the French). One implication of this *Combat* is that the fighting, though thrilling in its violence, necessitated the imposition of a European colonial order to ensure its cessation.

In complete contrast to Chassériau's imagery of masculine violence, the painter made a series of feminised interiors – bath-scenes and harems – based on the Jewesses of Constantine and the idea of Islamic households he could not directly visit. These works of the 1850s show the artist's melding of Delacroix's colour with an Ingresque conception of the female body: classical in posture, frank in its nudity, and contained within a graceful arabesque outline. RB

[1] See Marc Sandoz, *Théodore Chassériau: catalogue raisonné des peintures et des estampes*, Arts et Métiers Graphiques, Paris, 1974, p. 284 and passim.

EUGENE FROMENTIN

17 A STREET OF LAGHOUAT (Une Rue à El-Aghouat) 1859

Oil on canvas 142 x 103 cm
Musée de la Chartreuse, Douai

Fromentin's glimpse of the parched city of Laghouat in the Sahara communicates a directness that belies its painting in Paris some six years after his last trip to Algeria. The omnipotent sunlight permeating the painter's famous written accounts of the desert is here defined in opposition to the shade which spills like a precious liquid over one side of the street. The vigorously handled ochre ground asserts atmospheric unity, giving warmth to the steep shadows, to the jagged slice of sky and to walls caught in the full force of the sun.

Announcing the oppressive heat which discourages movement outdoors in the middle of the day, Fromentin's main group also illustrates the reversal of western pictorial conventions he discovered in his eastern subjects. Seen with disconcerting clarity in the half-light, the men's pale robes attract the eye away from the surrounding glare.

Baudelaire, who admired the work at the Salon of 1859, lingered on the apparent comfort of 'these men extended in the blue shadows' whose expressions, he thought, revealed 'the happiness inspired by boundless light'. The critic recognised the work's enticing somnolence as a product of Fromentin's 'restful contemplation' and was duly transported to his own private memories and associations.[1] Fromentin's distance from his subject, indeed, seems vital to his work's appeal, apparently influencing the trancelike mood, the ascending perspective and the ornately crumbling surfaces which enclose the figures and the viewer in a summation of the remembered site.   PR

[1] Charles Baudelaire, 'Salon de 1859', in Claude Pichois (ed.), *Charles Baudelaire: critique d'art*, Gallimard, Paris, 1992, p. 310.

EUGENE FROMENTIN

18 WINDSTORM ON THE ESPARTO PLAINS (Coup de vent dans les plaines d'alfa) 1864

Oil on canvas 116.8 x 162.8 cm
The Najd Collection, courtesy of the Mathaf Gallery, London

Fromentin followed his success at the Salon of 1859 with a series of North African scenes that were most favourably received when dramatising the extremes of the exotic climate. This exceptional example from the Salon of 1864 animates the plains of esparto grass – accused of being unbearably monotonous in Fromentin's travel book, *A Summer in the Sahara* – with a romantically intense windstorm. Fromentin's invention soars in the group of horsemen who cower under the frills of buffeted burnouses. Designed in brief outline by a preliminary drawing, the climactic pattern of these draperies evidently afforded the stimulus for the composition. With skilful *mise-en-scène*, Fromentin leaves a wide gap on the right side of his image to add dynamism to the shapes in the oncoming blast.

This bracing picture of the desert appealed to the eminent realist critic, Théophile Thoré, as well as to the more conservative Léon Lagrange, who had reservations, however, about its gloomy colour.[1] The vigorously applied greys of the sky, forming a rich contrast to the side-lit figures, are unusually dark for Fromentin and suggest a debt to the expressive landscapes of such older contemporaries as Théodore Rousseau and Narcisse Diaz de la Peña.   PR

[1] Léon Lagrange, 'Salon de 1864', *Gazette des Beaux-Arts*, July 1864, p. 20.

EUGENE FROMENTIN

19 THE LAND OF THIRST (Au Pays de la soif) 1869

Oil on canvas 103.5 x 144 cm
Musées royaux des Beaux-Arts de Belgique, Brussels, inv. 3424

The Brussels *Land of thirst*, usually regarded as the second version of the ambitious composition in the Musée d'Orsay, was the culmination of Fromentin's effort to elevate Orientalist anecdote to the level of history painting. The title recalls the last words of *A Summer in the Sahara*: 'I will salute with a profound regret that menacing and desolate horizon which has been so rightly called – *Land of thirst*'.[1]

In his travel book, written fifteen years before this painting was made, Fromentin had implied his intent to compose his memories of the desert in a monumental synthesis. He had recounted a grim anecdote: the death from thirst of eight men and their animals who, in the summer of 1845, were surprised by the desert wind halfway between Laghouat and Ghardaia.

The barren landscape affords what looks to be the last resting place for the ragged party dispersed from its convoy. The group, which is surmounted in the Orsay version by a figure gesturing towards the horizon in dehydrated memory of Gericault's *Raft of the Medusa*, is allowed not even that vain hope in the Brussels work, whose flat landscape and unconscious bodies are watched only by circling birds. The lost men are divided from the viewer by the sheer face of rock that drops under the foot of the nearest figure.

Although neither version of *The land of thirst* was exhibited in Fromentin's lifetime, the work was hailed as a masterpiece after his death.[2] While the fatal image gives a falsely bleak impression of his *oeuvre*, its extreme vision of North Africa accords with the terms used in his travel writing and reaches for the pinnacle of French painting in the romantic and neo-classical genealogy of its expiring bodies.   PR

[1] Eugène Fromentin, *Une Eté dans le Sahara*, Plon, Paris, 1877 (1854), p. 283.

[2] Louis Gonse, 'Eugène Fromentin', *Gazette des Beaux-Arts*, January 1880, pp. 53–4.

EUGENE FROMENTIN

20 TAILORS IN FRONT OF THE MOSQUE (Tailleurs devant la mosquée) c.1850s

Oil on canvas 65 x 55 cm
Musée National des Arts d'Afrique et d'Océanie, Paris

Fromentin's intimate scene probably records a memory of the 'industries with next to no tools'[1] that he found being practised in the old quarters of Algiers in 1852, but its descriptive element is mitigated by references to French romantic and Dutch sources typical of mid-19th-century eclecticism.

The Dutch genre masters, rediscovered in France with the rise of Realism in the 1840s, furnished Fromentin with his humble subject and with his discrete composition, which leads from a tiled foreground to a set of subdivided spaces and shady inner rooms. 'We live in the picture, we walk about in it, we look into its depths.'[2] The empathetic response to the Dutch school recorded in *The Masters of Past Time* is expressed with equal candour by a painting such as this, despite its substitution of eastern colour for bourgeois sobriety.

The exotic character of Fromentin's image also reveals his knowledge of earlier art, specifically that of Delacroix. The repeated opposition of red and green promotes a luminosity which looks back to the palette of the *Women of Algiers* (fig. 5), while the fluttering draperies swirl and ruffle in incongruous baroque rhythms derived from Delacroix's history paintings.

Originality is present in Fromentin's refined application of such decorative touches as the intricate patterning of the faience tiles in the foreground and of the striped cloth to the right, which indicate the delicate imprint left on the painter's imagination by his direct experience of his subject.   PR

[1] Eugène Fromentin, *Une Année dans le Sahel*, Plon, Paris, 1877, p. 26.

[2] Eugène Fromentin, *The Masters of Past Time*, trans. A. Boyle, Phaidon, Oxford, 1981, p. 103.

LEON BELLY

21 GAZELLE HUNT (La Chasse à la gazelle) 1857

Oil on canvas 79 x 145 cm
Private collection

The *Gazelle hunt* was probably motivated by Belly's excursion into the Sinai desert in the spring of 1856, in the company of the painter Narcisse Berchère:

> *From the Wells of Moses we've followed a large plain, partly of sand, partly covered with large pebbles...On the left in the far distance, a chain of low, harsh, fractured mountains. This vast landscape, arid and abandoned, is always of the suavest colour; it seems that nature, so severe here and offering nothing that can refresh the senses, has been provided by way of compensation with the most seductive qualities of light and colour.*[1]

Belly found the Sinai Arabs 'truly sensitive to the beauty of nature – their physiognomies become fine and intelligent when one speaks to them of it'.[2] His picture offers a lyric conception of Arab life. The leading figure is clearly a man of high standing; apparently unarmed, he gives an easy gesture of command to the footman managing his salukis, which strain after the quarry visible in the distance. A desert breeze stirs the camel-riders' fine garments while, just below the ridge, a clutch of men struggling with horses is visible. This unorthodox composition, with its frieze-like figures silhouetted against a blue sky, has a freshness of gesture and vividness of lights and darks that improves on the standard Fromentin hunt.   RB

[1] Letter of 30 April 1856 to his mother, quoted in Conrad de Mandach, 'Léon Belly (1827–1877)', *Gazette des Beaux-Arts*, 4th series, vol. 9, February 1913, p. 144.

[2] ibid.

LEON BELLY

22 WATERBUFFALOES BATHING IN THE NILE 1861

Oil on canvas 99.2 x 143 cm
The Najd Collection, courtesy of the Mathaf Gallery, London

[1] Caroline Juler, *Najd Collection of Orientalist Paintings*, Manara, London, 1991, p. 20.

[2] Letter of 1 April 1856, in Conrad de Mandach, 'Léon Belly (1827–1877)', *Gazette des Beaux-Arts*, 4th series, vol. 9, February 1913, p. 146.

[3] Letters of 27 February and 1 April 1856, cited in Mandach, pp. 144, 145.

[4] See e.g. Léonce Bénédite, 'Exposition rétrospective: Belly (Léon)', *Société des Peintres Orientalistes Français*, 5th exh. cat., Galeries Durand-Ruel, Paris, 1898, pp. 17–18.

This scene of peaceful animal husbandry on the banks of the Nile is set near the village of Giza, site of the Great Pyramids. The sober Belly literally turned his back on antiquity and assimilated Egypt to the rural landscapes around Barbizon (where he had studied with the animal painter Troyon and was befriended by Rousseau and Millet). As was their practice, Belly applied an intensive scrutiny to this one area, calling it 'his "quartier général" and depict[ing] its stark terrain of tall palms, mud flats and winding streams many times'.[1]

Belly wrote of Giza: 'this country is admirable in the sense that one finds here in all their simplicity the basic elements of earth, water and air. Interesting incidents are distributed with a sobriety which gives them an accent of astonishing force…'.[2] Belly's great powers of observation were particularly attuned to the Egyptian light, which he described as being 'grey during the heat of the day', with brilliant skies that were 'colourless due to an excess of light'.[3] In the 1890s his supporter Léonce Bénédite went on to argue that Belly's investigations of light in the exotic climate had paved the way for those of the Impressionists in France.[4]   RB

RICHARD DADD

23 CARAVAN HALTED BY THE SEA SHORE 1843

Oil on canvas 90.2 x 151.1 cm
Private collection*

This work was first exhibited at the Liverpool Academy in 1843, as *Group of water carriers, men and camels, at a spring on the sea shore at Fortuna, near Mt Carmel, Syria*.[1] Dadd passed through Fortuna (Dor) with his patron, Sir Thomas Phillips, some time between the 13th and 20th of November 1842. He recorded the event in a letter to his friend W. P. Frith, writing from the steamer *Hecate* lying off Jaffa:

> *The water carriers (women) are very capital subjects for the brush; and they rush along with great celerity under pitchers of water of no small size…indeed you would have become perfectly rabid at the sight of their groups round the wells on the seashore, with, perhaps, a string of camels grunting and growling, the whole recommended to you by the overture of the sea roaring in.*[2]

Dadd's description of the scene as one of noise and confusion is very different from the effect of his meticulously arranged picture: solemn figures and camels spread across the crescent of shoreline in static pyramidal groups, delineated with the impact of a set of cut-out figures. However, Dadd has used an unusual combination of corals, greens, blues, sandy brown and yellows to soften this effect, imparting a subdued and dreamy atmosphere to the picture. Disparities in scale and focus add to the surreal effect of the receding water-carriers, shaped like minarets against a pale sky, and the turban-clad figures staring out of the picture with an air of uneasy watchfulness. Contemporary reviewers praised the painting when it was first shown: 'admirable in design…a work of rare and singular merit'.[3] It is the only known oil painting to have been completed by the artist between his return from the East and the patricide he committed in the autumn of 1843. The painting once belonged to Franz Ferdinand of Austria and was sold in Vienna after his assassination in 1914.[4]   UP

[1] See 'Catalogue. No. 91. Caravan Halted by the Sea Shore', in Patricia Allderidge, *The Late Richard Dadd*, exh. cat., Tate, London, 1974, p. 77.

[2] Dadd letter, 26 November 1842, in W. P. Frith, *My Autobiography and Reminiscences*, London, 1888, vol. 3, pp. 186–7.

[3] *Art Union*, October 1843, quoted in Allderidge, p. 77.

[4] Information from the Mathaf Gallery, London.

JOHN FREDERICK LEWIS

24 THE HHAREEM 1849 (EXH. RA 1850)

Watercolour and body colour 88.6 x 133 cm
Private collection*

The hhareem, the most important harem painting executed by Lewis, has a fascinating history. Before 1978, the small version of this painting (cat. 25), now held in the Victoria and Albert Museum, was thought to be the original painting cut down. In 1978 Rosemary Treble disproved this assumption when she discovered a photograph of the original, reproduced in the 1908 catalogue of the Franco-British Exhibition, which revealed subtle differences between the two versions.[1] After 1909 the painting was purchased by the great Japanese art collector, Kojiro Matsukata. It was then held by the 15-Bank from 1927 to 1928, and from there went into a private collection before going to its current owners.[2] This exhibition marks the first time this magnificent painting has been exhibited with the version from the Victoria and Albert Museum.

The central narrative of *The hhareem* is the spectacle of an Abyssinian slave being introduced into the harem of a Mameluke bey.[3] Poised like a magician revealing his latest astonishing trick, a black guardian (a eunuch) unveils the slave, who holds onto the last piece of her drapery in modest recoil. On the left the master of the harem, surrounded by his three wives, is transfixed by the spectacle and oblivious to the responses of the others in the room. This scene was no doubt intended to evoke both voyeuristic pleasure in the male viewer and perhaps also some measure of sympathy for the humiliation of the new slave. In this painting the figures are grouped in a double pyramidal structure. In the group on the right, the eunuch and drapery form a backdrop behind the Abyssinian slave, making her a central focus in the composition, while the

[1] Rosemary Treble, *Great Victorian Pictures and their Paths to Fame*, Fine Arts Council, London, 1978, pp. 51–2. Treble notes the subtle differences between the original and the copied fragment. *Souvenir of the Fine Art Section, Franco-British Exhibition*, 1908, comp. Isidore Spielmann, illus. *The Harem of a Bey*, no. 471, adjacent to p. 172.

eunuch's amused glance redirects our attention back to the bey on the left as we await his decision. Lewis has cleverly ordered the scene by using these devices to create two central focal points that echo the painting's narrative. The veiled woman seated in the background, a fellah, is the slave dealer's wife.[4] Her presence reminds the viewer of the prohibitions of the harem: the slave dealer cannot enter this space, consequently his wife is there in his place, but because she is another man's wife she must remain veiled in front of the master of this harem.

The painting offers the viewer a variety of pleasures, the foremost being the spectacle of the languid harem women. Assuming that these pleasures were for the male spectator, the critic for the *Illustrated London News* wrote: 'This is a marvellous picture, such as men love to linger around, but such as women, we observed, pass rapidly by'.[5] Lewis's extraordinary skill in the watercolour medium provides numerous other visual and tactile pleasures. In a further display of his virtuosity Lewis has created wonderful effects of dappled light which augment the complex patterns of fabrics and carpets and highlight the varied textures, evident for instance where the shadow of the *mashrabiyya* or lattice window falls across the fur of the gazelle in the foreground right, and where it forms geometric patterns across the moiré skirt of the gown worn by the Circassian wife. There is also some astonishingly elaborate work where the mosque is seen through the lattice in the background.

When exhibited at the Old Watercolour Society in 1850 this painting received an exuberant response from the British art critics.[6] They were delighted at what appeared to them to be an ethnographically accurate painting which catered to a western fantasy of the harem while giving 'no offence to Western feelings of decorum'.[7] Lewis's authority as an Orientalist was established by reference to his ten years of living in Cairo. What this claim for the ethnographic realism of this painting overlooks is that Lewis would never have had access to harems. His painting is an amalgam of studies of Cairene domestic interiors (it is thought to be a study of Lewis's own house in the Ezbekiya district), studio props, costumes, vases and other objects. Perhaps he also relied on the account of harem visits by women travellers, whose published diaries were numerous, or his wife, Marion, who as a woman could have visited harems in Cairo. Lewis often used his wife as a model for his harem paintings and may well have done so in this instance. Commenting on the third wife in *The hhareem*, the *Athenaeum* critic wrote: 'she is evidently a study from an Englishwoman, an introduction which injures the uniformity of the composition'.[8] This critic implies that the exoticism of the scene has been disrupted with this reminder that the painting is a studio reconstruction. The critic's concern might also be prompted by the sense that Victorian propriety has been offended by the suggestion of a respectable British woman as the inhabitant of a harem.   MR

[2] I would like to thank Satoko Asada for translating this information about the painting's history in Japan from the catalogue of *The Old Matsukata Collection*, 1989, cat. no. 8, p. 53. (The painting was exhibited in 'The First Exhibition of the Matsukata Collection', Tokyo, 1928, no. 53 and 'The Sixth Exhibition of the Matsukata Collection, Tokyo, 1934, no. 80.)

[3] The ethnic ascriptions of the figures in this painting are drawn from Lewis's detailed account of the painting in the *Royal Scottish Academy Catalogue of the 27th Exhibition*, 1853, no. 494.

[4] Lewis wrote: 'The Girl who is being unveiled by the black guardian, is also upper country, and brought into the Hhareem by the wife of the slave owner who is a fellah, and is seated in the middle distance, habited in the out-door dress of the common people'. *Royal Scottish Academy Catalogue of the 27th Exhibition*, 1853, no. 494.

[5] *Illustrated London News*, 4 May 1850, pp. 299–300.

[6] 'On the whole we look on this drawing as one of the most remarkable productions of this age of English Art, and in all probability calculated to open up a new field for emulation', *Athenaeum*, no. 1175, 4 May 1850, p.480.

[7] *Athenaeum*, no. 1175, 4 May 1850, p. 480.

[8] ibid.

JOHN FREDERICK LEWIS

25 THE HHAREEM c. 1850

Watercolour and body colour 47 x 67.3 cm
The Board of Trustees of the Victoria and Albert Museum

This painting is a later version of the lower left section of Lewis's famous painting *The hhareem* of 1849 (cat. 24). The Abyssinian slave and her black guardian, who create the central drama in the earlier painting, have been omitted in this later work (the only traces of their presence being the drapery and hand of the eunuch on the extreme right). What assumes central focus is the Turkish bey and his three wives, whose lively facial expressions indicate their responses to the (now absent) newcomer. While the master is evidently transfixed by the sight of the new slave, the two older wives (Georgian and Circassian) nearest him convey a wary appraisal of the new slave which suggests their apprehensions at a potential rival. Lewis informs us that the Georgian woman at the top of this grouping is the 'Sit el Gebir',[1] or ruling lady of the harem, whose superior position in the household hierarchy has been secured because her child, nestled at her feet, is the master's eldest son. Below these two is the third wife, a Greek woman, whose more innocent look suggests that she too may be a recent introduction (perhaps a victim of the jealousies and intrigues of the others). This painting affirms stereotypical western notions about the rivalry among women and the power imbalances of the polygamous family structure. It is uncertain whether or not this version has been cut down;[2] what seems to favour such a theory is the fact that the meaning of the entire scene is premised on the action that is absent – the unveiling of the new slave.   MR

[1] *Royal Scottish Academy Catalogue of the 27th Exhibition*, 1853.

[2] Charles Newton, Curator at the Victoria and Albert Museum, notes that all the edges of this painting have been cut with a knife (personal communication).

JOHN FREDERICK LEWIS

26 STUDY FOR 'THE HAREM' c. 1850

Pencil and watercolour 35.7 x 49.3 cm
National Gallery of Victoria, Melbourne. Bequeathed by Mrs Lewis 1908

Fig. 28
JOHN FREDERICK
LEWIS
The harem n.d.
oil on panel
88.9 x 111.8 cm
Birmingham City
Museums and Art
Gallery

This sketch is a study for *The harem*, held by Birmingham City Museum and Art Gallery.[1] In contrast to *An eastern beauty* (cat. 27), which is one of Lewis's many preliminary single-figure sketches, *Study for 'The harem'* is a rare drawing which reveals Lewis's compositional working processes. Unlike the characteristic precision of the final painting, the sketch indicates its figures in a provisional manner, suggesting that Lewis was experimenting with their placement. In the final painting Lewis dropped the oval format suggested by this sketch and shifted a number of the female figures so that they are more clearly positioned in line with the architectural planes of the room – a change which lends a greater sense of order to the final painting. For example, in the finished work the servant holding the mirror is moved backwards so that her mirror is in line with the framing edge of the carved wall panel, and her back in line with the edge of the wall behind. Similarly, the standing woman behind her has been turned so as to be parallel with that wall, and the upright woman on the divan to the right has been moved in line with the very corner of the recessed window.

This watercolour sketch was donated to the National Gallery of Victoria in 1907 by the executrix of Marion Lewis, Lewis's wife. After her death a number of Lewis's sketches were donated to Cape Town, Ottawa, New Zealand and Australia (Sydney, Adelaide and Perth).   MR

[1] The precise dating of the final painting is uncertain, but it is likely to be the early to mid-1860s. See Harley Preston, 'The harem – painting behind the scenes', *Art Bulletin of Victoria*, no. 28, 1987, p. 88.

JOHN FREDERICK LEWIS

27 AN EASTERN BEAUTY before 1851

Watercolour on paper 38.1 x 33 cm
Peter Nahum at The Leicester Galleries, London

In this delightful sketch Lewis's delicate lines and the washes of colour lend a refined air to the young woman who is depicted seated cross-legged on a divan. As is characteristic of Lewis's preliminary sketches of women, attention is paid to the face, costume and upper body, while hands and feet are omitted. This sketch is most likely one of the numerous sketches of women Lewis made in Cairo and is typical of the sketches that were part of the extensive archive Lewis brought back to England in 1851. This exotic archive (which included costumes, photographs, porcelain objects, fezzes, tarbooshes, Arabic musical instruments and even Turkish scimitars) provided the inspiration for the Orientalist tableaux Lewis was to produce for the rest of his career.[1]

Given the pervasive social constraints, Lewis's subjects were not in fact the respectable Islamic harem women of Cairo, but more likely women from the fringes of society. Unfortunately, there are no extant accounts of Lewis's strategies for engaging models, but William Holman Hunt describes how he resorted to finding models in a local brothel in Cairo in 1854. One of the problems Hunt encountered was the Moslem prohibition against creating a human likeness, which he dismissed as a 'stupid superstition'.[2] MR

[1] The contents of his studio collection are given in the listings of the posthumous sale held at Christie's on 7 May 1877. See Major-General Michael Lewis, *John Frederick Lewis R.A. 1805–1876*, F. Lewis Publishers, Leigh-on-Sea, 1978, pp. 41, 50.

[2] Diana Holman Hunt, *My Grandfather: His Wives and Loves*, Hamish Hamilton, London, 1969, p. 131.

JOHN FREDERICK LEWIS

28 LIFE IN THE HAREM, CAIRO 1858

Watercolour and body colour 60.7 x 47.7 cm
The Board of Trustees of the Victoria and Albert Museum

In contrast to the high drama and busy narrative of Lewis's *The hhareem*, *Life in the harem, Cairo* is a quiet, intimate harem painting. Resting on a divan, the harem woman has her eyes closed in a state of reverie, while her hand gently holds a posy of flowers that rests on her lap. The Victorian audience for this painting was familiar with the idea that in eastern harems nosegays, or posies, were used to communicate illicit messages; thus the posy here would suggest that the young woman is dreaming of a lover outside the harem.[1] Her reverie is about to be disturbed by the entry into the room of a woman carrying a tray of refreshments on which are two porcelain coffee cups and two rosewater flasks or sweetmeat containers.[2] The woman is accompanied by a young black servant boy. The divan extends beyond the lower edge of the painting, while the other end (complete with peacock-feather fan) is reflected in the mirror, a pictorial device which inscribes the space in front of this scene into the work. Emphasis on the space in front of the painting – the viewer's position – is further reinforced by the young woman entering with refreshments who looks beyond the seated woman with a welcoming smile. The combined effect of this welcoming smile and mirror device creates an intimacy between the viewer and the harem scene, as the viewer is invited to imagine that he is seated on the vacant end of the divan.   MR

[1] Joan Del Plato, 'From slave market to paradise: The harem pictures of John Frederick Lewis and their traditions', PhD thesis, University of California, Los Angeles (UMI, Ann Arbor), 1987, p. 248.

[2] Charles Newton, Curator at the Victoria and Albert Museum, has made these precise observations about the objects on the tray (personal communication).

JOHN FREDERICK LEWIS

29 THE CARAVAN AT EDFOU c. 1861

Watercolour 17.5 x 45 cm
Pan Arabian Co., courtesy Peter Nahum at The Leicester Galleries, London

In 1850 the artist John Frederick Lewis made an excursion into Upper Egypt, sketching camels and desert scenes along the way. This watercolour depicting a caravan at Edfou relates to that journey and also to a larger oil version of the same subject which Lewis exhibited at the Royal Academy in 1861, titled *Edfou, Upper Egypt* (Tate Gallery, London). Lewis, unlike English topographical watercolourists such as David Roberts, rarely included views of ancient monuments in his Egyptian work. However, in the 19th century the temple at Edfou was considered one of the most beautiful monuments on the Nile. The largest temple erected by the Ptolemies, it was also one of the best preserved, dating from 237 BC to 57 BC. In depicting the site, Lewis's panoramically horizontal composition has been focused around three architectural elements representing the ancient, modern and medieval world respectively. From left to right, he juxtaposes the heavy sloping masonry of the pylon gate and half-buried colonnades of the temple of Horus against the centrally placed curve and counter-curve of the lighter tent structure in the Bedouin encampment, and balances it with the distant mosque and minaret rising out of the flat plain, bisected by the blue horizontal of the river Nile.

The fresh, bright colours, minutely realised effects of light, heat and distance, as well as the saddled camels, echo the oil painting he exhibited in 1859, entitled *Waiting for the ferry boat*.[1] In his 1859 *Academy Notes*, Ruskin criticised that picture, asking:

> if we must *live in the East, is no landscape ever visible but a dead level of mud raised two feet above a slow stream?...The Sphinx, and the temples, and the hieroglyphics...and everything that we want to know about... – shall we never have any of these?*[2]

Perhaps it was in answer to Ruskin's criticism that Lewis depicted this different landscape at Edfou, combining motifs of architectural and historical interest with the endless sunburnt sands.   UP

[1] See Major-General Michael Lewis, *John Frederick Lewis R.A 1805–1876*, F. Lewis Publishers, Leigh-on-Sea, 1978, p. 38.

[2] Ruskin, quoted by Richard Green, *John Frederick Lewis R.A. 1805–1876*, exh. cat., Laing Art Gallery, Newcastle-upon-Tyne, 1971, p. 31.

JOHN FREDERICK LEWIS

30 STUDY FOR 'THE HOSH (COURTYARD) OF THE COPTIC PATRIARCH'S HOUSE IN CAIRO' c. 1864

Oil on wood 36.9 x 35.6 cm
Tate Gallery, London. Purchased 1900

In this sunny courtyard scene Lewis connects two of the key themes that were to inspire him throughout his career – the desert life of the Bedouin people and domestic life in Cairo. In the mid-ground a Bedouin messenger waits patiently near his camels while the Coptic Patriarch in the shade of the covered recess dictates to his secretary letters which the messenger is to convey to a desert convent. The enormous acacia tree that forms a canopy over the crowded courtyard provides the opportunity for Lewis to explore the effects of dappled shadow on the paving in the mid-ground, while his fascination with reflective surfaces is evident in the glassy pond reflecting its own magnificent tiled edge. This delightful painting is animated by a clever illusionistic depiction of birds in various stages of flight dotted across the front of the picture plane. It is an extraordinarily busy work, which one critic described as crowded with 'materials for twenty pictures',[1] while another asserted that the 'multiplicity of details...have a bewildering effect'.[2] By contrast, the critic for *The Times* provides a delightful interpretation of the auditory effects of this painting: 'pigeons flutter and coo, and ducks dabble and quack, and goats nibble and bask and baa, and slave girls chatter, and the old Patriarch goes droning on at his dictation through all'.[3]

The Coptic Church is one of the most ancient branches of Christian belief. In 1849 Robert Curzon wrote that 'The Copts look to their patriarch as the chief of their nation'.[4] The setting for this painting has been identified as the courtyard of the painter's own house in the Ezbekiya district of Cairo, which may have been owned by the Patriarch himself.[5]   MR

1 *Art Journal*, 1864, p. 166.
2 *Illustrated London News*, 7 May 1864, p. 454.
3 *The Times*, 30 April 1864, p. 14.
4 Robert Curzon, *Visits to the Monasteries in the Levant*, Century Travellers, London, 1983 (1849), p. 117.
5 MaryAnn Stevens (ed.), *The Orientalists: Delacroix to Matisse*, exh. cat., Royal Academy of Arts, London, 1984, p. 205. Edward Lane noted that the Coptic Patriarch owned a considerable number of houses in Cairo; Edward W. Lane, *The Manners and Customs of the Modern Egyptians*, ed. E. Rhys, J. M. Dent, London & E. P. Dutton, New York, 1908 (1836), p. 539.

JOHN FREDERICK LEWIS

31 INDOOR GOSSIP, CAIRO 1873

Oil on panel 30.5 x 20.3 cm
The Whitworth Art Gallery, The University of Manchester

Lewis portrays a familiar western stereotype of feminine vanity in this harem painting where a young woman adjusts her earring in front of a mirror while conversing with her seated companion. Lewis imbues the scene with an element of intrigue by introducing into the painting a woman who listens to their conversation from an adjoining room – indicated by the slither of space on the left side; perhaps this eavesdropper will report their conversation to the master of the harem. As is so often the case in Lewis's work, this element, which changes the painting's meaning, is not immediately evident. The painting was exhibited at the Royal Academy summer exhibition in 1874 with a companion painting, *Outdoor gossip, Cairo*, which depicts three men conversing in an open doorway near a small barred window behind which, barely visible, are women in a harem, again a device to appeal to the western viewer's curiosity about the seclusion of women in Islamic cultures.

The intense colouring of the women's brocaded fabrics and the complex patterning created where the shadow of the *mashra-biyya* or lattice window falls on the wall and fabrics lends a jewel-like quality to *Indoor gossip*, an effect intensified by the mirror reflection of the lattice shadow and woman's profile. Such mirror effects were favoured in Lewis's later intimate harem paintings.

Fig. 29
JOHN FREDERICK LEWIS
Outdoor gossip, Cairo
1873
Private collection

Response to this painting varied. Endorsing the ethnographic accuracy of the range of Orientalist paintings Lewis exhibited in 1874, the critic for the *Illustrated London News* wrote that they are 'wonderful as illustrations of Cairene life, manners, habits, costumes and architecture in a thousand minutiae'.[1] In contrast, the *Athenaeum* critic described the costumed figures in *Indoor gossip* as the product of 'the apparently inexhaustible wardrobe of the artist's *atelier*' and stated, 'we wonder he does not tire of painting these subjects, these hackneyed materials. His work here is but exquisitely brilliant mannerism'.[2]   MR

[1] *Illustrated London News*, 9 May 1874, p. 446.

[2] *Athenaeum*, 30 May 1874, p. 739.

HENRIETTE BROWNE (MME JULES DE SAUX)

32 THE BUDGERIGAR (La Perruche) 1875

Oil on canvas   147.4 x 91.5 cm
Russell-Cotes Art Gallery and Museum, Bournemouth

In *The budgerigar*, exhibited at the Paris Salon of 1875, Henriette Browne depicts a woman in eastern costume gently holding a bamboo stick on which an exotic bird is perched with wings spread as if it has just alighted. Behind her on the left, settled on a copper bowl, are two other exotic birds. In western harem paintings birds were popular icons often symbolising female sexuality, however such symbolism is muted in this painting, in which the birds function as an elegant ornament for this respectable lady. With an emphasis on modesty and gentility, Browne's woman has little in common with the harem paintings by her French male counterparts – Gérôme, Débat-Ponsan or Ingres. The emphasis on the effects of light which highlights the magnificent sheen of the yellow fabric of the woman's dress in this painting is reminiscent of Lewis's fascination with exotic fabrics in his harem paintings. Lewis's *Caged doves* of 1864 is a thematically analogous painting with its focus on a solitary woman and her harem pet. However Browne's painting is more oblique in its meaning than the obvious symbolism of Lewis's painting, which suggests that the harem interior is a gilded cage for both woman and bird. Browne has chosen an unusual setting for this work, evidently a studio painting. *The budgerigar* is intriguing because despite the Oriental carpet and bowl in this work there are only a few of the usual accoutrements that would confirm it as a harem painting, and the fringed fabric draped behind gives little information of the location of this scene. Browne's attention to the facial features of the woman aligns her painting with the portrait tradition, however the title gives no indication of the sitter's identity.   MR

WALTER CHARLES HORSLEY

33 GREAT BRITAIN IN EGYPT, 1886—1887

Oil on canvas 122.5 x 154.9 cm
The Art Gallery of New South Wales, Sydney. Purchased 1889

In 1875, having recently completed his training at the Royal Academy Schools, Walter Charles Horsley left England for India, travelling via Turkey. He was employed by the London *Graphic* as one of its special artists to record the visit to India of HRH the Prince of Wales. While there he was also commissioned by the Nawab of Bahawalpour to paint a series of sporting portraits. Three years later he travelled to Cairo. Inspired by that journey, *Great Britain in Egypt, 1886* was first shown at the London Royal Academy in 1887 with two other Cairo subjects by Horsley. It was singled out and used to illustrate the *Art Journal* review of the exhibition at Burlington House: 'No. 1047, *Great Britain in Egypt, 1886*, is as good a thing as Mr. Walter Horsley has done for some time'.[1]

Horsley enjoyed painting anecdotal details designed to amuse or interest his European audience, as in this Kiplingesque depiction of the British in Egypt. Representing the divergent cultures acting out an Imperial master–servant relationship, Horsley played on the contrast between the military correctness of the soldiers of the Empire and the relaxed informality of the indigenous civilian populace, who appear to regard them with some bemusement as imported curiosities. Horsley was a patriot, but not above extracting some amusement from the spectacle of these stalwart English soldiers imperturbably 'taking tea', their delicate complexions at risk from the punishing heat of a foreign sun. However, the two off-duty soldiers in 'walking out dress'– a non-commissioned officer from a Scottish regiment and a regular of the York and Lancaster Regiment – also seemed designed to remind his audience of much-publicised victories in the 1882 Egyptian campaign (such as the Battle of Tel-el-Kebir depicted by Alphonse de Neuville and Lady Elizabeth Butler, and in the illustrated pages of the *Graphic*).[2] Perhaps it was the Imperial theme that prompted Horsley to send this particular picture to Melbourne for the Centennial International Exhibition in 1888, marking the hundredth anniversary of British settlement in Australia. The work was purchased from this exhibition and entered the then National Art Gallery of New South Wales permanent collection in 1889.[3]   UP

[1] *Art Journal* (London), vol. 5, 1887, pp. 247, 279.

[2] See P. Harrington, *British Artists and War*, Greenhill Books, London, 1993, pp. 211–17. He argues that the rebellion in the Sudan was of less interest to the British public than the cost of garrisoning Egypt, and notes that W.C. Horsley and J. E. Hodgson both painted several scenes relating to the British occupation of Egypt. Horsley's included *A friendly power in Egypt* and Hodgson's, *Off duty* and *Far from home*, in which both artists concentrated on everyday scenes in the life of the garrison's soldiers rather than battle heroics.

[3] See Renée Free, *Art Gallery of New South Wales Catalogue of British Paintings*, Art Gallery of New South Wales, Sydney, n.d. (1987), p. 90.

EDWARD POYNTER

34 THE VISIT OF THE QUEEN OF SHEBA TO KING SOLOMON 1890

Oil on canvas   234.5 x 350.5 cm
The Art Gallery of New South Wales, Sydney. Purchased 1892*

When this great picture, *The visit of the Queen of Sheba to King Solomon*, was first exhibited in London in 1890 it was immediately acclaimed by the critics as the largest and most important of Poynter's later career. The grandiose subject matter was in keeping with the ambitious size of the painting, for it illustrated the Old Testament story of the Queen of Sheba's visit to the fabled court of King Solomon, a choice which allowed the artist to demonstrate his scholarly research as well as his technical skill. As one contemporary writer observed: 'the subject is above all things pictorial, and modern archaeology has at least given scope for a great deal of plausible guessing as to what "Solomon in all his glory" was really like'.[1]

The painting depicts the sumptuous reception hall of the king, who receives his royal visitor amid a throng of richly attired courtiers, wives, musicians and servants. The Bible recounts that 'when the Queen of Sheba heard of the fame of Solomon...she came to test him with hard questions'.[2] Her bold confrontation with the great Solomon has been variously interpreted by later Jewish, Christian and Islamic writers,[3] and much recent scholarship has focused on the legendary queen's symbolic challenge to the 'time-honoured rules of gender'.[4] Poynter, however, chose to illustrate the moment of the king's triumph: Solomon has answered 'all her questions' and the overwhelming impact on the queen of:

all the wisdom of Solomon, the house that he had built, the food of his table, the seating of his officials and the attendance of his servants, their clothing, his cupbearers, and his burnt offerings...[ensured] there was no more spirit in her.[5]

In this recreation of the biblical scene, the splendour and masculine authority of the Jewish kingdom is deliberately contrasted against the exotic feminine allure of the 'queen of the South'.[6] Walter Armstrong's pamphlet on the painting, written to accompany the London exhibition, makes clear this distinction:

Mr Poynter has dressed the Jewish king and his servants in comparatively quiet colours, and for jewels has given them ornaments of gold and enamel, similar to those found in Pharaonic tombs. On the other hand, [Queen] Balkis herself blazes with gems. Her costume, if costume we can call it, resembles that of a Hindoo goddess...Behind the queen stands her black chamberlain; and she is attended by two girl slaves holding fans, the universal emblem of royalty in the East...Nearer the frame come more Ethiopians kneeling, and bearing specimens only of the presents which she brought with her...All these blaze with barbaric colour, suggestive of the lowest civilization of Sheba.[7]

The youthful queen's appearance caused some discussion when the picture was first exhibited, with several writers commenting on her eastern exoticism, in particular her 'Indian type of olive beauty', her semi-nudity (with 'barbaric gems...strewn about her naked arms and bosom') and the lotus flowers in her hand.[8] These lengthy reviews also testify to the fact that Poynter's choice of subject matter was uncommon in British painting of this period. One possible source for the artist may have been his French master, Charles Gleyre (1806–74), who had executed a painting entitled *La Reine de Saba* in 1838–39.[9] Certainly, the story of the Queen of Sheba was immensely popular with the French Romantics, and Poynter's opulent figure could reflect the influence of

works such as Flaubert's *La Tentation de saint Antoine* (1856–57, 1874) and Gounod's opera *La Reine de Saba* (1862), which transformed the biblical figure into an Oriental *femme fatale*.[10]

Contemporary critical attention also focused on the accuracy of the artist's reconstruction of Solomon's palace, with its extraordinary wealth of architectural detail. The biblical text only described certain key features: the costly stone foundations, the pillars and beams made of cedar from Lebanon, the use of gold and brass as decoration, and the king's 'great throne of ivory', with its six steps flanked by twelve lions.[11] For additional information, Poynter turned to recent archaeological discoveries in Syria, Assyria and Persia, an approach which was in keeping with the scholarship of the day, which argued that authentic evidence of the biblical past could be sought in these excavations. Thus, when considering the 'House of Solomon', the contemporary architectural theorist, James Fergusson, unhesitatingly declared: 'we shall find that the buildings at Persepolis and Nineveh throw very considerable light on the arrangements of that palace'.[12]

Poynter clearly shared these views: his picture's vivid architectural ornament is based on Assyrian and Persian examples; the twelve large golden lions and smaller lion 'carpet weights' are modelled on examples in the British Museum that were excavated at Nimrud by the great archaeologist (and friend of Poynter) A. H. Layard.[13] Other sources include ancient Egyptian musical instruments and a magnificent peacock-shaped Persian incense burner. However, the artist was also willing to supplement historical accuracy with his own well-informed imagination; thus the ornate throne and elaborate

Fig. 30
EDWARD POYNTER
*Study for the head of
the Queen of Sheba*
late 1880s
black and white
chalk on buff paper
22.5 x 19.5 cm
The Art Gallery
of New South Wales,
Sydney

costumes are from his own designs. As one modern scholar, Patrick Conner, has argued, it is this eclectic mix of art and archaeology that creates such a powerful distillation of 'all that was most striking and characteristic in an alien civilization'.[14]

Poynter began the picture in 1883, but the sheer size of the canvas, combined with his painstaking working methods, resulted in it taking over six years to complete. In line with his academic training, the artist undertook numerous preliminary drawings for the figures, drapery and accessories – over seventy are recorded – as well as studies of the entire composition, including a highly finished oil sketch.[15] Several critics remarked that Poynter even had a small architectural model of the palace, 'complete in every detail', made to scale, which allowed him to 'paint with certainty the effects of light and reflection, complicated as they were by the great complexity of the crowd of figures which filled the picture'.[16] The painting was finally exhibited in 1890 at Thomas McLean's Gallery in the Haymarket, in a somewhat unfinished state. It subsequently went on a tour of the provinces, before returning to London in 1892, where it was purchased by the National Art Gallery of New South Wales, Sydney.

While praised as 'one of the most elaborate pictures of its class ever painted',[17] some writers described Poynter's *Queen of Sheba* as 'a return to his earlier dramatic spirit'.[18] This referred to the fact that the artist first began painting imaginative reconstructions of the ancient world in the 1860s. Indeed, Poynter and Alma-Tadema were generally acknowledged as the leaders of the new trend for historical paintings in Egyptian or Graeco-Roman settings. This taste for the material reality of antiquity was, of course, closely related to the demand for a more 'truthful' kind of Orientalist biblical painting – one which evoked the ancient Near East by means of geographically accurate locations, the correct racial types and authentic accessories.[19] Poynter's *oeuvre* encompassed both these subjects although, by the 1890s, a grand Old Testament spectacle such as *The visit of the Queen of Sheba to King Solomon* may have seemed a little old-fashioned. Certainly this is suggested by the mixed reviews which greeted the picture's arrival in New South Wales.[20]

The artist himself regarded the painting very highly, and sought – unsuccessfully – to have the work exhibited at the 1893 International Exhibition in Chicago. It was subsequently selected by Poynter 'as the one by which he wished to be represented' at the London Guildhall's exhibition of living artists in 1900.[21] Nevertheless, this major painting remained the least appreciated of Poynter's late works, its antipodean location meaning that it was chiefly known to the British public through engravings.[22] But Britain's loss was Australia's gain, as the artist's nephew, Malcolm Bell, declared: 'the splendid *Queen of Sheba's Visit to King Solomon*...to England's irreparable loss, has gone to far-away Sidney [sic] to set a noble example of imaginative and technical achievement before the artists of Australia'.[23]   AI

1 'Mr Poynter's 'Queen of Sheba', *The Times,* 17 May 1890, p. 17.

2 I Kings 10: 1.

3 For an excellent survey of the subject see J. B. Pritchard (ed.), *Solomon and Sheba,* Phaidon, London, 1974.

4 J. Lassner, *Demonizing the Queen of Sheba,* University of Chicago Press, 1993, p. 1; see also M. Warner, *From the Beast to the Blonde,* Chatto & Windus, London, 1994, pp. 97–146.

5 I Kings 10: 4–5.

6 In the New Testament, the Queen of Sheba is not mentioned by name, but as 'The queen of the South… [who] came from the ends of the earth to hear the wisdom of Solomon' (Matthew 12: 42). She is known as Bilqis in Islamic writings, and Queen Balkis in later Christian texts; Pritchard, pp. 99, 139.

7 *Note by W. Armstrong on the Meeting of Solomon and the Queen of Sheba by Edward J. Poynter,* London, 1890, p. 3; subsequently printed by Charles Potter, Government Printer, Sydney, 1892.

8 *Saturday Review,* 21 June 1890, p. 768; see also *Athenaeum,* 31 May 1890, p. 710; *The Times,* 17 May 1890, p. 17.

9 C. Gleyre, *La Reine de Saba,* oil on canvas, 54 x 43 cm, c. 1838–39, Musée cantonel des Beaux-Arts, Lausanne. This source first suggested by Renée Free in *Victorian Olympians,* exh. cat., Art Gallery of New South Wales, Sydney, 1975, p. 25.

10 See T. Reff, 'Images of Flaubert's Queen of Sheba in later nineteenth century art', in *The Artist and the Writer in France: Essays in Honour of Jean Seznec,* eds F. Haskell, A. Levi & R. Shackleton, Clarendon Press, Oxford, 1974, pp. 126–33; Pritchard, pp. 138–41.

11 See I Kings 7: 1–12; I Kings 10: 17–22.

12 J. Fergusson, *The Palaces of Nineveh and Persepolis Restored,* Spottiswoode & Shaw, London, 1851, p. 224.

13 O. Jones, 'Assyrian and Persian ornament', in *The Grammar of Ornament,* London, 1856, pp. 28–30; A. H. Layard, *Discoveries in the Ruins of Nineveh and Babylon,* London, 1853, pt 2, pp. 359, 601–2; *note by N. Armstrong,* pp. 2–3.

14 P. Conner, 'Wedding archaeology to art': Poynter's Israel in Egypt', in *Influences in Victorian Art and Architecture,* eds S. Macready & F. H. Thompson, Society of Antiquaries, distr. Thames & Hudson, London, 1985, p. 118.

15 *The Queen of Sheba's visit to King Solomon,* oil on canvas, 36.8 x 54 cm, c. 1884, Maharaja Fatesingh Museum, Baroda, India. Exhibited at the 1891 Royal Academy, no. 305. See also Renée Free, *Art Gallery of New South Wales Catalogue of British Paintings,* Art Gallery of New South Wales, Sydney (1987), p. 157.

16 F. H. Jackson, 'The work of Sir E. J. Poynter, P.R.A.: viewed mainly from the decorative side', *Architectural Review,* vol. 2, 1897, p. 164. See also H. Sharp, 'A short account of the work of Edward John Poynter R.A.', *Studio,* vol. 7, 1896, p. 15.

17 C. Bell, 'Sir Edward John Poynter', *Dictionary of National Biography,* London, 1927, p. 440.

18 (M. H. Spielmann), 'Edward J. Poynter P.R.A.', *Magazine of Art,* vol. 21, 1897, p. 120.

19 See K. Bendiner, *An Introduction to Victorian Painting,* Yale University Press, New Haven, Conn., 1985, pp. 65–77; M. Warner, 'The question of faith: Orientalism, Christianity and Islam', in MaryAnne Stevens (ed.), *The Orientalists: Delacroix to Matisse,* exh. cat., Royal Academy of Arts, London, 1984, pp. 32–4.

20 See Art Gallery of New South Wales Press Clippings 1884–1896, Art Gallery of New South Wales, Sydney, pp. 82–3.

21 See Free, *Art Gallery of New South Wales Catalogue,* p. 157.

22 Photogravure after *E.J. Poynter's The Queen of Sheba's Visit to King Solomon,* published by Raphael Tuck & Sons, London, 1892, copyright owned by Thomas McLean, dedicated to the Trustees of the National Gallery of New South Wales.

23 M. Bell, *The Drawings of Sir E.J. Poynter, Bart., P.R.A.,* George Newnes, London (1905), p. 7.

LAWRENCE ALMA-TADEMA

35 EGYPTIANS 3,000 YEARS AGO 1867–68

Oil on canvas   64.5 x 90 cm
Auckland Art Gallery, New Zealand. Purchased by the Mackelvie Trust 1921

This picture, which is inscribed 'to my friend Andrew Gow', is a replica of Alma-Tadema's famous painting, *Pastimes in ancient Egypt*, exhibited in Brussels in 1863, then re-worked and exhibited at the Paris Salon in 1864. Awarded a gold medal at the Salon, the picture was subsequently damaged by a gas explosion at the dealer Gambart's house in London in 1866.[1] It was probably after this incident that Alma-Tadema decided to paint a replica. He tended to paint his second versions smaller than the original and the Auckland picture is no exception, being smaller than the restored 1863 version now in the Harris Museum and Art Gallery, Preston. Alma-Tadema's replicas were never exact copies; they were separate versions of an earlier subject with whose composition he often experimented, introducing small changes. To make an exact copy would be to infringe copyright of the original, which he sold with the work.

The subject of this painting was important to Alma-Tadema's career, as it was his first successful painting of an Egyptian theme. He was influenced in its conception by the distinguished Egyptologist Georg Ebers. Other sources he consulted included photographs of recent archaeological discoveries and John Gardner Wilkinson's book, *The Manners and Customs of the Ancient Egyptians*, published in London in 1837 – a text that was also consulted by Edwin Long. According to Swanson, Alma-Tadema's imaginative reconstruction of an 18th-Dynasty entertainment being given in the presence of a Nubian ambassador, and hosted by a priest named Phatmes, included an amalgamation of the following archaeological sources: architecture taken from the Temple of Gerf-Horfeyn, an ancient harp in the Louvre, a wall painting of Thutmos in the Bibliothèque Nationale and the sarcophagus of Phatmes in the Leiden Museum.[2] UP

1 Vern Swanson, *The Biography and Catalogue Raisonné of the Paintings of Sir Lawrence Alma-Tadema*, Garton & Co., London, 1990, pp. 146–7.

2 ibid., pp. 131–2.

LAWRENCE ALMA-TADEMA

36 CLEOPATRA 1875

Oil on canvas mounted on an oval panel 54.6 x 66.7 cm
The Art Gallery of New South Wales, Sydney. Gift of Sir Herbert Thompson (Egyptologist) 1920*

Cleopatra, the last queen of Egypt, attracted many 19th-century painters as a subject. She was seen as the epitome of the *femme fatale* who used her sexual wiles to achieve power over men. In this cameo-like portrait, Alma-Tadema poses his bare-shouldered model in profile against a gold ground, inspired by lines from Shakespeare's *Anthony and Cleopatra* (Act II, sc. ii) which are inscribed on the painting's frame: 'For her own person, it beggar'd all description; / She did lie, in her pavilion, cloth-of-gold of tissue'. In all, the artist painted three versions of this subject. This was the first, and he exhibited it at the Royal Academy in 1876. It was bequeathed to the Art Gallery of New South Wales by Sir Herbert Thompson, the eminent Egyptologist and son of Alma-Tadema's surgeon and pupil, Sir Henry Thompson.[1]

Alma-Tadema painted Cleopatra again in 1877 (cat. 37) and in 1883 he produced a full-scale picture, *The meeting of Antony and Cleopatra*. Using the same pose, he represented her seated on her throne in the royal barge, against the lavish background of the cloth-of-gold pavilion, and holding a crook and flail, symbols of her queenship.[2] The face of Cleopatra in the Art Gallery of New South Wales picture has similarities with a marble bust of Cleopatra VII (c. 68–30 BC) in the British Museum. It is a strikingly sensuous painting that combines the artist's favourite historical interests with characteristically fastidious brushwork and his decorative flair for posing elegant female subjects.   UP

[1] Renée Free, *Art Gallery of New South Wales Catalogue of British Paintings,* Art Gallery of New South Wales, Sydney, n.d. (1987), p. 7.

[2] Vern Swanson, *The Biography and Catalogue Raisonné of the Paintings of Sir Lawrence Alma-Tadema*, Garton & Co., London, 1990, p. 219.

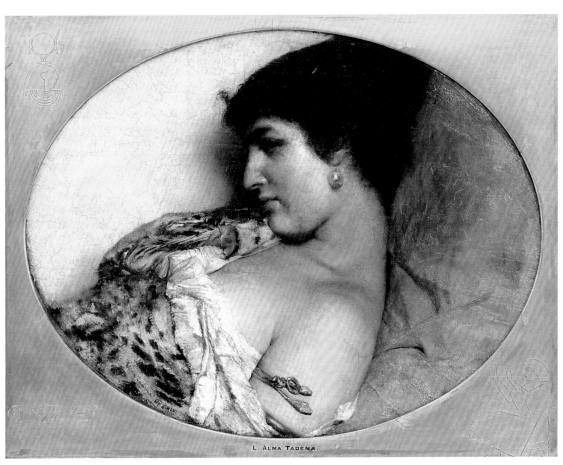

L. ALMA TADEMA.

LAWRENCE ALMA-TADEMA

37 CLEOPATRA 1877

Oil on panel 19 x 26.7 cm
Auckland Art Gallery, New Zealand. Purchased by the Mackelvie Trust 1916 ■

Although similar in pose and accessories to the 1875 version (cat. 36), this painting of Cleopatra is not identical. It is smaller and the model appears less fleshy, with her head tilted a little more forward. According to Swanson, it is possible that this picture was commissioned from Alma-Tadema by George Herschel, as the first known correspondence between the two relates to its acquisition by Herschel.[1] The distinctive gilded frame with its temple form and Egyptian motifs was designed to complement the picture and is consistent with the artist's antiquarian interests. Alma-Tadema's scholarship was informed not only by the extensive collections available to him at the British Museum but also by his friendship with the German Egyptologist Georg Ebers, who was the author of several best-sellers, including *Egypt in Word and Picture* and the historical romance, *An Egyptian Princess*.   UP

[1] Vern Swanson, *The Biography and Catalogue Raisonné of the Paintings of Sir Lawrence Alma-Tadema*, Garton & Co., London, 1990, p. 198.

EDWIN LONG

38 AN ANCIENT CUSTOM 1876

Oil on canvas 101.6 x 142.2 cm
Private collection, courtesy Peter Nahum at The Leicester Galleries, London

Combining his interests in religion, the Bible and the new science of archaeology, Edwin Long visited Egypt and Syria in 1874. Inspired by that journey, he produced a series of astonishingly detailed reconstructions of the ancient Near Eastern world, peopled with exotic, lightly draped young women. *An ancient custom* not only displays Long's antiquarian interests but also his gifts as a colourist. The scene is bathed in a softly glowing light that intensifies the contrasts of pale and dark skin, gleaming jewellery and red lips with black hair, creamy white and deep blue robes with the red, woven wall-hanging. Long first exhibited this picture at the Royal Academy Summer Exhibition of 1877, at which time it was described as 'Two figures nearly life size; a Nubian girl on her knees painting the eyebrows of her young Egyptian mistress'.[1] The mistress, pale-skinned and more lavishly dressed than her black servant (a favourite Orientalist trope), is seductively posed on a leopard-skin rug, beside familiar emblems of female vanity – a polished metal mirror and an ornamented cosmetic box. The stone relief behind her was probably based on a fragment from the North Palace, Nineveh – *Lions in a garden* dated 645–640 BC – which Long could have studied in the British Museum.[2]

The *Art Journal* reviewer of the Royal Academy Summer Exhibition commented that 'The merits of Mr Long's work lie in his archaeological knowledge'.[3] However, Long's archaeological researches were not intended to recreate specific historical sites, but to provide grandly imaginative settings for the small human dramas that were his real interest. He routinely amalgamated details drawn from historically separate sources within a single image. Long's approach to depicting women in his historical tableaux was closest to Alma-Tadema's; they even chose similar titles. For example, Alma-Tadema's *An antique custom*, set in a Roman bath, was completed in the same year. However, according to Long, *An ancient custom* was 'the original study' for a larger-scale biblical subject representing Queen Esther at her toilette which he completed in 1878.[4] Importing the background motifs from the Persepolis reliefs and Layard's work at Nineveh, Long this time created an even grander architectural setting (a replica of *Queen Esther* is in the National Gallery of Victoria). Nineteenth-century reviewers wrote lingering descriptions of Long's exotic eastern beauties, particularly admiring their 'eyes of liquid fire', mouths 'like a crimson flower', and rounded limbs 'shown through gauze vestments'.[5]   UP

[1] See Mark Bills, 'An ancient custom', in *Edwin Longsden Long RA*, London (in press). He notes that, according to the artist, a second, smaller version of *An ancient custom* was completed in 1877 for engraving.

[2] Information from Alison Inglis.

[3] *Art Journal* (London), 1877, p. 197.

[4] E. Long, *The Times*, 7 June 1879, p. 8.

[5] *Sydney Morning Herald*, 1 September 1894, reviewer commenting on Long's *Queen Esther* then on display in Sydney at the National Gallery of Victoria Loan Exhibition.

WILLIAM STRUTT

39 THE NUBIAN BARBER PLIES HIS SIMPLE TRADE WHEN EGYPT'S HAUGHTY KINGS IN SPLENDOUR REIGNED 1888

Watercolour, pencil and gum on paper 61 x 52 cm. Thirty Victoria Street, Sydney

In 1878 Strutt made the acquaintance of a party of Nubian (Upper Egyptian) hunters who were visiting London with the Munich wild-animal dealer, Hagenbeck. By his own account, they brought with them 'everything that could possibly illustrate in the most complete manner the habits...and toilettes of these most interesting people'. He went on to remark: 'Mixing with the swarthy Nubians and their animals, I could almost fancy myself at Kardofan or Khartoum'.[1] This work is based on the careful studies Strutt made while visiting the Nubian animal keepers at the Alexandra Park grounds. Strutt had spent twelve years (1850–62) in Australasia, painting subjects from the local life and making ethnographic studies of the indigenous people. A former pupil of Paul Delaroche and Horace Vernet in Paris, he continued to portray the peoples and customs of foreign cultures after his return from the colonies. This grandly titled watercolour combines historicism and the fashion for Orientalist subject matter with closely detailed observation.

Bathing his figures in a mysterious light that reveals Egyptian paintings and reliefs behind them, Strutt projected the real Nubians he had studied into an imaginary historical Nubia 'when Egypt's haughty kings in splendour reigned'. This tendency to see in the contemporary Near East survivals of ancient, noble types and customs was a feature of British Orientalism, which also relied heavily on the archaeological fragments that could be studied in the British Museum. Strutt, like Poynter, Long and Alma-Tadema, researched his antiquarian subjects painstakingly, piecing together carefully

drawn studies, literary references and the allure of places 'far away and long ago' to confect a Fantasy Orient that confirmed his English-speaking audience's expectations. First shown in England at Nottingham Art Gallery in 1881, Strutt sent the picture to Adelaide two years later, to Wivell's Art Gallery, where a contemporary reviewer noted that: 'The pose of the figures is capitally rendered, although the positions are extremely difficult. The background shows the vestibule column and wall of an ancient Egyptian palace, on which are the characteristic hieroglyphics'.[2] Purchased by a Sydney collector, this work was shown at the Loan Exhibition held at the National Art Gallery of New South Wales in 1897, and catalogued as *The Nubian barber*.[3]
UP

[1] Strutt, quoted in Heather Curnow, *William Strutt*, exh. cat., AGDC, Sydney, 1980, p. 54.

[2] *South Australian Advertiser*, 25 July 1883.

[3] Heather Curnow assisted Sotheby's, Sydney, to document this work for its sale in April 1995; Maud Page also researched Strutt's papers in the Mitchell Library, Sydney, for Frank McDonald at Thirty Victoria Street.

JEAN-LEON GEROME

40 THE SNAKE CHARMER (Le Charmeur des serpentes) c. 1880

Oil on canvas 84 x 122 cm
Sterling and Francine Clark Institute, Williamstown, Mass., USA

Intense colour, seductive as a jewel, dominates in Gérôme's homage to the magnificence of Ottoman architecture and design. Yet the grand interior, deep and dream-like as a swimming pool, is in a state of gradual deterioration. It is the moral messages contained in such contrasts – of splendour and decay, past glories and present neglect – that have brought this beautiful painting to recent critical attention.

The snake charmer has been held up as an exemplar of Orientalism by Edward Said (who used it for the cover of his seminal book on Orientalism) and by the art historian Linda Nochlin.[1] For Nochlin, *The snake charmer* is a fantasy concoction based on cultural misrecognition dressed up as documentary realism. The magic-weaving spell of the charmer or the storyteller is the quintessential stuff of an *Arabian Nights* fantasy. There is a touch of taboo, too, as well as mystery, in the anticipatory atmosphere of this all-male scene, hinted at by the phallic snake coiled around the naked, muscled body of the young boy–performer. This sublimated homoeroticism creates a more subtle sexual display than that found in Gérôme's comparable scenes of exotic entertainments featuring women, where the body is in full frontal view.

Gérôme presents a catalogue of racial types, elaborate costumes and varied emotional reactions among the pictured audience. Their intense involvement with the performers contrasts with the imaginary detachment of the undisclosed western observer. Interestingly, their gazes are mostly directed towards the old pipe-player (a minor figure from the viewer's vantage point) rather than the boy and his snake. This may be seen as a device to deflect desire for the nude, or simply as a way of keeping the eye active over the surface of the picture by creating a complex triangulation of lines of vision between us, the performers and their audience. For, above all, Gérôme seeks to satiate the eye through the amassing of intricate visual detail, exemplified by the almost overpowering sumptuousness of the blue-tiled decoration.   CJ

[1] Linda Nochlin, 'The imaginary Orient', *Art in America*, May 1983, p. 119.

JEAN-LEON GEROME

41 MOORISH BATH (LADY OF CAIRO BATHING) (Bain turc ou bain maure: deux femmes) 1870

Oil on canvas 50.8 x 40.8 cm
Courtesy Museum of Fine Arts, Boston. Gift of Robert Jordan from the Collection of Eben D. Jordan

Hammams or baths were essential Islamic institutions that enabled Muslims to perform the Koranic requirements of ritual purification. For western artists they provided exotic eastern locales in which to paint nudes and explore contrasting skin tones against glistening marble and tiled architectural settings. This bath scene is considered the first of at least twenty in Gérôme's *oeuvre*. A generic composition, it was begun in London as a gift but, 'as a model for the Nubian was lacking', it was completed in Paris.[1]

Both bath scenes by Gérôme in this exhibition depict a fair-skinned mistress attended by a dark-skinned slave. Black slaves were often, but not exclusively, employed as servants in Islamic societies. (Under Koranic law, born Muslims could not be slaves.) However, in a 19th-century context, the juxtaposing of black and white bodies implied varying racial and sexual interpretations. In an established western visual arts tradition, the representation of a black servant served to sexualise the setting. By the mid-19th century, scientific discourse associated the sexual appetite of the black woman with lesbian sexuality. This association was further enhanced by the belief, commonly held by western audiences and fostered by numerous European travel accounts, that lesbian relationships occurred in the women's baths. Aesthetically pleasing, Gérôme's eroticised bathers had a popular appeal and sold very well.   SA

[1] Information from the object file of the Boston Museum for Fine Arts, cited by Gerald Ackerman, *The Life and Work of Jean-Léon Gérôme*, Sotheby's, London & New York, 1986, p. 89.

JEAN-LEON GEROME

42 THE ALMEH (WITH PIPE) 1873

Oil on canvas 53 x 40.5 cm
The Nadj Collection, courtesy of the Mathaf Gallery, London

Kuchuk had just left her bath...her front hair was platted [sic] in thin braids that were drawn back and tied together; the lower part of her body was hidden in immense pink trousers; her torso was entirely naked under purple gauze...She is a formidable looking creature, large-breasted, fleshy, with slit nostrils, enormous eyes, and magnificent knees; when she danced there were formidable folds of flesh on her stomach.[1]

Gérôme made four images of Egyptian *almehs*, female entertainers specialising in dance, in 1872–73. The Cairene almeh's strikingly coloured costume of ballooning trousers and transparent blouse was noted by both Lane and Flaubert, who was describing his famous erotic encounter with the courtesan Kuchuk-Hanem in Egypt in 1850.[2] Like Kuchuk-Hanem, Gérôme's *Almeh (with pipe)*, here seen soliciting trade from the street, doubles as a prostitute. Gérôme's primary emphasis is on the seductiveness of the meticulously painted costume, artfully enhanced by the provocative pose. The almeh's face and arms, one raised above her head and the other resting on her hip, are semi-concealed by dusky veils of green and black chiffon, leading the eye to dwell on the luminous skin exposed on her breasts. Her body inclines forward, with one slippered foot invitingly extended. The voluptuousness of her belly is emphasised by the trousers billowing out beneath the knot of fabric on the hips. The long pipe reinforces the message of languor and sensuousness. Gérôme adds intrigue to a potentially obvious image by placing the model to one side of the stone doorway. This lures the imagination into the dark reaches of the passage behind her, where the shrouded figure of the procuress stands. This decrepit woman, and the broken patterned grille over the doorway above her, function as intimations of the material and moral decay that often haunted European fantasies of the Orient as a paradise of limitless erotic pleasure.   CJ

1 *The Letters of Gustave Flaubert 1830–1857*, ed. Francis Steegmuller, Faber & Faber, London, 1981, p. 116.

2 William Lane, *The Manners and Customs of the Modern Egyptians*, 1836, p. 386, quoted in Richard Ettinghausen, 'Jean-Léon Gérôme as a painter of Near Eastern life', in *Jean-Léon Gérôme*, exh. cat., Dayton Art Institute, Dayton, Ohio, 1972, pp. 19–20.

JEAN-LEON GEROME

43 THE BATH (Le Bain) c. 1880–85

Oil on canvas 73.6 x 59.6 cm
Fine Arts Museums of San Francisco. Mildred Anna Williams Collection 1961.29

While Gérôme is known to have visited bathhouses in Egypt and Turkey, the architectural details of this work may derive from several disparate sources.[1] The striking green tiles were possibly inspired by the famous ceramics used on the Green Mosque in the Turkish city of Bursa. The stalactite squinch supporting the unseen dome is typical of those found throughout the Islamic world.

The modelling and positioning of the figures in both of Gérôme's bath paintings highlight racial hierarchies. The white models, who in fact were French, are soft and pliant and representative of a pampered, leisured class. In contrast, the bodies of the black models are hard and muscular, demonstrating a familiarity with physical labour.

In the foreground a pair of *nalin* or pattens, decorated with inlaid mother-of-pearl, can be seen. Pattens were worn in the bathhouse to protect bathers from slipping on the wet marble surfaces and elevated them above the dirty water and corrosive depilatories swirling around on the floor. Stools or up-ended buckets were used for seats in the bathhouse, not the reed boxes depicted here. These props are possibly bird cages and appear in a number of Gérôme's paintings, including his first Salon exhibit, *The cock fight* of 1847.

As well as being a visual feast, this bath scene has an inviting tactile quality. The architectural surfaces gleam in the bath's hot steamy atmosphere and the sense of touch is directly illustrated by the black slave's handling of the porcelain-like body of the white woman. SA

1 Paul Lenoir, *Le Fayoum, Le Sinai et Pétra: expédition dans la moyenne Egypte et l'Arabie Petrée sous la direction de J. L. Gérôme*, Paris, 1872, pp. 186, 173, cited in MaryAnne Stevens (ed.), *The Orientalists: Delacroix to Matisse*, exh. cat., Royal Academy of Arts, London, 1984, p. 141; Caroline Juler, *Najd Collection of Orientalist Paintings*, Manara, London, 1991, p. 129.

JEAN-LEON GEROME

44 HAREM IN THE KIOSK c. 1875–80

Oil on canvas 76.2 x 115 cm
The Najd Collection, courtesy of the Mathaf Gallery, London

Gérôme made three trips to Constantinople, signalled as the location of the *Harem in the kiosk* by the Golden Horn seen on the horizon. This picture dates from his last trip in 1875. Gérôme's subject is a rather unconventional representation of the harem. The Turkish harem, in particular, held a special place in the European male's imagination as a place of Oriental indolence, luxury and licentiousness, a fantasy which Gérôme himself did much to sustain in his many scenes of harem women bathing. The tenuous relationship that this fantasy had to the reality of the harem tended to be pointed out by European women, from Lady Mary Wortley Montagu to the French painter Henriette Browne, who, unlike men, were actually able to visit harems. Gérôme's depiction of harem women seen from afar in a public place was the closest a European man might get to the reality, enabling the painter to go some way towards debunking the myth. The usual atmosphere of cloying eroticism associated with the private chamber or the steamy confines of the bath is replaced by one of easy sociability out of doors. The women are seen taking in the fresh early morning air against an exquisite backdrop of opalescent, pastel-toned sky and water. Their purity and respectability are underlined by their pristine white headdresses and the presence of their children leaning over the side of the kiosk. Nevertheless, the fantasy themes of claustration and the master's wrathful possessiveness are still much in evidence, with the fearsome guard confronting the viewer's gaze directly, barring access to the women separated from us in their elegant, floating prison.   CJ

JEAN-LEON GEROME

45 BONAPARTE BEFORE THE SPHINX c. 1867–68

Oil on canvas 92.7 x 137 cm
Hearst Castle™/Hearst San Simeon State Historical Monument™

Gérôme made the first of many trips to Egypt in 1856. This is one of four or five images he did of Napoleon in Egypt, dated in Ackerman's authoritative book on Gérôme to 1867–68.[1] A later replica was apparently also produced. According to a visitor in 1886 Gérôme liked this painting so much he had it hanging in his bedroom.

The painting bears the alternative title of *Oedipus*. In classical mythology, Oedipus in exile travelled to Thebes, a city terrorised by a monstrous Sphinx, half-woman and half-lion. All those who passed were required to answer riddles posed by the Sphinx or be devoured. Cunning Oedipus solved the riddle, killed the Sphinx and so liberated the Thebans, who, in their gratitude, crowned him king. A sophisticated French Salon audience would have been able to draw the classical parallels Gérôme intended here with Napoleon's attempted conquest in 1798 of Egypt, then ruled by the Ottoman Empire. However, such a parallel resembled wishful thinking. The artist's patriotism is shown in his choice of a moment early in the campaign when French victory over the combined Turkish and English forces still seemed possible.

In the picture Napoleon is seen taking the measure of his own destiny against the magnitude and antiquity of the Great Sphinx, guardian of the Necropolis at Giza, a short distance from Cairo. Behind Napoleon are the shadows of his mounted entourage of generals and, in the distance, spreading out in great serried ranks on the plain of Giza, is Napoleon's mighty army gathering for battle. The general allegedly inspired his troops with a sense of their historic mission by declaring 'Soldats! du haut de ces pyramides quarante siècles vous contemplent!' (Soldiers! Forty centuries look down upon you from these pyramids!). The French won the Battle of the Pyramids against the Turkish Mameluke troops and Napoleon proceeded to Cairo. But only days later the British, led by Admiral Nelson at sea, defeated the French and gave Egypt back to the Turks.

Happier results flowed from the ambitious artistic and scientific expeditions which accompanied Napoleon's doomed military campaign. The most famous is a French soldier's discovery of the Rosetta Stone, the key to deciphering Egyptian hieroglyphics. Publication by the French of massive illustrated tomes accurately documenting Egyptian treasures revived a European craze for Egyptian-inspired art and design, visible at the Paris Exposition of 1867, contemporary with this painting.[2] CJ

[1] Gerald M. Ackerman, *The Life and Work of Jean-Léon Gérôme*, Sotheby's, London & New York, 1986, p. 222.

[2] Peter A. Clayton, *The Rediscovery of Ancient Egypt: Artists and Travellers in the Nineteenth Century*, Thames & Hudson, London, 1982, esp. pp. 14–26.

JEAN-LEON GEROME

46 ARABS CROSSING THE DESERT c. 1870

Oil on canvas 41.2 x 56 cm
The Nadj Collection, courtesy of the Mathaf Gallery, London

Gérôme marries the popular romantic subject of the Arab cavalier, memorably portrayed by Delacroix and Fromentin, with the more stately ethnographic or religious genre of the caravan, treated by Belly and Girardet. While the latter commonly feature the camel rather than the horse, here camels are relegated to the background, and are clearly lower down the hierarchy. Gérôme's theme is the relationship between the noble Arab and his steed, an exclusively masculine bond which is underlined by the absence of women and children. The calm, static, frieze-like composition provides an extreme contrast with the frenzied turbulence of the images of equestrian combat by Delacroix and Chassériau, also in the exhibition. There is none of the theatrical commotion, no wild eyes and flaring nostrils of starting horses, of the romantic paintings. Instead, Gérôme's fatalistic Bedouin horsemen setting out in the early morning across the Sahara convey the idea of a more essential drama – the survival of the fittest. Here the respected enemy is Nature, pitted against the supreme will and adaptability of the nomad who makes the desert, most inhospitable of places, his home. Stoic endurance and slow, but inexorable, progress are the tactics of his assault. Horses and riders have their eyes fixed on a far point on the horizon, rationing their energies for the journey. The viewer observes the procession from a point on the ground, looking up. At close range to the leader and his two hooded offsiders, we catch their costume and facial expressions in saturated colours and sharp detail, in contrast to the dusty haze that envelops the rest of the picture.   CJ

FREDERIC LEIGHTON

47 PORTIONS OF THE INTERIOR OF THE GRAND MOSQUE OF DAMASCUS 1873–75

Oil on canvas 158.1 x 122 cm
Harris Museum and Art Gallery, Preston

The diminutive stature of the two children in the foreground of Leighton's painting highlights the impressive scale of the Damascus mosque. Leighton conveys the grandeur of the mosque through the strong verticals of the magnificent carved *minbar* or pulpit, the hanging lamps and the delicately rendered geometric ornamentation of the wall tiles and mosaic floor. The Islamic mosque was a subject of curiosity for many 19th-century European artist–travellers because entering these places of worship was notoriously difficult and official permission needed to be obtained. In 1843 the Egyptologist John Gardner Wilkinson recommended that the visitor to mosques in Cairo adopt Turkish dress, which would enable him 'to examine, and even draw the interior, without molestation'.[1] Leighton's painting is derived from a number of sketches made on the spot during his journey to Damascus in 1873. Notwithstanding the fact that Leighton entered the Damascus mosque, in this painting he has inaccurately depicted the two men praying in different directions and the two young girls unveiled on the mosque's central floor.[2]

This was Leighton's third journey to the East, from which he was to bring back not only many accoutrements that appeared in his paintings, but also tiles and even a 17th-century *mashrabiyya* or lattice window. These were later incorporated into Leighton's 'Arab Hall', built as an extension to his home in Holland Park Road, London in 1877–79. Leighton was assisted in his search for Syrian pottery and tiles in Damascus by the Reverend William Wright, to whom he had been introduced by his friend, the well-known Orientalist traveller Richard Burton (infamous for having entered the sacred Islamic cities of Mecca and Medina in 1853 disguised as an Indian Muslim doctor).   MR

[1] Sir John Gardner Wilkinson, F.R.S., *Modern Egypt and Thebes: Being a Description of Egypt Including the Information for Travellers in that Country*, John Murray, London, 1843, p. 229.

[2] MaryAnne Stevens (ed.) *The Orientalists: Delacroix to Matisse*, exh. cat., Royal Academy of Arts, London, 1984, p. 202.

OSMAN HAMDY BEY

48 KORAN INSTRUCTION 1890

Oil on canvas 80 x 60 cm
The Nadj Collection, courtesy of the Mathaf Gallery, London

A member of the Ottoman intellectual élite, Hamdy's Orientalist paintings provide a unique view of a culture from within. In this work, a *Hodja* or religious teacher reads the Koran (which means 'to recite') to a fellow Muslim at the entrance of the Green Mosque, built in 1420 at Bursa, the first Ottoman capital.[1] Epitomising the perfection attained in the first period of Ottoman art, this mosque was celebrated for the dark turquoise and green tiles, meticulously depicted here, decorating the antechamber to the prayer hall.

An air of piety is captured by the light illuminating the figures receiving the word of God in the foreground, and emanating from the window on the *qibla* wall, which marks the direction of Mecca, in the background. The strategic placement of the large candle flanking the Hodja, and the hanging lantern in line with the pupil and window further connect the idea of light with prayer. While the use of light and shade impart depth to this work, a subtle flattening of form suggests both an appreciation of Ottoman miniature painting and a deference to Islamic injunctions prohibiting sculpted representations which seek to imitate God's creations.

Hamdy, like his teacher Gérôme, based many of his architectural works, including this one, on his own photographs. His figures, taken from sketches of models who posed in his studio, were added later.[2] They convey a mood of serene and tranquil faith in the knowledge that God, as the Koranic inscription above them declares, is forgiving and beneficent.   SA

[1] Caroline Juler, *Najd Collection of Orientalist Paintings*, Manara, London, 1991, p. 170.

[2] ibid.

ALBERTO PASINI

49 SYRIAN HORSE MARKET (Marché aux chevaux, Syrie) c. 1890

Oil on canvas 51 x 65 cm
The Art Gallery of New South Wales, Sydney. Purchased 1894

The Piedmontese painter Alberto Pasini was inspired by the rich legacy of Ottoman architecture. He made careful sketches of urban buildings, and the typical street, courtyard and market scenes that he encountered during his wide-ranging travels through Moorish Spain, Turkey, Egypt, Persia, Lebanon and Syria. His modestly scaled pictures of Near Eastern subjects were closer in spirit to the view-painting tradition of landscape art than to the figure traditions on which Orientalist genre painting was usually based. The groups of figures in his pictures, while deftly drawn, are incidental to Pasini's love for portraying the play of light over crumbling stucco surfaces, the subdued sheen of faience tiles, the textures of weathered carvings, and inscriptions on old buildings.

This picture was based on the artist's trip to Syria in 1873. It is a studio elaboration of details sketched, and buildings remembered, combined with Pasini's recurrent and skilfully deployed formula of men, shiny horses and modestly veiled women (some of them holding jaunty parasols). Such pictures, with their quasi-photographic representation of architecture, airy sunshine and crisp colours, had made Pasini internationally popular with buyers. He was perhaps the best-known non-French Orientalist exhibiting at the Paris Salon. His Parisian dealer was Goupil, whom he shared with Gérôme, and who sold many of his paintings to American collectors.[1] When representatives of the National Art Gallery of New South Wales purchased this work in Paris in 1894 and had it shipped to Sydney, the local press recorded its arrival with the prosaic statement, 'The Syrian Horse Market is an Eastern scene, by Pasini, heavy in architecture, and carefully painted'.[2]   UP

1 See Lynne Thornton, *Les Orientalistes: Peintres Voyageurs*, ACR, Paris, 1993, p. 144.

2 *Daily Telegraph*, 22 December 1894.

EDOUARD DEBAT-PONSAN

50 MASSAGE IN THE HAMMAM (Le Massage, scène de hammam) 1883

Oil on canvas 127 x 210 cm
Musée des Augustins, Toulouse

A visit to the hammam or bath was considered *de rigueur* for travellers to the East. The accuracy of the details in this painting suggests that Débat-Ponsan visited one during his trip to Constantinople the year before the work was exhibited.

The hammam experience is often described as a drama in five acts. The first act, the seasoning of the body, is achieved through sweating. The massage scene depicted here is the second act of the bathing ritual. In front of an Iznik faience a woman is massaged on a marble slab in the steam room. An art critic who reviewed the 1883 Salon exhibit described the woman being massaged as 'clearly display[ing] the languidness induced by the hammam, a state of inertia that contrasts sharply with the vigorous liveliness of the powerful hands that are freely kneading and pulling her'.[1] This procedure is followed by an exfoliating scrub before the bather washes at one of the marble basins, like the one illustrated in the background. Turkish hammams (unless they are thermal baths) generally do not have communal immersion pools; still water is believed to contain *ifrits* or evil beings. Instead, using a shallow bowl like the copper one shown next to the basin, the bather pours water over the body from the free-flowing water collected in the basins. In the final act the bather returns to the outer chamber to rest.   SA

[1] Cited by Lynne Thornton, *Women as Portrayed in Orientalist Painting*, ACR, Paris, 1985, p. 71.

PAUL-DESIRE TROUILLEBERT

51 THE HAREM SERVANT (Servante du harem) 1874

Oil on canvas 130 x 97 cm
Musée des Beaux-Arts, Nice. Fonds National d'Art Contemporain

Described by Philippe Comte as 'one of the best examples of that Orientalism of the bazaar so dear to our taste for kitsch', Trouillebert's painting is at once provocative and withdrawn.[1] The combination of the harem servant's exposed breasts with her intense, inscrutable stare is unsettling. Our gaze locks with hers as she enters or prepares to leave the room. Her secret world appears to be as tightly entwined as the coil of the narghile, which she may be about to offer the viewer.

Trouillebert's brief excursion into Orientalism provides popular decorative appeal rather than an authentic ethnographic study. The choice of an Oriental setting for his French model may have been further inspired by the works of his teacher, Ernest Hébert.[2] The artefacts, such as the narghile and tray, decorated with calligraphy, are realistically rendered, and the necklaces and jewellery adorning the unusual headdress demonstrate some familiarity with eastern goldsmithing designs. In Turkish harems servants were sometimes known to display the wealth of their owners in this fashion. The depiction of the two chained armbands, however, serves to remind the viewer of her servile status.

The most compelling aspect of this work rests in the disquieting tension the artist has created by contrasting the vulnerable bare-breasted body with the enigmatic look the harem servant bestows upon the viewer.   SA

[1] Philippe Comte, *Les Peintres orientalistes (1850–1914)*, Musée des Beaux-Arts, Pau, 1983, n.p.

[2] ibid.

LEON BONNAT

52 AN ARAB SHEIKH c. 1870s

Oil on canvas 65 x 72.5 cm
The Walters Art Gallery, Baltimore, Maryland, no. 37.173

Bonnat's Orient is the darkened studio where a model in Arab costume poses among props – a sword, divan and saddle – that would have been collected on the artist's single trip to Egypt and the Holy Land in 1868–69. This sheikh, at once a powerful exercise in mimesis and a staged exotic stereotype, exemplifies the conflict between documentation and imagination that was identified by the realist critic Castagnary as a problem for modern Orientalism.

An eminent exponent of the *juste milieu* between academic idealism and the comparative spontaneity of the contemporary avant-garde, Bonnat exploited stark chiaroscuro and illusionistic handling to extract a new *frisson* from his religious and exotic subjects. His withered *Job*, using the same venerable model as is depicted here, was praised at the Salon of 1880 for 'trenchant precision' and 'prodigious relief'.[1] Bonnat's fallen reputation in the 20th century has more readily reflected the opinion of Jules Laforgue, who dismissed him in 1886 as a mere producer of photographs.[2]

In spite of its vivid textures, differentiated by subtle adjustments of focus that refer to the artist's early study of Velasquez in Madrid, Bonnat's superficial aesthetic promotes an artificial effect. The room in Paris, illuminated by the steady shaft of light from a skylight, seems incongruously remote from the southern milieu its assembled contents purport to conjure.   PR

[1] Emile Michel, 'Le Salon de 1880', *Revue des Deux Mondes*, 1 June 1880, p. 666.

[2] Jules Laforgue, 'Souvenirs d'un Salon', in Mireille Dottin (ed.), *Laforgue: textes de critique d'art*, Lille University Press, 1988, p. 122.

EMILE GLOCKNER

53 A FINE BLADE c. 1900

Oil on canvas 127.5 x 99 cm
The Najd Collection, courtesy of the Mathaf Gallery, London

Flaubert wrote in 1850 that Byron's Orient was 'the Orient of the curved sword', adding, 'I prefer the baked Orient of the bedouin and the desert'.[1] Glockner's compelling but quiet image of a white-robed Bedouin pensively stroking the wicked curve of a long-bladed knife of Ottoman origin, combines the menacing romance of Byron's Turkish Orient with the luminous beauty and emptied-out stillness of the Egyptian desert regions that had attracted both Flaubert and Fromentin. His romantically back-lit portrayal of an Arab connoisseur of weapons, expertly assessing the quality and finish of his 'fine blade', can also be compared with Bonnat's painting of *An Arab sheikh* (cat. 52). Both artists employed quasi-photographic techniques to provide somewhat ambiguous images of ethnic stereotypes, combining documentary accuracy with a theatrical flair for the specifics of pose, gesture and expression.

According to Caroline Juler, this is a fine painting by an artist whose Orientalist subjects are rare. However, we know relatively little about Glockner's working practices. In this regard, Juler points out that this figure could either be based on Bedouin tribesmen that Glockner met on a visit to Egypt, or be drawn from a model posed in his studio in Dresden. She also notes a further interesting ambiguity:

> *Though the background is blank, Glockner has painted the man's features and the light and shade on his clothes as if he were in an outdoor setting with the sun at his back, or inside near an open door or window. Only the edges of his fingers, nose and arms catch the light while the rest of his body is in shadow.*[2]

It is the mysterious nature of the effects of light that ultimately determines our response to the figure's broodingly powerful presence.   UP

[1] Gustave Flaubert, quoted by D.A. Rosenthal, *Orientalism*, exh. cat., Memorial Art Gallery of the University of Rochester, New York, 1982, p. 113.

[2] Caroline Juler, *Najd Collection of Orientalist Paintings*, Manara, London, 1991, p. 157.

LUDWIG DEUTSCH

54 THE NUBIAN GUARD 1895

Oil on panel 51.8 x 33.7 cm
Private collection*

Viennese-born artist Ludwig Deutsch, who made his career as an Orientalist working in Paris, was an outstanding ethnographic painter of the Islamic world. This harmonious and richly coloured painting on panel is one of his most memorable works. It was painted from a Nubian or Sudanese model who posed for the artist in his French studio. During the 1890s and early 1900s Deutsch completed a series of pictures which he titled variously 'sentinel', 'palace guard' or 'harem guard', repeating, with minor variations, polished images of picturesquely costumed ethnic models standing guard at the entrances to marbled palaces. Rudolf Ernst, who was a close friend of Deutsch in Paris, painted a similar series. In this painting, Deutsch's *Nubian guard* wears glistening red slippers and an Ottoman helmet, is brandishing a long Ottoman *alam* or staff, and has a cluster of typical Near-Eastern weapons tucked into his belt (all items which feature in other works by the artist and probably drawn from his own collection of Islamic artefacts).[1]

Deutsch gives this stern figure – by implication a harem guard – a strong sense of character and expression. His features are painted with heightened naturalism and a precision of detail that characterises every part of the picture. The carefully painted marble finishes and geometrical decorations on the wall behind the figure are also reminiscent of the palace in *The tribute* (cat. 55). However, Deutsch creates a fresh impact in this work with his sonorous colour notes, especially the vivid slash of red drape set against the malachite green of an embossed bronze door. It is his skilful arrangement of colours and shapes, as well as his confident handling of bold colour contrasts, that gives such authority to this statuesque single-figure composition.   UP

[1] See Caroline Juler, *Najd Collection of Orientalist Paintings*, Manara, London, 1991, p. 50, for a discussion of other works from this series and associated artefacts used by the artist.

LUDWIG DEUTSCH

55 THE TRIBUTE c. 1897

Oil on panel 70 x 96.5 cm
The Najd Collection, courtesy of the Mathaf Gallery, London

Ludwig Deutsch specialised almost exclusively in scenes from the Islamic world, and was able to recreate many types of environment, from rough architecture and humble folk to noble households with elegantly clad figures, as in *The tribute*. Like many of his works, it was undated, but was exhibited at the Salon des Artistes Français in 1897. The subject of palace guards was one of the artist's most characteristic themes, which he has amended here with ceremonially clad figures silhouetted against a palace façade. According to Caroline Juler:

> *The scene is set in the interior of a palace whose architecture Deutsch may have based on the Mosque of Sultan Hassan in Cairo. Deutsch's figures, each one a study in different ethnic types, approach a darkened entrance carrying gifts for an unseen ruler. The picture is another sparkling essay in precision, the whole surface clear and sharp, and Deutsch has given it a particular nobility, as if the men were part of an ancient frieze.*[1]

Similar arrangements of intricately carved geometrical decoration, marble columns, steps and beautiful inlays of coloured tiles feature in many of Deutsch's pictures. However, the horizontal format makes this an unusual composition in the artist's *oeuvre*, the dignified procession of the figures moving towards the darkened doorway adding solemnity to the scene. Deutsch's picturesque scenes appear frozen and fixed forever, yet also function like film-stills, implying continuity of the actions depicted. Many European writers and painters had romanticised the East as 'timeless', and Deutsch followed this tradition. His was a fantasy of *Arabian Nights* pageantry translated into a quasi-photographic language of representation. He was careful to clothe his fantasies with authentic accessories such as ornately crafted weapons, *objets d'art* and exquisitely made and coloured costumes, and set them against the stately grandeur of Ottoman and Mameluke buildings.   UP

[1] Caroline Juler, *Najd Collection of Orientalist Paintings*, Manara, London, 1991, p. 50.

LUDWIG DEUTSCH

56 THE SCRIBE 1904

Oil on panel 51 x 37 cm
The Najd Collection, courtesy of the Mathaf Gallery, London

Deutsch depicted more than one version of this subject, a public letter-writer in Cairo, who is shown sitting in the street outside his house waiting for passing trade and posed in the meditative attitude of a thinker.[1] One of the traditional professions in the Near East, public scribes earned a living by reading as well as writing. Always well-educated, they were respected persons in Islamic cities, where a high value was placed on literacy and the subtleties of elegant calligraphy. The demand for public scribes in Cairo was widespread among all classes, because the daily business of the city was conducted in two languages: Arabic, the language of the mass of the people; and Turkish, the language of the State.

A number of directly executed oil sketches indicate that Deutsch visited Egypt, probably during the 1880s and 1890s. However, he painted most of his prolific repertoire of Orientalist subjects in France. Working mainly from the studio on rue Navarin that was listed as his official address in the Salon catalogues from 1885 to 1905, Deutsch employed Arab and African models who were working in France. He posed them with Islamic artefacts from his extensive personal collections, including furniture, ceramics and metal-work, as well as the carpets, silk robes, sashes and slippers that made repeated appearances in his pictures. Deutsch's passion for accuracy meant that the closely observed ornamentation detailed in favourite architectural backgrounds, which he also used more than once, was sometimes taken from photographs. In this, as in his choice of subjects and their careful realist rendering, Deutsch was strongly influenced by Gérôme. The carved, high-backed wooden dais, narghile, inlaid table, beautiful tile work and carved decoration around the doorway of this typical Ottoman house in Cairo are all convincingly rendered details that combine to make Deutsch's depiction of the scribe and his surroundings palpably real.   UP

[1] See Caroline Juler, *Najd Collection of Orientalist Paintings*, Manara, London, 1991, p. 45.

RUDOLF ERNST

57 REFRESHMENT c. 1890s

Oil on panel 60 x 48.7 cm
The Najd Collection, courtesy of the Mathaf Gallery, London

As is frequently the case with Ernst's pictures, *Refreshment* is undated. Like many of his works, it is brilliantly coloured and painted with eye-catching technical virtuosity. Ernst's fascination with the traditional arts and crafts of the Near East, especially decorated ceramic tiles and textiles, is also apparent here. Vivid shades of red, yellow and blue sparkle across the surface of his picture, like a closely woven tapestry, and the various textures and surfaces come alive under his skilful brush. Both servant and master are richly dressed and barefoot, their dark skin contrasted with the jewel-like patterning of their sumptuously decorated surroundings. *Refreshment* demonstrates Ernst's exuberantly eclectic approach to his subjects, combining an intricate overlay of designs from different sources – Algerian, Turkish, and Hispano-Moresque.

Caroline Juler has surveyed these sources in her analysis of the painting:

> *The background wall with its Alhambra-style window frame is covered with ceramic tiles whose patterns, though based on Ottoman designs, seem too regular to have come from the potteries of Iznik, Diyarbakir or Damascus, but copies of Turkish tiles like these were produced in Tunisia and elsewhere in North Africa. Ernst's reclining figure lies on a sofa covered by a Turkish Kilim and the dark cushion cover by his left hand also has a Turkish pattern. The carpet on the floor is taken from a Kazak 'eagle's claw' type...The servant wears an Egyptian head-dress with 19th century Turkish clothes and an Algerian woman's scarf around his waist. One half of the Alhambra vase can also be seen to the right.*[1]   UP

[1] Caroline Juler, *Najd Collection of Orientalist Paintings*, Manara, London, 1991, p. 89.

RUDOLF ERNST

58 THE FORTUNE TELLER c. 1890

Oil on panel 80.6 x 60 cm
The Najd Collection, courtesy of the Mathaf Gallery, London

Rudolph Ernst, like his friend Ludwig Deutsch, was a Viennese-born Orientalist who settled in Paris during the 1870s. During the 1880s, when he made his first journeys to Moorish Spain, Morocco and Tunis, Ernst began to exhibit pictures of mosque interiors and outdoor scenes of street traders, painted with photographic exactitude. During his extensive travels, which later included visits to Egypt and Turkey, he sketched, took photographs and collected a wide range of artefacts. Ernst's eclectic approach to his sources meant that he sometimes mixed them together in his pictures with less regard for the authenticity of his settings than his compatriot Ludwig Deutsch. According to Caroline Juler:

> *in* The fortune teller, *Ernst portrayed a traditional Arab custom of predicting a person's future by reading their palm print in the sand. The fortune teller's carpet is modelled on a Turkish coupled-column prayer rug, and the entrance behind him shows the neglected but still graceful façade of an Ottoman house with its intricate carving above the door.*[1]

Ernst painted many colourful pictures of the traditional professions and customs of the Ottoman world: storytellers, money-changers, brass-workers, various kinds of street vendors and wandering musicians. Most of these pictures, although rendered with technical precision, were not scenes witnessed on his travels, but studio compilations based on memory, imagination and models dressed in costumes and posed with various artefacts from the artist's collections.   UP

[1] Caroline Juler, *Najd Collection of Orientalist Paintings*, Manara, London, 1991, p. 86.

ALFRED DEHODENCQ

59 JEWISH BRIDE IN MOROCCO (Mariée juive au Maroc) N.D.

Oil on canvas 92.2 x 73.9 cm
Musée des Beaux-Arts de la Ville de Reims

The idea that Dehodencq is the link between Eugène Delacroix and Edouard Manet is well founded. A painter whose admiration for the former is clear in many of his Tangiers subjects (Jewish weddings, crowd scenes), Dehodencq's popular paintings of Spain helped inspire the Spanish phase of the young Manet.[1] Dehodencq's realism, his careful observation of costume and ethnic type, and his fluent brushwork relate him to Manet.

Indeed *The Jewish bride* has echoes of Manet's *Olympia* in the frank stare of the bride at the spectator, and the presence of the African servant at her side. Yet the idea of focusing on the formal costume of a Jewish woman had been explored by Delacroix in elaborate watercolours of 1832, and in his etching *Jewess of Algiers* (cat. 7). Delacroix even published an article explaining the wedding ceremony, with the bride's need for an upright seated posture 'immobile as an Egyptian statue', and elements of costume seen here, such as the broad cloth belt and the *jemar* or mitre cap from which the 'ram-buckle' ornaments hang.[2]

Whether Dehodencq's picture shows an actual bride or simply a young woman in festive costume (as seems more likely),[3] the painter has used the humanising devices of direct engagement with the spectator as well as virtuoso brushwork to offset the severity inherent in any formal costume study.   RB

[1] See Claude Roger-Marx, 'La Conquête picturale de l'Afrique du Nord, II–Alfred Dehodencq', *La Revue de l'Art*, vol. 57, 1930, p. 298.

[2] Delacroix (1841), cited in *Delacroix in Morocco*, exh. cat. (Institut du Monde Arabe), Flammarion, Paris, 1994, p. 156 (see ill. p. 157).

[3] Many details of her costume are also present in Delacroix's portrait of Mme Ben-chimol; see *Delacroix in Morocco*, p. 179.

ALFRED DEHODENCQ

60 MOROCCAN STORYTELLER (Le Conteur marocain) c. 1877 (Salon of 1877; Exposition Universelle 1878)

Oil on canvas 146 x 110 cm
Musée National des Arts d'Afrique et d'Océanie, Paris

Exhibited in the Paris Salon towards the end of his career, Dehodencq's *Moroccan storyteller* displays his ability to compose multiple-figure groups of exceptional liveliness. We see here an exchange between indoors and outdoors, the public and the private realms so separate in Maghrebian society. To the left a seasoned itinerant entertainer offers his services (his wife is just visible in the shadows); to the right a family of Jewish women and children consider his offer – the children with distinct nervousness, the women with degrees of anticipation and pleasure.

Dehodencq's much-commented upon prowess in grasping the diverse traits of the Moroccan peoples is evident here (Gautier had remarked his 'astonishing ethnographic aptitude').[1] Black Africans usually appear as talented musicians, dancers or storytellers in his pictures; Jewish people as a mildly exotic bourgeoisie whose elaborate ceremonies en- liven the domestic sphere. Here warmth and good humour are displayed in the exchange between performer and patron. Storytellers have considerable status in Maghrebian society, and the African's fine jellaba and imposing bulk attest to his success (compare with Delacroix's *Two studies of a Moorish musician*, cat. 4). The work exemplifies Dehodencq's 'eloquent grasp of attitude and gesture, that execution full of verve... and that profound intelligence of types which gives to a work...the value of a durable document'.[2] RB

[1] Gautier, quoted in Gabriel Séailles, 'Alfred Dehodencq', in *Société des Peintres Orientalistes Français*, 2nd exh. cat., Galeries Durand-Ruel, Paris, 1895, p. 21.

[2] ibid., p. 22.

HENRI REGNAULT

61 HASSAN AND NAMOUNA (Hassan et Namouna) c. 1870

Watercolour, gouache and black pencil on paper 56.5 x 79 cm
Collection Alain Lesieutre, Paris

One of the last works before Regnault's untimely death, this splendid watercolour gives an idea of his expertise in the medium as well as his obsession with all things eastern. 'It is the Orient that I call for, that I demand, that I want', he wrote after taking up his scholarship to Rome, 'only there, I believe, will I feel that I really am something'.[1]

Hassan and Namouna is one of three finished watercolours Regnault painted and presented to his fiancée, Geneviève Bréton, during the Siege of Paris (he had returned from Tangier in mid-winter to fight the invading Prussian army). According to Duparc:

> *To extricate Regnault from the sadness which enveloped him, his friends tried to get him to take up his brushes again…The studio of M. A. Goupil was decorated for him with rich Oriental hangings, sparkling silks, carpets with vivid and varied colours; Regnault set to work and did these three marvellous watercolours that everyone admired…[2]*

The most authoritative of those admirers in matters Oriental was Théophile Gautier, who wrote:

Fig. 31

HENRI REGNAULT, *Hassan and Namouna* (engraving after a drawing, repr. in Marx, *Henri Regnault*, p. 81)

> *On a divan laden with brocade, silk and leather is seated or, rather, reclines a young man, nude to the waist, tanned almost like a mulatto, with his arm pressed against his knee in a bold and artful movement. He is a strange figure – a sort of loosely rolled turban covers his brows with its broad folds, and projects a mysterious shadow over his eyes. One might say he was an Oriental Manfred or Don Juan who perhaps has known another civilisation and is looking for new diversions. His thin and nervous body, consumed with ardour, reminds us of the hero of Namouna, of Alfred de Musset's Hassan, who went off to brighten his scepticism in the land of the Sun, quitting his cigar for hashish.*

> *The painter probably did not intend this interpretation, but his watercolour suggests it: the boredom with luxury, the desire for the unknown, the weariness of 'artificial paradises', as Baudelaire calls them, can be read on this drawn countenance, still young despite all the excess.*

> *Stretched out on the thick carpets strewn on the ground, her shoulders resting against the divan, is a young woman enveloped in a hooded black gandourah open to her breast, whose whiteness is that of the moon emerging from a dark cloud. Nonchalantly she lets her henna-tinted fingers stray across the strings of the guzla accompanying her song, which she exhales like a sigh from her distracted lips. Nothing is more separate than these two beings, young and beautiful both, yet placed at either ends of a divan.*

[1] Letter to M. de Montfort (Rome, April 1869), in Arthur Duparc (ed.), *Correspondance d'Henri Regnault*, Charpentier, Paris, 1872, pp. 261–2.

[2] Duparc, pp. 402–3.

[3] Théophile Gautier, *Oeuvres de Henri Regnault exposées à l'Ecole des Beaux-Arts*, Paris, 1872, pp. 32–3 (this and Duparc quoted in sale catalogue of Beaussart Lefèvre, Paris, 29 April 1994, no. 20).

[4] See Roger Marx, *Henri Regnault, 1843–1871*, J. Rouam, Paris, 1886, pp. 63–4.

The luxury which surrounds them has a muted richness, a sort of funereal gravity, despite the violence of the tones held in the shadows through a superb mastery of coloration. Although nothing more than curtains and door-hangings, all the art of the Orient is manifest in these magnificent textiles...yet there is something tragic under this accumulation of splendours. This room could serve as the backdrop to some scene of jealousy or murder. Blood would leave no mark on these carpets of sombre purple.[3]

Regnault's charcoal and wash figure study seems closer to this dramatic intent than the final version, in which the pair of lovers threaten to 'disappear under the charming luxury of accessories'.[4]   RB

HENRI REGNAULT

62 THE ALHAMBRA, GRANADA: ENTRANCE TO THE HALL OF THE TWO SISTERS
(Alhambra de Grenade, entrée de la salle des deux soeurs) c. 1869

Watercolour with gouache highlights on paper 61 x 49 cm. Musée du Louvre, Paris

The Alhambra (from the Arabic *al-Hamra*, 'the Red') is the palace built in Granada, southern Spain, by the Nasrid caliphs at the high-point of their culture during the 13th and 14th centuries. A great masterpiece of Islamic architecture, it enjoyed cult status among poets and artists during the 19th century. John Frederick Lewis's appetite for the East began with his *Sketches and Drawings of the Alhambra* (1835), a volume superseded by the lavish *Plans, Elevations and Sections of the Alhambra* by Owen Jones and Jules Gourey (1836–45).[1]

It was partly to study Islamic ornament on behalf of his father, director of the Sèvres ceramics factory (and a pioneer of photography) that Regnault arrived in Granada with Clairin (q.v.) in 1869. His diligent analyses of tile colours and his photographic work were overshadowed by his ardour: 'Ah! my friend, if you could see the Alhambra!…There is nothing so beautiful, so delirious, so intoxicating as that!'.[2] 'We kneel before the genius of the Moors, every day we discover new splendours, the most incredible, the most hypnotic combinations of design in the doors and ceilings. What imagination in these ornaments…it's a labyrinth in which you lose yourself'.[3]

Regnault saw that using the palace as a backdrop for paintings on the life of the Moors of old would necessitate 'watercolours of fantastic difficulty' such as this one, bought posthumously by the State.[4] The famous honeycomb ceiling beyond this grandly sumptuous gateway inspired his *Summary execution* of 1870. In both, the blazing colour of golden sandstone is the symbol of a way of life whose drama and artistry Regnault could only imagine.   RB

[1] See Michael Darby, *The Islamic Perspective*, World of Islam Festival Trust, London, 1983, pp. 27, 43ff.

[2] Letter to M. Butin (1869), in Arthur Duparc (ed.), *Correspondance d'Henri Regnault*, Charpentier, Paris, 1872, p. 302.

[3] Letter to his father (October 1869), in Duparc, pp. 316–17.

[4] Phrase of Regnault to Butin, in Duparc, p. 303; on the Alhambra watercolours and the State see Roger Marx, *Henri Regnault 1843–1871*, J. Rouam, Paris, 1886, pp. 62–5, 87.

Georges Clairin

63 ENTERING THE HAREM late 1870s

Oil on canvas 82 x 65 cm
The Walters Art Gallery, Baltimore, Maryland, no. 37.82

Clairin's *Entering the harem* caters to an audience familiar with the tropes of Orientalist representation, arranging parts borrowed from Delacroix (the foreground still-life of exotic bibelots) and Regnault (the theatrical Moorish setting) in a smooth pastiche. The western male viewer's vicarious identification with the commanding sheikh, whose paler skin is framed in this work by the blackness of two attendants, was an important stimulus to the popularity of harem scenes in 19th-century representation. Clairin's allusion to the harem as a site of erotic fantasy remains implied rather than stated, with the locus of sensual pleasure transferred from the body's image to the tactile and visual appeal of rich stuffs, glittering metals and ornamental décor. Penetration becomes a matter of the sheikh's entrance through the curtained arch which separates the viewer from the private space of his household.

Clairin was particularly admired by his contemporaries for his bravura colourism, lavished here on the silken gleam of the sheikh's sleeve and the boldly abstract decorations of the architecture which describe his imagined Orient as a place at one remove from the coarser texture of reality. PR

GEORGES CLAIRIN

64 THE GUARD ND.

Oil on canvas 116.8 x 58.4 cm
Private collection*

Assertive handling borrowed from Impressionism and a palette dominated by yellows, oranges and reds assist Clairin in his description of a chic and not very forbidding Nubian guard. With the setting reduced to flat shapes whose vigorous handling only momentarily mimics the textures of carpet and old stone, attention is drawn to the juxtaposition of saturated and blanched colours forming a patchwork on the picture surface. The draped archway of Clairin's *Entering the harem* (cat. 63) recurs here as a piece of formalist pattern, with the blank wall cutting a decorative arc through a swathe of densely patterned fabric.

Clairin's memory of Manet is suggested by the structural use of black lines, tilted slightly off the perpendicular, to make details such as the guard's weapons and the hanging carpet's border reinforce his picture's flatness. The painter's academic training emerges only in the carefully finished head whose elegant placement high in the composition supports the implied eroticism of the flamboyant costume. This would seem to be a late addition to Clairin's gallery of eastern types, displaying a confidence in the arrangement of the props and in the adumbration of the dandifed figure that represents the Orient as a mere category of the French pictorial imagination. PR

BENJAMIN-CONSTANT

65 THE KING OF MOROCCO LEAVING TO RECEIVE A EUROPEAN AMBASSADOR c. 1880

Oil on canvas 135.3 x 106 cm
The Najd Collection, courtesy of the Mathaf Gallery, London

Benjamin-Constant visited Morocco in 1872 when he accompanied Charles Tissot, the plenipotentiary French minister, and the painter Georges Clairin (q.v.) on a diplomatic mission from Tangier to Marrakesh.[1] Like Delacroix forty years before him, Benjamin-Constant availed himself of official protection in order to travel securely in Morocco. He stayed primarily in Tangier for eighteen months, collecting Islamic artefacts and making sketches that inspired numerous paintings completed after his return to Paris. In the 1870s and 1880s the many Orientalist subjects among his exhibits at the Salon excited considerable controversy. In reviewing the Salon of 1876, Emile Zola described Benjamin-Constant as 'a good pupil of Cabanel, tormented by the long shadow of Delacroix'.[2]

Indeed the theme of this painting explicitly recalls a famous Delacroix in the Musée des Augustins in Benjamin-Constant's home town of Toulouse: *The Sultan of Morocco and his entourage*, 1845. The immense horsehoe arch of the portal evokes the fortified walls of Meknès as painted by Delacroix, but whereas in the latter's work the mounted figure of the sultan and his entourage is immediately before the viewer, in Benjamin-Constant the grand personage can only be glimpsed in the shadows of the gate, riding slowly towards the brilliantly lit centre stage.

Such a composition exemplifies what one writer has called the 'solemn and monumental entries' typical of Benjamin-Constant.[3] In the artist's related *Execution of the last rebels*, 1880, the sultan presides over a foreground of bloodstained bodies – an expansion on the violent thematics of his late friend Henri Regnault. Such theatrical massacres in harems or palace grounds became the source of Benjamin-Constant's notoreity. In this more documentary work, however, the violence is limited to the flash of exultant rifle-shots behind the sultan, and the uncertain fate of the prisoners on the right. The picture presumably recreates Sultan Sidi Mohammed (1859–73) welcoming Charles Tissot in 1872, an event the artist may have observed.

'M. Benjamin-Constant owes his career to a theatrical and robust talent', wrote Ary Renan, 'I would class him amongst the last of the Romantics (without intending any insult)'.[4]   UP & RB

[1] See Caroline Juler, *Najd Collection of Orientalist Paintings*, Manara, London, 1991, p. 29.

[2] Emile Zola, 'Salon de 1876', in *Mon Salon, Manet, Ecrits sur l'art*, Garnier-Flammarion, Paris, 1970, p. 258.

[3] See Régine Cardis-Toulouse, 'Benjamin-Constant et la peinture orientaliste', *Histoire de l'Art*, no. 4, December 1988, p. 82.

[4] Ary Renan, 'La Peinture orientaliste', *Gazette des Beaux-Arts*, 1894, cited in Cardis-Toulouse, p. 86.

GUSTAVE GUILLAUMET

66 THE SEGUIA, BISKRA (La Séguia, Biskra) 1884

Oil on canvas 100 x 155 cm
Musée d'Orsay, Paris. Acquired 1885

Biskra, an ancient oasis settlement dating at least to Roman times, was by the late 19th century a popular destination for European tourists in Algeria. Near the Arab town with its rammed-earth buildings and intricate system of *seguias* or irrigation channels feeding date-palm groves, a strip of modern hotels and the blight of a casino could be found.[1] Ignoring the latter, Guillaumet, a veteran of twenty years spent painting the desert regions of Algeria, evoked the harsh beauty of traditional oasis life in this canvas. Scattered figures give a sensation of quiet and of space, while the morning light plays across the brown earth and sun-baked walls.

A keen observer who exalted the time-honoured rituals of North African agriculture like some Barbizon painter in the desert, Guillaumet indicates the operation of the seguia system: the cut walls of the man-made channel on the right contrast with the meandering main stream, itself traversed by a water channel contained in a hollowed-out log. In the background, observed a critic, 'one sees a band of pale emerald green softened by the distance, and a palm grove outlined against a sky that is cloudless, yet almost white with warm vapours. Three girls come to draw water with their jugs, and one must add, with Guillaumet, [that] "the elegance of the amphora completes the grace of the woman".'[2]

A composition of immaculate discipline (at twenty-three Guillaumet had been runner-up for the landscape prize at the Ecole des Beaux-Arts), this late work, shown at the Salon of 1885, was considered one of the two or three finest by a master who had single-handedly revived the standing of the Orientalist school:

> *By the picturesque choice of subject, the elegance of its silhouettes, the finesse of the light, the exactness of its values, the delicacy of the reflections absorbed by the shadows, by the skill in laying out the terrain and the assurance of its design, finally by the sobriety and deftness of its execution, this painting is an incomparable work. It has suavety, it has poetry, and a true air of classical beauty.*[3] RB

1 The writer Isabelle Eberhardt, who travelled in remote Algeria dressed as a male Arab, bemoans Biskra's adulteration in *Prisoner of Dunes: Selected Writings*, trans. Sharon Bongert, Peter Owen, London & Chester Springs, 1995, p. 92.

2 E. Durand-Gréville, 'Gustave Guillaumet', *L'Artiste*, vol. 57, no. 1, May 1887, p. 351.

3 Léonce Bénédite, 'La peinture orientaliste et Gustave Guillaumet', *La Nouvelle revue*, vol. 50, January 1888, p. 336.

GUSTAVE GUILLAUMET

67 WOMAN OF BOU SAADA (Femme de Bou-Saâda) 1880s

Oil on canvas 31 x 46 cm
Private collection, courtesy Galerie Jean-François Heim, Paris

One of the rare individual figure studies by Guillaumet, this work has the visual weight of an icon. The pyramidal composition, of doubled triangles, sits solidly in its frame. In a masterly and unusual motif, the woman's right leg juts directly towards the viewer, although drapery disguises the impact of its foreshortening. The Berber model's strongly featured face and her gaze turned sharply away from the viewer gives a vivid sense of inner life (and possibly resistance to the painter's scrutiny). Although seated, the woman's powerful right arm and febrile hands, one clutching a shawl while the other fingers its blood-red woollen strands, imparts a sense of impending movement. Guillaumet's energetic brushwork helps convey this impression.

Thematically the painting is related to Guillaumet's late series of seated women weaving in the Rembrandtesque gloom of poor Bou Saâda houses (Musée d'Orsay, Paris). But, by providing only bright studio walls and the floor as background, Guillaumet abstracts his sitter from such a genre context, elevating her to the status of the portrait. Seated on the ground, unlike a European, she is nevertheless endowed with dignity and grace.

The overall motif is close to that of the sculptural monument to Guillaumet, *Girl of Bou Saâda* (fig. 32)[1], in which a Berber girl scatters flowers over an effigy of the artist. The artist's premature death was widely lamented: 'La jeune école française perd en lui un artiste hardi, fidèle et convaincu', wrote the Symbolist Ary Renan.[2] Made by his former teacher Barrias, the memorial was set up in Montmartre Cemetery after being displayed at the Salon of 1900. RB

Fig. 32
BARRIAS
*Girl of Bou Saâda,
tomb of the painter
Guillaumet* 1900
Montmartre Cemetery,
Paris

[1] Thanks to Jean-François Heim for suggesting this connection.

[2] 'In him, the new French school has lost a dedicated, bold and committed artist'; Ary Renan, 'Gustave Guillaumet', *Gazette des Beaux-Arts*, 2nd series, vol. 35, May 1887, p. 404.

127

FREDERICK A. BRIDGMAN

68 THE EMBROIDERER (La Brodeuse) after 1900

Oil on canvas 48.3 x 64.7 cm
The Najd Collection, courtesy of the Mathaf Gallery, London

An American pupil of Jean-Léon Gérôme, Frederick Bridgman made his first Algerian tour in 1872 and thereafter visited North Africa almost annually. Describing a trip in the winter of 1885–86, Bridgman wrote that 'my impressions of North Africa can never be dispelled'.[1] He exhibited Orientalist subjects regularly at the London Royal Academy, the Société des Peintres Orientales Français, and in New York. This is his most intimate painting of a North African subject: a gentle depiction of a barefoot woman wearing billowing red silk harem pants and daydreaming over her embroidery while sitting beside a tame gazelle – a symbol of innocence – in the leafy courtyard of an Algerian villa. The model for the embroidering woman appears in a number of Bridgman's works, as do gazelles. His early work was close to that of Gérôme, but Bridgman later became an admirer of Renoir. His idyllic image of the secluded life of a North African woman is intimate, sunlit and freshly coloured, making an interesting comparison to Renoir's painting of an Algerian girl (cat. 72).

In 1884 the *Magazine of Art* urged artists to go to Algiers, declaring: 'fortunately for the artist, it has preserved most of its characteristic features to this day with true Oriental conservatism'. This text, like Bridgman's imagery, described the private world hidden behind the public façade of its white-walled villas:

> *a large patio, or court…In the centre a fountain sends up a thin spray of water, and at the foot of each twisted column that supports the slender white horseshoe arches, which rise airily from the four sides of the court, a few vines and passion flowers, or the Bougainvillea, flushing into tender mauve at its extremities, clamber to the floor above; while orange, lime, or pomegranate trees cast refreshing shadows…ever flashing and changing beneath the soft light thrown from the sunny walls above.*[2] UP

[1] Bridgman, quoted by Caroline Juler, *Najd Collection of Orientalist Paintings*, Manara, London, 1991, p. 27.

[2] 'Algiers', *Magazine of Art*, vol. 7, Cassell, London, Paris & New York, 1884, p. 178.

Etienne Dinet

69 THE SNAKE CHARMER (Le Charmeur de vipères) 1889

Oil on canvas 175.6 x 180.4 cm
The Art Gallery of New South Wales, Sydney. Purchased 1890

Dinet's painting *The snake charmer* was purchased in Paris in July 1890; destined for the collection of the National Art Gallery of New South Wales, it was shipped to Sydney in its original frame. Painted in Laghouat in Algeria in 1889 and first exhibited at the Salon in Paris the following year, it received favourable comment from the French critics.[1] George Lafenestre declared that 'Algeria is a good school for colourists' and Dinet 'among the first to express the extraordinary and unexpected effects of the sun on figures in the open air'. He explained that Dinet worked in Africa 'in order to sate himself with light' and admired:

> *his large picture,* The snake charmer, *where all the figures, dazzled by an intense light, squint and grimace in the heat, which also causes observers to squint; but if one can endure this blinding dazzle, one sees that the figures under this excessive radiation are wonderfully individualised and vividly real.*[2]

Dinet's *The snake charmer* depicts full-length figures in the middle distance, unlike his later works where he tended to prefer half-length close-up views of figures and focused more on the depiction of human emotions. Although individual reactions among the group of figures watching the snake charmer have been vividly differentiated, their overall significance remains subservient to Dinet's fascination with the vibrant luminosity of Algerian light. In Algeria Dinet freed himself from the slick finish that was a requirement of his academic training in order to paint directly observed scenes with vigour and freshness. In *The snake charmer* his approach to form is broad; he uses his brush and colours to accentuate the play of shadows and highlights across various surfaces and to animate his realistic depiction of scene. The draperies seem to trap and intensify light; brown skin glistens with white reflections; the yellowish sand not only merges into the blue-toned shadows cast down by the figures but also reflects a bright light upwards like a mirror. Dinet nuances contrasting colour values to suggest the 'glare' of full sun, balancing cool blues, whites and greys against warm yellows, orange and touches of red.

The realism of Dinet's painting of dazzling sunlight and heat was to prove important for generations of Australian painters who came to admire his work hanging in the permanent collection at the Art Gallery of New South Wales. Lionel Lindsay later wrote: 'I cannot but think that the magnificent Dinet *The snake charmer* in the Sydney Gallery, helped Streeton in realising the atmosphere of summer. Sunlight has rarely been so magnificently rendered as in this characteristic group of Arabs'.[3] Lindsay himself visited Dinet in Bou Saâda in 1929 and reminded him that Sydney owned this important early work. Dinet told him how he had painted the snake charmer in a town south of Bou Saâda, that it 'was done...in the open' and that 'the old man was afterwards bitten by one of the little horned vipers and died'. Lionel guessed that after so many years Dinet's recollection of the work had faded, saying, 'I don't think he remembers how good the picture is in its marvellous truth of light'.[4]

Years later, Lloyd Rees confirmed that Dinet's *The snake charmer* was much admired by Australian artists and was also one of the pictures from the Gallery collection they most talked about. He remembered it particularly in the period just after the First World War, when he first arrived in Sydney and: 'A new sense of realism was coming into artistic thinking. This was admired as a painting of light, rather than of subject'.[5]   UP

1 For a list of Salon reviews see Denise Brahimi & Koudir Benchikou, *La Vie et l'ouevre de Etienne Dinet*, ACR, Paris, 1984, cat. no. 144.

2 Georges Lafenestre, 'Les Salons de 1890', *Revue des Deux Mondes*, Paris 1890, vol. 3, p. 925.

3 Lionel Lindsay, *The Art of Arthur Streeton*, special number of *Art in Australia*, Angus & Robertson, Sydney, 1919, p. 12.

4 Lionel Lindsay letter, 27 March 1929, inserted in autographed copy of Dinet's *Khadra: Danseuse Ouled Nail*, given to him by Dinet in Bou Saâda, 26 March 1929; Mitchell Library collection, Sydney.

5 'Victorian favourites, a conversation: Elwyn Lynn and Lloyd Rees', *Art and Australia*, vol. 22, no. 1, Sydney, 1984, p. 52.

ETIENNE DINET

70 SLAVE OF LOVE AND LIGHT OF THE EYES: ABD-EL-GHERAM AND NOURIEL AIN,
   AN ARAB LEGEND (Esclave d'amour et lumière des yeux: Abd-el-Gheram et Nouriel-Aîn, légende arabe) 1900

Oil on canvas 47 x 54 cm. Musée d'Orsay, Paris. Acquired 1901

Probably the best-known of all Dinet's works owing to postcards, prints and copies by other artists, Dinet's *Slave of love* was purchased by the French Minister of Fine Arts for the Musée du Luxembourg in 1901.[1] Despite its relatively small size, the work's intense detail and highly romantic theme guaranteed its popularity with the museum public of the earlier 20th century.

The importance of this work in the history of Orientalism is that, like many of Dinet's figure scenes, it documents a perception of Arab life that is profoundly sympathetic and made – to an extent unprecedented for a Westerner – with an 'inside' knowledge of a local culture. Dinet's passion for the Algerian desert life led him to become fluent in Arabic, make a home in the oasis town of Bou Saâda, and convert to Islam in 1913. From 1889 he studied Arab culture under the guidance of the young M'Zabite writer,

Sliman ben Ibrahim, who became his lifelong companion (despite the latter's two marriages). The subject of this picture is revealed in one of their several collaborative books, *Pictures of the Arab Life*, in which Sliman relates it to the lyrical tradition of Arab love stories:

> *'Clair de Lune'…See these young lovers from my country…Their two entwined bodies seem to me to possess one unique soul which suffices for them both to live. The joy of their reunion makes them forget everything…*
>
> *The moon is the faithful companion of Saharan lovers, it is compassionate and helpful.*
>
> *A cruel fate had separated Abd-el-Gheram, the Slave of Passion, and Nouriel Ain, the Light of the Eyes.*
>
> *Immense and empty spaces stretched between their two hearts, but they found a means to reunite in the contemplation of the moon. Every evening…their eyes gazed upon the moon, at the place they felt the cherished eyes of the other fixed at that same hour…*[2]

Fig. 33
LEHNERT &
LANDROCK
Couple, Algeria
c. 1911
Photograph
Collection Angela
Tromellini, Bologna

Inspired by embracing couples in Islamic miniatures (and possibly photographs such as shown in fig. 33), Dinet binds the figures to their background with a soft pink moon-light relayed by oleander blooms and the girl's translucent veil. Her abundant silver jewellery, studied from Berber models, is echoed in the medallion to the right.[3] The lovers' smiling faces, almost saccharine by today's standards, nevertheless reveal a portrait-like specificity and inwardness all too rare in Orientalist art.   RB

[1] See Denise Brahimi & Koudir Benchikou, *La Vie et l'oeuvre de Etienne Dinet*, ACR, Paris, 1984, cat. no.319, p. 234.

[2] Etienne Dinet & Sliman ben Ibrahim, *Tableaux de la vie arabe*, Henri Piazza, Paris, 1922 (1906), pp. 119–20.

[3] This reads 'Etienne Dinet, painted in 1900 at Biskra'; Brahimi & Benchikou, p. 234.

AUGUSTE RENOIR

71 ARAB FESTIVAL, ALGIERS. THE KASBAH (Fête arabe, Alger. La Casbah) 1881

Oil on canvas 73.5 x 92 cm
Musée d'Orsay, Paris. Gift of the Biddle Foundation in memory of Mrs Margaret Biddle 1957

[1] Renoir (with Gérôme) was an honorary president of the Société des Peintres Orientalistes Français, where he exhibited from 1893 to 1900; in *Exposition Nationale Coloniale: Exposition rétrospective des orientalistes français*, Marseilles, 1906, his *Fête au camp* is listed as no. 53.

[2] See MaryAnne Stevens (ed.), *The Orientalists: Delacroix to Matisse*, exh. cat., Royal Academy of Arts, London, 1984, p. 222; and John House, *Renoir*, Hayward Gallery & Arts Council of Great Britain, London, 1985, p. 226.

[3] Renoir, quoted in House.

[4] 'When one has seen Algeria one loves it. The farmers are making enormous fortunes, properties are increasing in value and in ten years Algiers will certainly be the most beautiful city in the world'; letter to Mme Bérard, formerly held at Archives Durand-Ruel, kindly provided by John House.

Traditionally considered the most important of the dozen canvases brought back from Renoir's visits to Algiers in the springs of 1881 and 1882, *Arab festival* was purchased by Claude Monet in 1900 and included in the retrospective of Orientalism at the Colonial Exposition of 1906.[1]

The occasion painted by Renoir has never been firmly identified; it may have been a religious celebration or, as seems more likely, a performance by itinerant North African musicians of the kind painted by Delacroix and Dehodencq (cats 4, 60).[2] In the centre of the canvas a ring of five dancers play tambourines and flutes before a large crowd. Men, women and children, wraith-like in their rendering, are scattered across a natural amphitheatre formed by the raw earth of the heights behind the kasbah (today built over). The corner of bleached towers, domes and cubes of 'Algiers the White', with the hazy blue sea beyond, helps anchor this highly unconventional composition.

The festive atmosphere of Renoir's picture is augmented by its very lack of specificity, indeed the painter's inability directly to paint the Algerian populace. Renoir recounted to Vollard: 'When I delivered this picture to Durand-Ruel, it looked like a heap of crumbled plaster. Durand-Ruel trusted me, and several years later the colour had done its work, and the subject emerged from the canvas as I had conceived it'.[3]

Although his letters reveal a Frenchman full of enthusiasm for the physical splendours of the colony and its rich potential,[4] like a regular Orientalist Renoir's aesthetic focus was the transforming quality of North African light. RB

AUGUSTE RENOIR

72 ALGERIAN GIRL (Algérienne) 1881

Oil on canvas 50.8 x 40.5 cm
Courtesy Museum of Fine Arts, Boston. Juliana Cheney Edwards Collection

A master figure painter among Impressionists, Renoir's urge to paint from live models in Algiers was frustrated by the traditional reluctance of Islamic people to have anything to do with painting, and the fact that such models as were available seemed to be very expensive:

Here I am installed in Algiers and negotiating with some Arabs to help me find some models…I have seen some incredibly picturesque children. Will I be able to get them? I'll do everything I need to for it. I've also seen some pretty women…The figure, even in Algiers, is becoming more and more costly to obtain. If you knew the quantity of bad painters there are here. It's crazy, and above all the English, who spoil the few women who are available. It's insupportable.[1]

In Paris between trips Renoir responded to the problem by resorting to the expedient of Delacroix: dressing sitters in Algerian costume. *Algerian girl,*[2] however, was probably painted on location, as was the masquerading daughter of a Parisian journalist in *Mlle. Fourcaud dressed as an Algerian.* If the sitter was not French, she might have been from the Jewish or Berber communities – although Renoir managed not to characterise her as such, assimilating her instead to the peaches-and-cream complexion and chubby physiognomy he used for Parisiennes (the European features seem unmistakable when compared with the contemporary *Woman of Bou Saáda* by Guillaumet, cat. 67). Her costume, with its iridescent over-skirt and tangerine-tinted jacket, is that of a well-to-do city dweller, and patent-leather shoes give the girl a cosmopolitan touch (Turkish women often combined items of European costume with traditional gowns).

It is surprising to see a conventional Orientalist subject rendered in the feathery patina of impressionist brushstrokes. Renoir's brilliant, lustrous colour, achieved by 'brushing the colour thinly across a dense layer of opaque white priming',[3] achieves a bejewelled decorative effect which advances even upon the Orientalist watercolours of Delacroix and Regnault. RB

1 Letter to Durand-Ruel, March 1882, in Lionello Venturi, *Les Archives de l'impressionnisme*, Paris & New York, 1939, vol. 1, pp. 124–5 (thanks to John House).

2 This work was probably the *Algérienne assise* exhibited at the 'Première exposition rétrospective et actuelle des peintres orientalistes français', Palais de l'Industrie, Paris, October–December 1893, cat. no. 397 (Durand-Ruel collection).

3 John House, *Renoir: Master Impressionist*, Queensland Art Gallery & Art Exhibitions Australia, Sydney, 1994, p. 88.

TOM ROBERTS

73 MOORISH DOORWAY 1883

Oil on canvas 48.3 x 33 cm
Joseph Brown Collection*

In the summer of 1883 Tom Roberts took a break from his art studies at the Royal Academy Schools in London to travel through Spain. Andalusia, where he lingered for three months, was romantic Spain, popularised by Washington Irving, Bizet and Gautier. When he went there in 1869 the young painter Henri Regnault said, 'My divine mistress the Alhambra calls me: she has sent me one of her lovers, the sun' (see cat. 62).[1] From the 1830s it was a favourite destination for French and English painters seeking sunshine and romantically picturesque motifs. Among the artists who travelled there were Roberts's mentor, Edwin Long, then president of the Royal Academy, Frederic Leighton and Jean-Léon Gérôme, who worked for a month in Granada together with the Italian Orientalist Alberto Pasini. During his 1883 visit to Granada, Roberts met one of Gérôme's pupils, Laureano Barrau, who encouraged him to make direct colour sketches in front of the motif.

In September, when Roberts arrived in Granada, he wasted no time in visiting the Alhambra and sketching the site 'where Moorish art reached its acme, and was glorious in its designs, colour and architecture'.[2] The following year he exhibited a Spanish subject at the Royal Academy titled *Basking – a corner in the Alhambra*.[3] It is not certain whether the painting *Moorish doorway*, which Roberts inscribed 'Granada' and dated October 1883, is related to that picture, but the implications of 'basking' and warm sunlight are consistent. In order to convey the sense of an exotic place, Roberts chose a picturesque 'postcard' motif for *Moorish doorway* and concentrated on convincingly rendering the textures of weathered masonry, its warm tonalities exposed under the glare of afternoon sunlight. It was in tackling such 'Orientalist' subjects in Spain that Roberts first captured the full intensity of dazzling light playing across forms in the open air. This experiment in rendering 'glare' through closely controlled tones and enlivening touches of the brush also prefigured the way in which Roberts would later approach the depiction of similarly hot, dry landscapes in the Antipodes.   UP

1 Regnault, quoted in Philippe Jullian, *The Orientalists*, Phaidon, Oxford, 1977, p. 115.

2 Dr William Maloney, who was with Roberts in Spain, quoted by R. H. Croll, *Tom Roberts: Father of Australian Landscape Painting*, Robertson & Mullens, Sydney, 1935, p. 12.

3 Royal Academy Exhibition, London, 1884, cat. no. 775.

TOM ROBERTS

74 UNTITLED (Seated Arab) c. 1884

Oil on canvas 45.9 x 30.9 cm
Private collection, Thirty Victoria Street

Roberts's painting of a seated Arab is unusual in the artist's *oeuvre*. It is closely related to academic realism and to the type of Orientalist ethnic figure developed by Bonnat (cat. 52) and Gérôme in particular. Roberts had visited Paris and joined Gérôme's classes at the Académie Julian before his return to Australia in 1885.[1] It is not known whether this painting dates from the brief period when he was under Gérôme's instruction, but it is certainly the closest he ever came to Gérôme's meticulous Orientalism. Roberts had also recently travelled in Spain and might have encountered such a quiet, back-street setting in the historic Moorish quarter of an Andalusian town. However, the 'Arab' painted here was most likely based on a studio model.

The sense of intrigue, mystery and exoticism is heightened by the softly atmospheric lighting and contrasting colour notes. X-rays show that there is little underdrawing and that the paint has been quite directly applied. The plunging view into the narrow alleyways of a supposed Moorish town is the most 'impressionist' part of the canvas. However, like Gérôme, Roberts turned the background into a foil for the seated figure and used it as a counterpoise to bring equilibrium to the composition. There was a long tradition in Dutch genre painting that associated images of smokers with allegories of the senses. Roberts's exploitation of the calm, blank area of whitewashed wall and his concern for visual balance hark back to the ordered compositions of the Dutch masters. Likewise, his emphasis on materiality – his revelling in the contrast between the shimmering, faintly striped green costume and the rough surface of old masonry. Such muted pearly tonalities might be compared with other pictures by Roberts from this time, such as the quiet single-figure study, *Woman on a balcony*, painted in Venice in 1884, or the multi-figured and more complex composition depicting his voyage home from Europe, *Coming south* of 1885–86.   UP

1 See Helen Topliss, 'Biographical outline', in *Tom Roberts, 1856–1931: A Catalogue Raisonné*, 2 vols, Oxford University Press, Melbourne, 1985, vol. 1, pp. 68–9. Roberts's card for the 'Académie Julian–Passage des Panoramas. J.L. Gérôme', lodged with the Roberts Papers, coupled with a letter from his friend Harry Bates (ML MS, vol. 3, A 2480), puts Roberts in Paris between October 1884 and February 1885.

ARTHUR STREETON

75 FATMA HABIBA 1897

Oil on canvas on paperboard 29 x 27.4 cm
Art Gallery of South Australia, Adelaide. Gift of Mr and Mrs Douglas Mullins 1997

Arthur Streeton inscribed this small, emblematic picture 'Cairo 1897'. It depicts a veiled woman, her eyes sparkling and slightly narrowed, as if in hidden laughter. *Fatma Habiba* has been momentarily frozen into a still, close-up, iconically frontal form that Streeton presents with un-swerving intensity, exploiting the contrast between her shrouded, triangular silhouette rising like a pyramid above an empty horizon, and the flare of sunlight that bounces off the chalky wall behind her. Streeton was fascinated by the ethnic diversity of the colourfully dressed inhabitants who thronged Cairo's crowded streets. In one of his letters home he described waiting for the Nile bridge to swing open and seeing:

> *quite 700 or 800 waiting with us for the bridge to open…as they've waited thousands of years before. Arabs, Egyptians, Berbers, Copts, and all sorts wait quietly – their long gowns of a dozen degrees of blue – women sit on donkeys, or squat on their dark haunches, dark-robed against the oranges they sell.*[1]

The image of the veiled woman was, for the Westerner, one of the most potent images of the mysterious Orient. What was hidden from the gaze tantalised the imagination, and Streeton, like his friend Conder, was drawn to the poetry of Omar Khayyám and the fantasy world of the *Arabian Nights*.[2] Although his letters home comment on the modern intrusion of 'the fresh-complexioned, soldier-boys of the Empire' in Cairo, he preferred to paint only the contemporary survivors of its old ways and 'everything else that used to constitute the playground of Cleopatra'.[3] The difficulty of finding local models willing to pose had long proved a challenge to Orientalist painters and Streeton takes up this challenge with an element of humour. His Egyptian *Mona Lisa* also smiles enigmatically, but only with her eyes.   UP

[1] Arthur Streeton, letter from 9 Waghe-el birghet, Cairo, reprinted in the 'Red Page', *Bulletin* (Sydney), 21 October 1899.

[2] In 1905 he exhibited an *Allegory from Omar* at the RA in London– 'Three figures of beautiful women, with flowing hair, stand in an almost golden light'; see review, 'Australian artists in London', *Daily Telegraph*, 8 June 1905.

[3] Streeton letter, reprinted in the *Bulletin*, op. cit.

ARTHUR STREETON

76 EGYPTIAN DRINK VENDOR 1897

Oil on canvas on paperboard 33.2 x 18.3 cm. Collection National Gallery of Australia, Canberra
Bequest of Henriette von Dallwitz and of Richard Paul in honour of his father, Dr Oscar Paul 1965

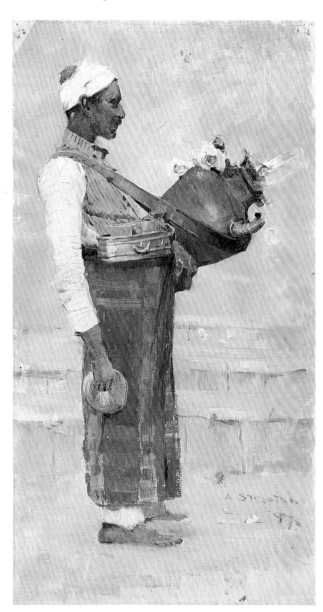

In 1898, being settled in London, Streeton wrote to Tom Roberts that he was sending to Australia:

> *a small parcel of my pictures for Jim Conroy – in case there is an Exhibition coming on in Sydney – they are figure studies of Arabs…Would you choose suitable frames at Callans for me –* cheap they must be *– & if the 3 Drink Sellers could be placed in one frame, they would prove more attractive I believe – & stand a better chance of sale…When these things are framed I'd be so glad if you'd blow the dust off the dark ones, & then give 'em a coat of thin spirit varnish – I tried oil on 'em here – & find they will improve by varnishing.*[1]

According to Mary Eagle, the diagram Streeton enclosed with these framing instructions for Roberts indicates that this is the 'Red one' specified in Streeton's preferred arrangement, left to right: 'Red one', 'Pale blue one', 'Dark blue one' – all to be framed in 'dark brown or oak green'.[2]

The bright Egyptian light descends vertically to stencil the profiled drink vendor against the buff-coloured stone walls of the old city, his vivid scarlet apron the strongest note in the harmony of tans, pinks and creamy whites that Streeton uses to distinguish the beautiful colour scheme of 'Red one' in his series of pictures of drink-sellers at outdoor cafés. Such motifs were primarily an opportunity for Streeton to make attractive impressionist pictures of light and what he hoped would be a marketable set of decorations. Leaving Cairo to set up a studio in London, where he arrived at the end of May 1897, Streeton had ambitions to paint a series of allegorical figure decorations as well as travel pictures and to hold 'an Exhibition entirely of decorations' which he believed would make his name in London.[3] This scheme came to nothing, so he gradually sent groups of his decoratively conceived Egyptian pictures back to Australia.   UP

[1] Streeton letter to Tom Roberts, 29 June 1898, in Ann Galbally & Anne Gray (eds), *Letters from Smike: The Letters of Arthur Streeton 1890–1943*, Oxford University Press, Melbourne, 1989, pp. 78–9.

[2] Mary Eagle, *The Oil Paintings of Arthur Streeton in the National Gallery of Australia*, National Gallery of Australia, Canberra, 1994, p. 120.

[3] Streeton letter to Walter Barnett, 6 October 1897, quoted in Eagle, p. 111.

ARTHUR STREETON

77 A SELLER OF DRINKS, CAIRO 1897

Oil on canvas on wood panel   42.2 x 21 cm
Private collection

This vividly decorative painting with its Arabic inscription, 'Mahommed Ali', is the most daring in composition and colour of Streeton's series of three Egyptian drink-sellers. It was probably based on an encounter with a street vendor in an outdoor café in Cairo, of which Streeton kept a souvenir photograph that is still in the collection of the artist's family (fig. 34).[1] The subject of the photograph stands in the same frontal position as Streeton's drink-seller, supporting a large stoppered jar, with a cup and fly-whisk in one hand, and wearing a striped apron. However, Streeton changed the direction of the stripes in his painted image, using bold verticals to contrast with the striped architecture behind.

Streeton sent a number of his 'sketches of the East' back to Sydney, where a small group was successfully shown at the Art Society of New South Wales 19th Annual Exhibition in 1898.[2] Among these works, which a reviewer described as: 'clever studies of water carriers, porters and other inhabitants of Egypt – strongly drawn and richly coloured',[3] were three small images gathered into a single frame and titled *Egyptian drink vendors*, catalogued number 51 and priced at twenty-one pounds. Other titles included: *The spice bazaar*; '*Ottoman Ali*', *breadseller*; *The citadel, Muhammad Ali*; and '*Hassan*' *the porter*. The Sydney critics generally welcomed Streeton's fresh Orientalist 'sketches', finding continuities with his approach to Australian light and atmosphere. The *Daily Telegraph* declared: 'Mr Arthur Streeton's Cairo sketches are a considerable source of strength. They are slight but remarkably clever and full of interest. At a glance one can see that, like the artist he is, he has gone for the local atmosphere rather than a transcript of any particular spot'.[4]   UP

[1] See Mary Eagle, *The Oil Paintings of Arthur Streeton in the National Gallery of Australia*, National Gallery of Australia, Canberra, 1994, pp. 111, 120.

[2] Letter to Frederick Delmer, c. October 1897, records that he sent them to his friend Jim Conroy in Sydney saying 'I think he can sell for me'; see Ann Galbally & Anne Gray (eds), *Letters from Smike: The Letters of Arthur Streeton 1890–1943*, Oxford University Press, Melbourne, 1989, p.75.

[3] *Sydney Morning Herald*, 10 September 1898.

[4] *Daily Telegraph*, 8 September 1898.

Fig. 34
A seller of drinks
Photo by Arthur
Streeton

ARTHUR STREETON

78 CAIRO STREET 1897

Oil on canvas on paperboard 33.4 x 17.1 cm. Collection National Gallery of Australia, Canberra
Bequest of Henriette von Dallwitz and of Richard Paul in honour of his father, Dr Oscar Paul 1965

Cairo street depicts a Cairo street scene of the Grand Bazaar, looking towards one of the entrances of the polychrome mosque, El-Shafei. In a letter home, Streeton had recorded his admiration for 'the grand large design of some of the mosques and the fine arches and fastnesses of the city'.[1] He took photographs and made sketches of the picturesquely winding passageways between the close-packed buildings in the old city, the flimsy awnings shading street vendors' displays, and the graceful white minarets towering into the blue sky. In this picture the imposing height of the portal to the mosque caught Streeton's eye; as he said, 'one looks up with the wondering eye of a child'.[2]

Cairo was not only a city of impressive buildings and busy commerce to Streeton, it was also a vivid poem of colour and light, scents and sensations that he wanted to capture in his work. He wrote:

> *There is an unusual brilliance in the morning air of Cairo and a distinctive pleasant fragrance, perhaps resulting from mignonette, clover piled on camels' backs, coffee, incense and other flavours of the Orient...and tall minarets of pink and white tower into the blue air, while below tourists swarm with their brilliant dragomen.*[3]

The sparkling clarity of Streeton's palette of white, rose and blue, the crispness of touch with which he applied his colours, and the economy of drawing with which he suggested crowds and commerce against the serene beauties of a timeless architecture makes this small but freshly perceived image one of his most convincing evocations of the atmosphere and bustling street life of Cairo. UP

[1] Arthur Streeton, letter from 9 Waghe-el birghet, Cairo, reprinted in the 'Red Page', *Bulletin* (Sydney), 21 October 1899.

[2] Streeton, unpublished family papers quoted by Mary Eagle, *The Oil Paintings of Arthur Streeton in the National Gallery of Australia*, National Gallery of Australia, Canberra, 1994, p. 116.

[3] Streeton, 'With Signora Bozzetti', unpublished Personal Narrative, Streeton family papers.

Fig. 35
A Cairo street
Photo by Arthur
Streeton

HILDA RIX NICHOLAS

79 ARAB MARKETPLACE, MOROCCO 1914

Oil on board 27.3 x 35.1 cm
Collection Ballarat Fine Art Gallery. Purchased 1977

Fig. 36
Hilda Rix Nicholas dressed as an Arabian woman
c. 1914

Rix Nicholas Archive, Delegate, New South Wales

Tangier and its Grand Soko or main marketplace fascinated Rix Nicholas: it was 'so much like an extraordinarily beautiful dream that [she was] afraid to wake up in the morning and find it all gone'.[1] Living on its perimeter at the Hotel Villa de France gave her easy access to the site, in which she found everything she wanted – all the sights, smells and sounds of the Orient were hers for the taking. It was a popular place for European painters. *Travel* magazine advised that it was 'the best spot to witness the real life of the Moors'; it was also a place where 'harmonious Eastern pictures' could easily be constructed if artists avoided the tourists and discordant western buildings.[2]

Elsie Rix liked the picture; she called it a 'perfect shimmer' and was impressed with her sister's rendering of the 'feeling of the heat making the colours vibrate'.[3] Working quickly and with little time to record facial features, Rix Nicholas concentrated on the overall impression of form, colour and pattern, in the process sacrificing individual character and gesture to the flow of paint that eddies about the forms. Like other European painters, Rix Nicholas was intrigued by the range of colourful and richly embroidered costumes she saw in the marketplace. She collected as many as she could afford, and in her Moroccan work they played a decisive part in her construction of the exotic East. She focused less on specific details than on the decorative ensemble of dress.   JP

[1] Hilda Rix Nicholas to a friend, Tangier, 5 February 1912, Rix Nicholas Archive, Delegate, New South Wales.

[2] George E. Holt, 'Intimate glimpses of Tangier', *Travel*, November 1913, p.10; Robert E. Groves, 'Morocco as a winter sketching ground', *Studio*, vol. 45, 1908–09, p. 25.

[3] Elsie Rix to her mother, Tangier, 1914, Rix Nicholas Archive, Delegate, New South Wales.

HILDA RIX NICHOLAS

80 THE MOTTLED CROWD, TANGIER 1912–14

Coloured pastel on paper 37 x 27.7 cm
Private collection

When Rix Nicholas exhibited her Moroccan drawings in Paris in 1912 the critics acclaimed her 'remarkable draughtsmanship' as well as her 'accurate and truthful impression of the many different types of Moroccan people'.[1] She completed a large number of drawings in Tangier and, like *The mottled crowd*, each one sparkles with a jewel-like clarity, the surfaces alive with fresh and exciting colour harmonies. Each one was constructed carefully: figures and backgrounds were taken from various places and then assembled in parts to create a kind of imaginary Oriental picture, as working in the marketplace was not always easy. Even though whispers of '*Katsouer*' (the maker of pictures) greeted Rix Nicholas when she entered the marketplace, the Arabs could just as easily 'go quite alter [sic] themselves [and] sometimes she has to use a lot of people for one man'.[2]

In this scene a single woman surrounded by oranges, baskets and earthenware pots occupies centre stage while the crowd standing in front of the gateway of Bab-el-Medina and the German Legation fills the upper part of the composition. Resisting the temptation to succumb to the rich assortment of colour and texture she saw in the marketplace, Rix Nicholas carefully controlled her composition and concentrated on representing the market crowd as a pattern of well-defined colours and shapes. JP

1 'L'Oeuvre de Mlle. E. H. Rix', *New York Herald* (Paris), 25 November 1912, Rix Nicholas Archive, Delegate, New South Wales.

2 Elsie Rix to her mother, Tangier, 28 February 1914, Rix Nicholas Archive, Delegate, New South Wales.

ETHEL CARRICK

85 ARAB WOMEN WASHING CLOTHES IN A STREAM (Laveuses Algériennes) c. 1911

Oil on canvas 68 x 81 cm
Private collection, courtesy Rex Irwin Art Dealer

Ethel Carrick, like her husband Emanuel Phillips Fox, delighted in working outdoors in full sunshine. The spontaneity of her approach is immediately apparent here, and the impression of the subject so generalised as to be rendered almost abstract at first glance. Arabs washing their clothes in streams was one of the themes dear to Etienne Dinet, Bou Saâda's resident artist. It seems to have caught Carrick's eye primarily as an opportunity for painting desert light bouncing off the surfaces of rock, water and brightly clothed figures in movement.

A contemporary travel writer described a strikingly similar scene to that which inspired Ethel Carrick:

> *A few artists know of Bou-Saâda, and come for the light…It is a light that burns out all detail in the landscape. It produces grand splashes of colour…The glare has something strange in it… The wide winding river (Oued) is a jumble of boulders. Zig-zag comes the stream, flowing hurriedly where narrowed, and, where the land indents, making a broad and sluggish pool. Where the water runs quick women are kneeling and washing clothes.*[1]

Painted at Bou Saâda in 1911, this picture was first shown at the Salon d'Automne in Paris. When Carrick exhibited *Arab women washing clothes in a stream* in Australia in 1913, the *Sydney Morning Herald* art critic commented on her command of 'swift, impetuous strokes of paint…glowing chromatics and rhythmical, sweeping lines'.[2]   UP

[1] J.F. Fraser, *The Land of Veiled Women*, Cassell, London, 1911, pp. 1, 2, 13.

[2] 'Pictures for the home', *Sydney Morning Herald*, 7 November 1913, p.7.

ETHEL CARRICK

86 NORTH AFRICAN STREET SCENE c. 1921

Oil on panel 33.2 x 21.8 cm. Collection Ballarat Fine Art Gallery
Gift to the State of Victoria from Major Basil R.F. McNay of Argyll, Scotland, nephew of the artist 1983

North African street scene remained in the artist's possession during her lifetime and was donated to the Ballarat Gallery as part of a larger gift to the Victorian Ministry of the Arts by Ethel Carrick's nephew, Major Basil R. F. McNay of Argyll, Scotland. Carrick was not in the habit of dating her work and, because early and later works were often exhibited together, dating some of her pictures is difficult. This *North African street scene* was initially catalogued and dated 1911, however the subject indicates that it was painted later, in Tunisia, probably at Kairouan. The exact date Carrick went to Tunisia has not yet been established, but she first exhibited a Tunisian picture at the Salon d'Automne in 1921.[1]

This small snapshot or postcard-like view emphasises the distinctive shapes of the local buildings as a sequence of unornamented blocky silhouettes against the clear sky. The deeper colours in the foreground frame the brightness of the desert light flooding the centre of the picture, and the movement of the backview figures streaming into the narrow gap between the buildings also serves to draw our eye into the scene – like an invitation to step into another world. Carrick's hint of eastern mystery was consistent with the exotic image of Tunisia that lured 1920s western travellers: 'Chaos of barbaric tongues...drifts of fragrance and strange scents...In the shadowy sinuosities of these streets anything might happen'.[2]   UP

1 Carrick showed *La Rue Saussier, Kairouan*, cat. no. 368, at the Salon d'Automne 1921 (information from Ruth Zubans).

2 *Tunisia*, travel brochure published by Compagnie Générale Transatlantique, New York, 1927, n.p.

ETHEL CARRICK

87 NORTH AFRICAN MARKET c. 1921

Oil on canvas 45 x 60 cm
Private collection, Thirty Victoria Street

Ethel Carrick's market scene depicts a view of one of the souks or bazaars in Kairouan. The same subject, seen from a lower viewpoint, was also photographed for John Foster Fraser's travel book *The Land of Veiled Women*, published in 1911 (see fig. 37). Fraser wrote:

> *Kairouan is too far away for the west to have tampered with the distinctiveness of the Orient; and beyond the Bab (gate), which looks across the plains Tunis-wards, is the Souk-el-Berrain (the market of the Strangers), where the black people from the south dance, and where snake charmers show their skill.*[1]

Fig. 37
J. FOSTER FRASER
The mart at Kairouan

Baked by the hot, dry sirocco wind, Kairouan's white-walled buildings reflected heat like a mirror. Ethel Carrick captured this particular intensity of light in the upper half of her picture, shading the foreground with mauve, and scattering bright flashes of colour among the moving crowd. Looking down on the scene from above, she focuses on the black-and-white striped horseshoe arch that punctuates the street, the irregular awnings jutting over it and the foreground clutter of fruit stalls.

Carrick had long been attracted to market subjects. She instinctively preferred a populated landscape to an empty one. However, it was the light that particularised each experience for her most – the impression or, as she put it, the 'song' that she tried to convey in her work. She exhibited some of her Tunisian subjects in Australia in 1925 and said in an interview at that time: 'It is hard work…painting all day in the heat and blinding sand. From an artist's point of view, however, it is worth while'.[2] UP

1 J.F. Fraser, *The Land of Veiled Women*, Cassell, London, 1911, pp. 212–13 (location identified by John Pigot).

2 'Life and pictures', *Register* (Adelaide), 14 July 1925.

GEORGE LAMBERT

88 THE ROAD TO JERICHO c. 1918

Oil on canvas 35 x 46 cm
The Art Gallery of New South Wales, Sydney. Purchased 1941

According to Anne Gray, this oil on canvas version of the artfully intertwining terrain of Lambert's *Road to Jericho* was probably based on his smaller oil on cardboard sketch (now in the collection of the Australian War Memorial) and made by the artist in 1918 after he had returned to England from Palestine.[1] Lambert's experiences as a war artist with the Australian Imperial Forces in Palestine had a profound effect on him. Working in the blistering heat, travelling on horseback, Lambert 'moved about the newly captured territory, down the narrow winding road from Jerusalem to Jericho, and painted some dazzling views, capturing the warmth and peace of the Jordan Valley'.[2]

Lambert later said: 'of all the places I visited, the region around Jericho was the most attractive from the artistic point of view'. His eyes were constantly drawn to the shimmering horizon, 'an inspiring background of hills…beyond the Jordan the Mountains of Moab, standing out in jagged serrated masses of colour in strong light and shade'.[3] The cerulean skies and sharp clarity of the light knife-edged the contours and ridge-lines, flattening distance and stylising forms. It was a landscape eminently suited to the pared-down, yet descriptive formalism of Lambert's Anglo Post-Impressionist style. His Palestine landscapes were later regarded as models for modernising the Australian landscape tradition – ideal for conveying the particular qualities of space, intense light, subtle colours and shimmering but sharp-edged horizons that were also characteristic of the ancient, monolithic and sparsely vegetated terrain of inland Australia.   UP

[1] Anne Gray, *George Lambert: Catalogue Raisonné*, Bonaray Press in assoc. with Sotheby's & the Australian War Memorial, Perth, 1996, cat. no. P280, p. 80.

[2] Anne Gray, *Art and Artifice: George Lambert, 1873–1930*, Craftsman House, Sydney, 1996, p. 94.

[3] Lambert, quoted by William Moore, *The Story of Australian Art*, Angus & Robertson, Sydney, 1934, vol. 2, p. 63.

THE ROAD TO JERICHO

EMILE BERNARD

91 THE HASHISH SMOKER (La Fumeuse de haschisch) 1900

Oil on canvas 86 x 114 cm
Musée d'Orsay, Paris. Acquired 1902

The only depiction of a woman smoking hashish in Bernard's painted *oeuvre*, *The hashish smoker* was produced in Cairo the year before his major retrospective at Vollard's gallery in 1901. Bernard had witnessed Arab men smoking hashish in Cairo's cafés, and described the '*voluptés calmes*' of their erotic daydreams in an essay of 1908 in terms so vivid as to suggest his first-hand experience of the drug.[1]

Self-consciously arranged to show off a simple striped robe and heavy jewellery, and situated in a generic private space, his model seems to be more a product of the studio than a figure of Egyptian life. Perhaps inspired by the houri which Bernard claimed would appear to male hashish smokers, his *fumeuse* recalls Baudelairean images of Parisian prostitutes high on alcohol and nicotine.

Bernard was rewarded for his precise observation of the model, tempered by his deference to the masters, by his work's purchase for the Musée du Luxembourg after its showing with the Société des Peintres Orientalistes Français in 1902. But his rejection of impressionist technique and his enthusiasm for Venetian painting, revealed in his sombre palette and old-fashioned glazing, damaged his long-term reputation. The modernist historian Jules Meier-Graefe, regretting Bernard's metamorphosis from progressive Symbolist to State-endorsed Orientalist, cited *The hashish smoker* as evidence supporting his disparagement of Bernard's part in *fin de siècle* modernism.[2] PR

1 Emile Bernard, 'Art arabe', *La Rénovation Esthétique*, May 1908, pp. 20–3.

2 Jules Meier-Graefe, *Modern Art: Being a Contribution to a New System of Aesthetics*, 2 vols, trans. F. Simmonds & G. Chrystal, London 1908, vol. 2, p. 68.

HENRI EVENEPOEL

92 ORANGE MARKET AT BLIDA (Marché d'oranges à Blidah) 1898

Oil on canvas 81 x 125 cm
Musées royaux des Beaux-Arts de Belgique, Brussels, inv. 6171

Arriving in Algeria for reasons of health, the young, progressive Belgian artist (and friend of Matisse) Henri Evenepoel was disgusted by the Europeanisation of Algiers. With his friend Raoul du Gardier he fled south to the town of Blida, 'in an exceedingly beautiful situation at the foot of the lesser Atlas mountains [and] celebrated for its orange groves…'.[1] In Blida, he wrote to his father:

> *The Arabs have been able to protect themselves from all the European ignominies, and retain under the folds of their burnouses a little of that heroic pride which makes them, although vanquished, the sole true masters of the orange trees, of the light, the centuries-old olive groves, the mosques…*[2]

Something of that pride is present in Evenepoel's *Orange market*, the first major painting he undertook. Renting as a studio a tiny room looking onto the marketplace, Evenepoel made use of his Kodak camera to study the market's specific figures.[3] But the main struggle was with the intense light: 'The sun in this place kills me!…I did my *Arab market* in full sunlight with orange tones. I look at it and say, that's not it, it lacks colour! Fine! I work over it again, I add all the colour that I can…'.[4]

Evenepoel utilises a format common to his multi-figure Parisian street scenes: a high horizon, level with the heads of both painter and key figures. Below this, the heavily swathed bodies and piles of fresh fruit form a patchwork of interlocking colours. The use of silhouette, summary detail and an orange-yellow palette relates this work to the contemporary explorations of Bonnard and Vuillard. His fresh approach to figuration released Evenepoel from the stereotypy of much Orientalism.   RB

1 'An excursion to Blida', *El Djezaïr*, no. 4, 1 January 1905.

2 Letter of 28 November 1897, in *Henri Evenepoel à Paris, lettres choisies, 1892–1899*, ed. Francis E. Hyslop, La Renaissance du Livre, Brussels, 1972, p. 163.

3 See Elaine de Wilde et al., *Henri Evenepoel, 1872–1899*, Musées royaux des Beaux-Arts de Belgique, 17 March–12 June 1994, pp. 113, 138, 183.

4 Letter of 2 February 1898, in Hyslop, p. 172.

CHARLES CONDER

93 FLOWERS IN A VASE AGAINST A BACKGROUND OF THE COASTLINE OF MUSTAPHA, ALGIERS 1891

Oil on canvas 46 x 55.3 cm
The Art Gallery of New South Wales, Sydney. Purchased with assistance from Katies 1982

1 Letter to William Rothenstein, in J. Rothenstein, *The Life and Death of Conder*, Dent, London, 1938, pp. 77–8. J. Rothenstein dates it 23 February 1892, but internal evidence suggests 23 December 1891, a little after the Christmas letter about 'ploom pudding', p. 75.

2 Letter to Tom Roberts, dated 22 May 1891, quoted in Rothenstein p. 67.

3 Dowson poem, quoted by Barry Pearce in 'Recent Australian acquisitions with notes on Charles Conder's Algerian convalescence', *Art and Australia*, vol. 22, no. 1, 1984, p. 62.

Conder painted *Flowers in a vase* while convalescing at Mustapha, Algiers, on an estate owned by his friend, Henri de Vallombreuse. He dated this work December 1891, and announced in a letter to William Rothenstein: 'I am painting two roses in a pot on a rose tile terrace and away in the distance the blue sea and Algiers. I only started to paint today…I have spent a good deal of my time on my bed'. He was melancholy – 'Absinthe coloured spectacles are delightful only I can never find mine when I want them' – yet was stimulated by the beauty of the place: 'One thing I like in all tempers and weathers are the gorgeous villas against the sea'.[1]

The high horizon in this painting with its narrow strip of sea, sky, bay and blossom, seems suspended in space. The artist's compressed viewpoint, as if indeed he painted it prone on his bed, gives the iridescent vase of flowers a surreal, almost narcotic intensity. The solitary white-robed figure leaning over the distant parapet and the attenuated shapes of the shadows, quasi-human, add to the picture's sense of strangeness. The central flowerpiece is an extraordinarily lyrical piece of painting. Earlier that year Conder had been impressed by Monet's radiant paintings of haystacks, which he described in a letter to Tom Roberts after a visit to Monet's exhibition at Durand-Ruel's Paris gallery: 'I only wish you could have seen some of his landscapes [,] *they lived*…He takes you among hayricks and sunsets in a most natural way', but Conder qualified his praise, saying that Monet 'scoffs at poetry'.[2] For Conder, weeping petals were a symbolist metaphor, like the refrain by one of his favourite poets, Ernest Dowson: 'The roses fall, the pale roses expire / Beneath the slow decadence of the sun'.[3] UP

CHARLES CONDER

94 MOONLIGHT AT MUSTAPHA 1892

Oil on canvas 38 x 46 cm
Courtesy Savill Galleries, Sydney

Conder's dreamy picture of moonlight in Algiers – painted in pale opalescent colours – depicts a garden terrace overlooking the sea. Inverting the European convention of the *coulisse* or darker foreground framing, Conder has used light to dematerialise or disembody the forms in his landscape. Moonlight was often associated with mystery and magic, but for Conder, struggling to regain his health and aware that his condition was life-threatening, it fused with a melancholy reverie in the spirit of Omar Khayyám's *Rubáiyát*: 'Ah, Moon of my Delight who knows't no wane, / The Moon of Heaven is rising once again / How oft hereafter rising shall she look / Through this same Garden after me – in vain'.[1]

The motif of a mysteriously robed faceless figure on a terrace overlooking the sea is repeated from Conder's earlier work in the same series (cat. 93), but he replaces warm golden sunlight with cool silvery moonlight, rendered in a daringly minimal palette. His admiration for Puvis de Chavannes may have inspired it, but there are no gods on Conder's stage-set landscape; its emptiness only evokes the transience of the physical world. Painted while Conder was staying in Mustapha, this work was first shown in a joint exhibition that Conder and his friend William Rothenstein held at the Galerie Père Thomas on the rue Malesherbes, Paris, in the spring of 1892. Conder also showed paintings of almond trees in blossom and some drawings inspired by the *Rubáiyát*. The critic for *L'Art Français* praised the delicacy of his works, and their originality, but added the proviso, 'in paleness they are the limit of what is permissible'.[2]   UP

1 *The Rubáiyát of Omar Khayyám*, 1st edn, trans. Edward FitzGerald, London, 1874, quatrain 74.

2 'Revue artistique hebdomadaire', *L'Art Français*, 2 April 1892, quoted in Ursula Hoff, *Charles Conder*, Lansdowne, Melbourne, 1972, p. 57.

HENRY OSSAWA TANNER

95 PALACE OF JUSTICE, TANGIER c. 1908

Oil on canvas 65.1 x 81 cm
National Museum of American Art, Smithsonian Institution, Washington, DC. Gift of Mr and Mrs John Baxter

Like most western artists, Henry Ossawa Tanner was transported to another time when he travelled in the Orient. 'It took little imagination', he recalled in 1909, 'to close one's eyes to the flight of time and see in those hurrying travellers the crowds that hurried Bethlehemward on the memorable night of the Nativity, or to transpose the scene and see in each hurrying group a "Flight into Egypt".'[1] It was one of Tanner's favourite biblical themes, and in the previous year in Algeria he painted this enigmatic moonlit scene, one of several imaginary 'Flights'.

Bathed in darkened shadows, the Holy Family are seen crossing the square in front of the Palais de Justice in the kasbah of Tangier, Morocco. It was a popular site with European artists and featured in numerous pictures in the 19th and early 20th centuries. Tanner probably based the composition on one of the many commercial postcards that were available in North Africa as it is doubtful whether he went to Tangier in 1908. Drawing on his imagination rather than fact for this picture, he portrayed a luminous and translucent site that evoked the biblical past. Proportions and scale have been altered to give the Palais de Justice a sense of malevolent grandeur, its size dwarfing the tiny figures as they pass beneath its walls. Shafts of pale yellow light coupled with the chilly blues, lavenders and mauves accentuate the feeling of clandestine flight, transforming what was probably a common enough scene into an eerie biblical narrative.   JP

[1] Henry Ossawa Tanner, 'The story of an artist's life', *World's Work,* vol. 18, 1909, p. 11774.

LUCIEN LEVY-DHURMER

96 THE MOROCCAN (Le Marocain) c. 1900

Oil on canvas 64.5 x 50 cm
Musée National des Arts d'Afrique et d'Océanie, Paris

Lévy-Dhurmer became known in Paris in the mid-1890s as a pastellist fixated on the human face whose variations on Renaissance portrait forms were heavy with private symbolism. After 1900 he travelled extensively in Spain, Morocco and his native Algeria, taking copious visual notes and gathering ideas for his exquisitely composed studio pictures.

The unidentified sitter for *The Moroccan* is placed before a fragmentary city view dominated by a *zaouis* or religious complex resembling that seen from a similar high angle in Mammeri's more complete view of the sacred city of Moulay-Idriss (cat. 109). Following the allusive interweaving of sitter and setting which distinguished Lévy-Dhurmer's wide-angle portraits of Rodenbach in Bruges and Loti in Constantinople, this work would seem to depict a scholar or an artist who was intimately connected with the framing site.

Thrown into relief by the dazzle of whited walls, the young man's face floats above an ascending wave of fabric and is balanced by architectural geometry as on an abstract field. The sudden spatial jump from the ambiguously positioned bust to the enticing view below produces a sense of weightlessness which asserts this as an imaginary construction, for all its acute detail and its impressionist palette, as mysterious as those which preceded it.   PR

LUCIEN LEVY-DHURMER

97 EVENING PROMENADE MOROCCO (Promenade du soir) c. 1930

Oil on canvas 81 x 65 cm
Private collection

This minimal image apparently describes two women of the harem taking the air at the close of day. Their strangely bodiless figures loom before the viewer, offering fragmentary glimpses of four painted fingernails and two pairs of eyes – blue, in the case of the taller – to suggest the prized complexion of a Circassian slave.

Broken handling, typical of Lévy-Dhurmer's later work, agitates his pink and blue palette to imply an ultraviolet sunset and to impart a sense of unreality to the colour of the massively simple robes and of the distant architecture.

Echoing familiar European responses to Muslim women, the artist takes a fetishistic interest in the visible parts of their bodies, but also, unexpectedly, distracts attention with large impenetrable surfaces of surrounding colour. Depicted eyes, which look back at the viewer as if through slits in the canvas itself, subvert the easy relation of represented object to viewing subject usual for Orientalist painting.

Lévy-Dhurmer's composition recalls similarly simplified pastels he made in Marrakesh and Rabat, but his very stylised forms invite a contemplation of abstract themes that are removed from specific associations.   PR

ALBERT BESNARD

98 THE PORT OF ALGIERS AT DUSK (Le Port d'Alger au crépuscule) c. 1893–94

Oil on canvas 100 x 80 cm
Conseil Internationale de la Langue Française, Paris

In its day, *The port of Algiers at dusk*[1] was one of the most famous of all Orientalist pictures – a view of the old port by Besnard, that celebrated technician whose mastery of atmospheric colour rivalled that of the Impressionists. According to Roger Marx: 'In *The port of Algiers* he has observed the sun form, as it dies, an orange shimmer on the surface of the blue water…His vision of the Orient is the most intense and the most unexpected since Delacroix's'.[2]

Painted during Besnard's winter trip to Algeria in 1893–94, the work captures the most picturesque corner of a site that obsessed French painters from the 1830 invasion until the mid-20th century: the port of Algiers. For three centuries before 1830 the harbour had been the unassailable stronghold of the Algerine corsairs. The lighthouse on the left was built on the ruins of a Spanish fortress, the Penõn, captured in 1529 by Khair-ed-din Barbarossa, who constructed the causeway connecting it to the mainland to give shelter to his galleys. By 1894 the French had greatly extended and modernised the harbour off to the right, but Besnard preferred to focus on this historic zone: the pool near the Admiralty, reserved for the traditional fishing boats with their lateen sails shown bobbing peaceably on the lustrous waters.

Purchased for the Musée du Luxembourg from the 1895 Salon de la Nationale,[3] *The port of Algiers at dusk* was evoked in discussions of Orientalism and reproduced in colour many times over.[4] RB

1 Thanks are due to Geneviève Lacambre for help in locating this work.

2 Roger Marx, 'Revue artistique: le Salon du Champ-de-Mars', *Revue Encyclopédique*, vol. 2, 1895, p. 171.

3 *Société Nationale des Beaux-Arts, Exposition de 1895*, Paris, 1895, p. vi, cat. no. 107, *Port d'Alger au crépuscule*.

4 Léonce Bénédite, curator of the Luxembourg since 1892 and president of the Société des Peintres Orientalistes Français, presumably chose the work. It appears in colour in *Art et Décoration*, Supplement for August 1906; Prosper Ricard, *Les Merveilles de l'autre France*, Hachette, Paris, 1924, opp. p. 192; and Gabriel Hanotaux et al., *Histoire de colonies françaises et de l'expansion de la France dans le monde*, Plon, Paris, 1929–33.

ALBERT BESNARD

99 FRUIT MERCHANT AT MADURA (Marchand de fruits à Madurah) 1911

Oil on canvas 190.5 x 125 cm
Musée d'Orsay, Paris. Acquired 1912

When Besnard's suite of sixty-five Indian paintings was exhibited at the Galerie Georges Petit in 1912, it was to a rapturous reception by critics, both French and foreign.[1] Even the impresario of the new Cubism, Guillaume Apollinaire, called it a 'beautiful exhibition...one of the most precious documents of art and of modern Orientalism'.[2] Painted back in France on the basis of drawings, watercolours and sketchbooks filled during a six-month tour of British India with his wife (the sculptor Charlotte Besnard), Besnard's virtuoso skills as a draughtsman and mural decorator enabled him to amplify the eastern décor with an acuteness of observation that broke with Orientalist conventions.

Fruit merchant at Madura typifies the daring figural composition of Besnard's Indian work: although the picture has the disguised geometry of a pyramidal structure, the cut-off framing of the cream-pelted zebu entering on the left and the bisected body of the man striding to the right give a sense of arrested motion, as in snapshot photography (a pictorial device pioneered by Degas, whom Besnard admired). So Besnard evokes the exotic procession passing before two statuesque women in saris, whose copper vessels are quietly being filled in the shadows of the merchant's booth. The intense colour and reflected light of Besnard's *Fruit merchant* thrilled his public: 'From the warm shadows, fawn and tanned in tone...[and] sustained by a bass of deep black, sound generous fanfares of fire-red and lemon yellow'.[3] Another critic evoked in this:

> *halt of the crowd in front of the stall of a* Fruit merchant at Madura...*the muted splendour of the red and black clothes of the purchasers, and the supple, luminous silhouette of a big fellow in a bright yellow turban, whose body, muscular and nimble, is modelled vigorously under the light (a magnificent picture which the State has happily been inspired to buy, and which we will see again at the Musée du Luxembourg).*[4]   RB

[1] See Roger Benjamin, 'The colonial mirage: Besnard in India, Matisse in Morocco' (inaugural Joseph Burke Lecture), *University of Melbourne Fine Arts Society Bulletin*, vol. 6, no. 3, December 1994, pp. 3–5.

[2] Guillaume Apollinaire, 'La Vie artistique. Albert Besnard', *L'Intransigeant*, 12 April 1912, in Apollinaire, *Chroniques d'art. 1912–1918*, ed. L.-C. Breunig, Gallimard, Paris, 1960, p. 314.

[3] Paul Jamot, 'La "Suite indienne" de M. Albert Besnard', *Gazette des Beaux-Arts*, 4th period, vol. 7, June 1912, p. 443.

[4] Georges Lecomte, 'Albert Besnard aux Indes', *La Grande revue*, vol. 73, 10 May 1912, p. 125.

ALBERT BESNARD

100 STUDY FOR THE DELHI BALLERINA (Etude pour la ballerine de Delhi) c. 1910

Watercolour on paper 58.2 x 45 cm
Collection Galerie Jean-François Heim, Paris

Of all the exotic spectacles Besnard studied in India, the dance was perhaps his favourite. He painted the bayadères or temple dancers in Thanjavur, a transvestite male dancer in Hyderabad, and a trio of women dancers at Jodhpur. In Delhi he studied the Hindu nautch dancers,[1] fixing upon this spectacular gesture of the pleated skirt splayed out with both hands (a motif also depicted by the Anglo–Australian Orientalist Mortimer Menpes). Besnard embraced the full intensity of Indian colour, revelling in the pink iridescence of the skirt, the gold bodice, and the ultramarine blue of the woman's shoulder and headdress. A pierced nose, and copious pearls and copper bangles complete the effect.

Besnard's title of *Delhi ballerina* (given to the larger tempera painting for which this is a study)[2] shifts in reference from the familiar Parisian ballet to the exoticism of eastern dance. Such dance had been popularised in France by the court dancers of the King of Siam, sketched by Rodin at the 1906 Colonial Exposition. Apparently Besnard was particularly impressed by the religious import of Indian dance: 'The Orientals have only to take one step before a dance becomes a homage to the divinity, and the rhythmic manifestation of amorous aspirations becomes the figuring of devotion to the all-powerful gods'.[3] RB

[1] 'Nautch' is a North Indian designation for the kind of professional temple dancers, trained from childhood and sometimes doubling as courtesans, who in the South were called 'Devadasis' ('servants of the gods') or 'bayadères' (Portugese–French); (thanks to Priya and Dr Saratchandran, Melbourne).

[2] This study is surely '*Etude pour la ballerine de Delhi* (aquarelle gouachée)', cat. no. 47, in *Exposition Albert Besnard*, Galerie Georges Petit, Paris, 23 April–13 May 1912; and the main canvas cat. no. 23, '*Une Ballerine hindou à Delhi* (détrempe)', ill. in colour in Pierre Mille, 'Le Peintre Besnard dans l'Inde', *L'Illustration*, Christmas number, 1911.

[3] Arsène Alexandre, 'Le Voyage aux Indes', preface to *Exposition Albert Besnard*, p. 17.

Leon Bakst

101 INDO-PERSIAN DANCE (Marchesa Casati) 1912

Gouache on paper 56.8 x 47.4 cm
Art Gallery of South Australia, Adelaide. Special Picture Fund 1934

Leon Bakst was dubbed 'the Delacroix of costume' by Péladan in 1911, after his strikingly original designs for the *Arabian Nights*-inspired Diaghilev ballet *Schéhérazade* took Paris by storm during its 1910 season.[1] Influenced by Persian miniatures and remembering the visit of the Royal Bangkok Ballet to St Petersburg in 1900, Bakst's costume and set designs combined brilliant contrasting colours with flowing lines and sumptuously decorated surfaces. They also heralded a new wave of colourful Orientalist-inspired clothes, jewellery and décor. When the jeweller Cartier set sapphires and emeralds together, the effect was pronounced 'Bakstian'. Similarly, fashionable women in London and Paris wearing harem trousers, donning turbans and lounging about on gorgeously patterned divans shared the vogue for fantasy Orientalism.

In addition to designing for the theatre, Bakst also made drawings of odalisques and Orientalist costume designs for friends. One of these was the Marchesa Casati, the daughter of a Milanese industrialist who had married into the Venetian nobility.[2] Bakst met Louisa Casati in Venice, where she lived in extravagant style, and he admired her tall, green-eyed, red-haired beauty. This Indo-Persian design could have been made for the Marchesa to wear to a fancy-dress ball, or possibly for her participation in the Diaghilev ballet *Le Dieu bleu*. In 1912 Bakst designed for *Thamar* and *Le Dieu bleu* costumes with similar stiff skirts and highly embroidered jackets. The erotic element in Bakst's designs prompted Gerald Siordet to declare them based on 'a passionate enthusiasm for the flesh, for the contours of form, for strange pose and counterpoise of limb, for furious, abandoned movement, that sets an Eastern stamp upon his art'. Another critic, quoted by Siordet, concluded that Bakst had 'rediscovered the delicious female line bequeathed by the early Orientals'.[3] UP

1 Péladan, 'Les Arts du theatre', *L'Art Décoratif*, no. 153, June 1911, p. 286.

2 Alison Carroll retitled this work from *Persian dancer* to *Indo-Persian dancer (Marchesa Casati)* following the inscription top left, and researched its subject for the AGSA in September 1985.

3 Gerald Siordet, 'Leon Bakst's designs for scenery and costume', *Studio*, vol. 60, no. 247, October 1913, p. 5.

RUPERT BUNNY

102 THE HAREM c. 1913

Oil on canvas 51.8 x 79.5 cm. Lionel Lindsay Collection, Toowoomba Regional Art Gallery
Courtesy of the Lionel Lindsay Art Gallery and Library Trust

Bunny's *Harem* is located in an imaginary garden-world, a courtyard enclosed by lush tropical palms, warm, yet shaded from the full intensity of the sun. It shelters a quiet group of seductively dressed females playing a leisurely board-game, their silk harem pants shimmering with colour, blouses casually open to display their bodies, their faces painted, their jewellery sparkling in the light. The relationship between Orientalism and an adventurous palette was often remarked. It prompted Matisse not only to write regarding colour, 'my revelation came from the Orient', but also to warn that: 'in the early Russian ballets, Bakst threw in colours by the bucketful. It was magnificent but without expression. It is not quantity which counts, but choice and organisation'.[1]

Bunny also relished the 'savage' colours that attracted Bakst and Matisse. Like Bakst, he put together strident combinations of orange and rose-pink, but he also linked contrasting colours rhythmically across the canvas, resolving discords and balancing hot and cool tones in patterned strokes. Bunny came from a very musical family, and his instinct was to approach colour musically. Matisse and Gauguin wove blocks of pure colour together like an Oriental carpet. Bunny did not flatten his colours to the same extent. In *The harem* he used colour rhythmically to flesh out a poetic feeling or idea that began as tiny pencil notations like '*La cassette de bijoux*' and '*les trois graces*' in his sketchbooks.[2] Typically, *The harem* was undated, although close in style and theme to a work in the National Gallery of Australia called *Fortune-telling*, which Mary Eagle dates around 1913.[3] It entered the Toowoomba collection on the advice of Daryl Lindsay, then acting in his capacity as an executor of the Bunny Estate as well as adviser to William Bolton, the collector who later bequeathed this work to the Toowoomba Gallery. UP

[1] H. Matisse, 'The path of colour', in Jack D. Flam (ed.), *Matisse on Art*, Phaidon, Oxford, 1973, p. 116.

[2] Thanks to Barbara Kane for researching the Bunny sketchbooks held at the University of Melbourne Museum of Art.

[3] Mary Eagle, *The Art of Rupert Bunny*, Australian National Gallery, Canberra, 1991, p. 156.

RUPERT BUNNY

103 SALOME c. 1919

Oil on canvas 81 x 65.5 cm
The Art Gallery of New South Wales, Sydney. Purchased 1968

Rupert Bunny has given his *Salome* an eastern atmosphere with accessories drawn from a variety of sources – Persian, Turkish and Indian – his exuberant mixture of patterns and colours evoking a geographically non-specific Orient of voluptuous excess. He draws attention to Salome's oddly angled arms and open bodice with stylised Nijinsky-like gestures, freezing her pose against the serpentine counter-movement of her feather headdress and the variegated pink, apple-green and gold silks that swirl and spiral around her. Isadora Duncan, whom Bunny met in Paris, was also renowned for the sinuous rhythms of her dances with vividly coloured scarves.[1]

Interest in Salome, a favourite symbol of *fin de siècle* decadence in French art and the embodiment of the *femme fatale* in Oscar Wilde's play, was revived in the early 20th century by the Strauss opera *Salome* (1905) and the Ida Rubinstein ballet, *Salome*, designed by Bakst, which premiered in Paris in 1912. Rupert Bunny imagines a Bakstian Salome, mid-dance, profiled against an elaborate Oriental hanging lamp and the blue backdrop of a garden view at evening. Asymmetrically positioned, she becomes the decorative focus of his uptilted and modernistically flattened composition. There is an interesting contrast to the underworld of Moreau's hieratic *Salome* (cat. 89) which was shown again in Paris in 1906 by Georges Petit, who was also Bunny's dealer.

Rupert Bunny rarely dated his works, and an exact date for *Salome* has not been established, but it was exhibited at the Salon d'Automne in 1919, the Salons having been suspended during the First World War. After 1913, when he ushered in a new series of brightly coloured, Fauve-influenced works, Bunny made numerous images of Oriental dancers. Working from imagination and memory, his motifs began as thumbnail sketches with titles like '*danse chromatique*' or '*orgie dans le harem*' – both sketchbook drawings which can be related to the composition of *Salome*.[2] Painting without models, Bunny often reworked earlier themes and reversed the *Salome* design in a 1921 monotype called *Eastern dancer*. UP

[1] According to Mary Eagle, *The Art of Rupert Bunny*, Australian National Gallery, Canberra, 1991, p. 8, Bunny also met Loie Fuller, Sarah Bernhardt, Rodin, Debussy and Oscar Wilde at his teacher Jean Paul Laurens's weekly salons.

[2] Thanks to Barbara Kane for researching the Bunny sketchbooks held at the University of Melbourne Museum of Art.

ANDRE SUREDA

104 BERBER WOMAN (MOROCCAN ATLAS) (Femme berbère (Atlas marocain)) N.D.

Tempera on board 63.5 x 51 cm
Musée Lambinet, Versailles

The fluent figure drawing that under-pinned Suréda's inventive approach to the Oriental subject is evident in this magisterial composition. It is not surprising that as Suréda's career took wing an influential critic could proclaim that 'not since the great Orientalists of Romanticism like Delacroix, Decamps and Dehodencq have we encountered such a gust of Algerian air, such sunlight, such magnificence of tones'.[1]

This work is above all reflective in character: some have situated the woman sitting cross-legged on a rooftop terrace at the close of day in a cemetery. Certainly the pensive expression revealed by her unpinned veil and the scented flower held between her fingers denote reverie or loss. By placing the visual focus low and having her headdress extend to the very top of the picture, Suréda imparts an air of monumental dignity to his sitter.

Berber woman appears to belong among the many portraits produced during and after Suréda's 1922–23 journey to Morocco. The critic Gustave Kahn wrote:

> *André Suréda has undertaken a great enquiry into Morocco, enumerating the ethnic varieties, proceeding by thousands of rapid pencil sketches that have led to hundreds of worked-up portraits of indigenous people…[He has] ceaselessly noted…the intimate life of Moorish women and the voluptuous character of daily existence, be it active or in repose…*[2] RB

[1] Gustave Kahn, 'Art: exposition des orientalistes français', *Mercure de France*, vol. 111, 1 March 1913, p. 197.

[2] Gustave Kahn, 'Art: exposition des peintres du Maroc, Galerie Georges Petit', *Mercure de France*, vol. 160, 15 December 1922, pp. 761–2.

ANDRE SUREDA

105 OASIS WITH TWO WOMEN AND A HORSEMAN (*L'Oasis avec deux femmes et un cavalier*) c. 1919

Gouache and charcoal on paper 63 x 48 cm
Musée Lambinet, Versailles

Like Renoir, like Matisse and Charles Dufresne, André Suréda was seduced by the decorative possibilities of North African vegetation, which he had studied as early as 1907 in the oasis and palm groves of Bou Saâda. In the gouache *Oasis* he demonstrates a keen eye for tropical plant types, with their pendulous fruits and distinctive flowers. The two female figures function pictorially to help accentuate the play between the verticals of the tree trunks and the arabesque curves of the palm fronds; the man passing on horseback centres the composition and gives it an ethnographic specificity.

This gouache is apparently a study for a painting Suréda exhibited in Algiers in 1920, in an exhibition devoted to the circle of painters around the Villa Abd-el-Tif.[1] The Algerine critics welcomed his contribution: 'The sensualism of Suréda is in full view, with all his qualities of floral seduction', wrote Barrucand, praising him as 'rich in memory and imagination, [and] always interesting'.[2] Edmond Gojon detected a link with traditions of Islamic miniature painting: 'The *Oasis* evokes, by its composition and its deliberate awkwardness, the designs of the Persian and Hindu miniaturists…'.[3] The theme of the oasis and seated women was so versatile that Suréda used it for a commission of mural decorations for the French North African pavilion at the 1925 Exposition Internationale des Arts Décoratifs in Paris. RB

[1] See Catherine Gendre, *André Suréda (1872–1930): dessins-estampes-illustrations*, Musée Lambinet, Versailles, 7 June–7 July 1983, p. 27.

[2] Victor Barrucand, 'Abd-el-Tif et ses amis', *La Dépêche algérienne*, 7 January 1920.

[3] Edmond Gojon, 'Abd-el-Tif et ses amis', *L'Afrique du Nord illustré*, 17 January 1920, p. 7, quoted in Gendre, p. 27.

ANDRE SUREDA

106 CAIDS' ENCAMPMENT (MOROCCO) (Campement des caïds (Maroc)) c. 1922

Oil on canvas 130 x 97 cm
Musée d'Orsay, Paris. Acquired 1923

Suréda's *Caids' encampment* is a key example of French colonial art of the 1920s, and symptomatic of the art world's interest in the new French protectorate of Morocco. The 'pacification' of the Moroccan interior delivered dramatic subjects to the painters' view, such as the Berber forts of the Atlas Mountains seen here and in many paintings of Jacques Majorelle.

In 1922–23 Suréda travelled in the southern Atlas with the assistance of Resident-General Lyautey and the novelists Jérôme and Jean Tharaud, who had commissioned the artist to illustrate their travelogue and chronicle of the French presence, *Marrakesh, or the Lords of the Atlas.*[1] A version of *Caids' encampment* is reproduced in the chapter entitled 'The Lord of Télouet', which describes a visit to the labyrinthine 19th-century kasbah of Télouet, stronghold of Si Madani Glaoui, the pasha of Marrakesh (whose successor was portrayed by Suréda). The Tharauds recount a celebrated visit to Télouet by the previous Sultan of Morocco, Moulay Hassan, who had been met by the Glaoui brothers:

> *bringing with them provisions of all sorts, and a large number of horses and mules to replace the exhausted animals of the sherifian* méhalla *[army]. In the kasbah the reception was sumptuous. Dances and songs, lavish* diffas, *nocturnal fêtes…The visit of the sherif gave to the Glaoui the prestige of a magnificent lord who was in favour at court.*[2]

Fig. 38
ANDRE SUREDA,
Encampment at Télouet (*Campement à Télouët*)
(colour woodcut by Schmied, in Tharaud & Tharaud, *Marrakech*, 1924 edn, opp. p. 133)

Whether reconstructing that distant event or the more recent visit of Lyautey's entourage with the Tharauds in 1920, Suréda adopts a somewhat primitivist manner in depicting the splendour of the camp before Télouet. Local women observe from a rooftop terrace while the dignitaries receive refreshment in their decorated tents.

For the Tharauds it was the visual impact of Morocco that had led Suréda to 'discover his personal manner of painting in grand sober tints, harmoniously composed'.[3] Exhibited in Paris in 1922 and 1923, *Caids' encampment* was purchased for the national collections and included in the retrospective of Orientalism at the 1931 Colonial Exposition. Gustave Kahn considered it a 'beautiful painting…most entertaining in its imagery of large white tents, at the foot of ancient walls tattooed with reflections'.[4] RB

1 Jérôme Tharaud & Jean Tharaud, *Marrakech, ou les seigneurs de l'Atlas*, Plon, Paris, 1920; deluxe edn with Suréda's 53 colour plates engraved on wood by François-Louis Schmied, Cercle Lyonnais du Livre, Lyon, 1924 (see Catherine Gendre, *André Suréda (1872–1930): dessins-estampes-illustrations*, Musée Lambinet, Versailles, 7 June–7 July 1983, p. 57).

2 Tharaud & Tharaud, 1920 edn, p. 132.

3 Jérôme Tharaud & Jean Tharaud, *André Suréda*, Paris, 1948, n.p.

4 Gustave Kahn, 'Art: exposition des peintres du Maroc, Galerie Georges Petit', *Mercure de France*, vol. 160, 15 December 1922, p. 762.

AZOUAOU MAMMERI

107 VIEW OF FEZ (Vue de Fez) c. 1920

Oil on canvas 70 x 92 cm
Musée d'Orsay, Paris. Acquired 1921

The scene Mammeri paints in this somewhat forbidding image was one of the notable picturesque sites in the ancient Moroccan royal capital of Fez. In a contemporary book, Prosper Ricard reproduced a photograph of Fez seen from a near-identical position, describing the 'cascade of terraces…from which the green domes of the sanctuaries and the tall minarets of the mosques emerge'. Mammeri's leitmotif is 'a salient of the old Almohad defensive wall, mutilated but still standing and, as such, a powerful symbol of the thousand-year-old city'.[1]

In his meticulous painting Mammeri plays with the powerful illusionism available by looking down the long wall of the ancient fortification. Such Moroccan cityscapes and pastoral scenes from his native Kabylia impressed the critics at Mammeri's first solo exhibition in Paris, one critic evoking the 'series of precise and fine paintings, burning landscapes of Fez, red ramparts and verdant countryside'.[2] Mammeri's supporter, Léonce Bénédite, purchased the *View of Fez* for the Musée du Luxembourg in 1921, making it one of the first paintings by an indigenous artist to enter the French public collections.[3]   RB

[1] Prosper Ricard, *Les Merveilles de l'autre France*, Hachette, Paris, 1924, p. 292.

[2] H. Genet, 'Petites expositions', *La Chronique des Arts*, no. 10, 31 May 1921, p. 75.

[3] *Dessins et peintures de Si Azouaou Mammeri*, pref. Léonce Bénédite, Galerie des Feuillets d'Art, Paris, 2–21 May 1921 (probably no. 3, *Les Vieux remparts de Fez*).

AZOUAOU MAMMERI

108 INTERIOR OF THE KAIROUIINE MOSQUE, FEZ (Intérieur de la Mosquée Kairouiine à Fès) c. 1927

Oil on canvas 55 x 42.5 cm
Institut du Monde Arabe, Paris

Mammeri's work has recently attracted the attention of art experts from the Arab world, and *Interior of the Kairouiine Mosque, Fez* is the first Mammeri purchased for the Institut du Monde Arabe in Paris. According to curator Brahim Alaoui, himself a Moroccan, the interest of this image is in part its presentation of Islamic piety from the perspective of a practising Muslim. It is possible to recognise precise signs of Islamic observance, such as the colours of the devotional flags visible to the right, and the way the Immam, the elected theological leader who directs prayer, occupies the niche of the mihrab with his back to the viewer. This is hardly a 'picturesque' device in the Orientalist tradition; rather, it closes off the view of the human subject. Painting or photographing the inside of a mosque, at least for westerners in Morocco, was strictly forbidden; but according to Brahim Alaoui, Mammeri would have been permitted this because of his high standing as a member of an 'important maraboutic family' whose own piety was unimpeachable.[1]

As texts of the day reveal, Mammeri, in order to practise the art of painting in the great religious centres of Morocco, consulted learned exegetes of the sacred text: 'who recognised that the famous passage of the Koran is generally misinterpreted. What is forbidden is the reproduction of images "which carry a shadow", that is, sculpted figures which are susceptible to becoming idols'.[2] Paintings such as this indicate that Mammeri wished to present himself to his French audience as a man of faith who had nevertheless chosen to master the modern European language of painterly representation. RB

[1] Interview with Brahim Alaoui, Institut du Monde Arabe, 6 November 1996.

[2] See 'Le Premier peintre musulman', *L'Illustration*, no. 4094, 20 August 1921, p. 162; the point derives from Bénédite's preface in *Dessins et peintures de Si Azouaou Mammeri*, Galerie des Feuillets d'Art, Paris, 2–21 May 1921.

AZOUAOU MAMMERI

109 VIEW OF MOULAY-IDRISS (Vue de Moulay-Idriss) c. 1930

Oil on canvas 100 x 130 cm
Private collection, courtesy Lynne Thornton, Paris

As the decade of the 1920s progressed, Mammeri's art gained in fluency. The brushwork became more flexible, and the use of colour (whose early severity had seemed to contradict French expectations of an 'Oriental' sensibility) became more generous.

Mammeri's hypnotic *View of Moulay-Idriss* and its dramatic emplacement in a gorge is reminiscent of El Greco's famous view of Toledo (where Mammeri had painted on a scholarship in 1924). The artist's physical vantage point was one favoured by professional photographers.[1] Mammeri framed the view with a dark *repoussoir* of angular rocks and silhouetted cactus plants while, in the shadows, two heavily draped figures stand immobile, as if mysterious guardians of the holy city, which was (and remains) closed to non-believers.

View of Moulay-Idriss is dedicated to the memory of Moulay Idris El Akhbar, who in the 8th century founded the first Arab realm in the Maghreb (his son Moulay Idris El Azhar founded nearby Fez). In the foreground of Mammeri's painting, rendered with great precision and giving every sign of its careful upkeep, is the: '*zaouis* of Moulay Idris El Akhbar...A *horm* or sacred place, forbidden to infidels, which houses the tomb of the saint, a mosque, and Koranic schools whose religious leaders are Idrissid sherifs, descendants of the illustrious ancestor'.[2]

As such, the view may have had added ethnic and religious resonance for the Kabyl Muslim Mammeri. He gave the painting special treatment by ordering a hardwood frame inlaid with patterns based on Berber tattoos. The frame evokes the professional interest that Mammeri had in Moroccan arts and crafts as regional inspector of Moroccan Art and Arts Industries, based in Marrakesh from 1929.[3] RB

[1] See photograph, *View of Moulay-Idriss*, in Prosper Ricard, *Les Merveilles de l'autre France*, Hachette, Paris, 1924, p. 326.

[2] Ricard, p. 322.

[3] Biographic information from Professor Driss Mammeri, Algiers (communicated by Lynne Thornton, October 1996). Mammeri was nominated to the position by Prosper Ricard.

MOHAMMED RACIM

110 DANCER (Danseuse) c. 1922

Gouache heightened with gold 24.5 x 18 cm
Private collection, courtesy Lynne Thornton, Paris

An early example of his figure painting, Racim's *Dancer* shows the legacy of his years working as a decorative illuminator in its exquisite floriated border, painted gold and red in pure Persian style.[1] The theme of delicacy, transparency and floral decoration continues in the main image, where a young woman dances under the arcades. Her dress is of diaphanous white gauze, and with each henna-tipped hand she draws a veil, in a gentle whiplash, through the perfumed summer air. The elements of her costume – the embroidered belt, peaked epaulettes and bejewelled diadem – seem fantastical, of almost Indian or Siamese inspiration.

Yet a fantasy dancer she is; the palace in which she performs is the Alhambra in Granada, Spain, whose distinctive Lion Courtyard can be seen behind her. The jewel of Andalusia, the Alhambra had a stronger claim on the nostalgia of the Moorish peoples (whose ancestors built it) than on European Orientalists like Henri Regnault (see cat. 62). Racim has rendered its architecture with careful, if not complete detail (he had first travelled to Spain on a Hispano-Moresque scholarship awarded by the Algiers government in 1919).[2]

This *Dancer* was apparently exhibited in 1923 at the Salon des Artistes Algériens et Orientalistes in Algiers,[3] a breakthrough exhibition at which the young Racim was awarded two prizes and accorded warm appreciation by the press. Victor Barrucand wrote: 'Nobody today, even in Teheran, composes the faithful rhythms of a Persian miniature better than he'.[4]   RB

[1] The Arabic signature in this and the other Racims reads 'Mohammed Racim, Bil el Djezaïr' (i.e. 'of Algeria'); information from Mustapha Orif, Algiers, whose *catalogue raisonné* on Mohammed Racim is in preparation.

[2] Orif, op. cit.

[3] Orif identifies it with no. 209, *Danseuse*, in the *25e Salon de la Société des Artistes Algériens et Orientalistes*, Algiers, February 1923.

[4] See Victor Barrucand, 'Peinture, au Salon des Orientalistes', and J(ean) B(evia), 'Les Récompenses, au Salon des Orientalistes', *La Dépêche Algérienne*, 17 February 1923.

MOHAMMED RACIM

111 THE RAIS (Le Raïs) c. 1931

Gouache heightened with gold 18.5 x 13.5 cm
Private collection, courtesy Lynne Thornton, Paris

Racim specialised in portraits of Algerian corsairs, not only the great Khair-ed-din Barbarossa, but also the Rais – a term best explained by Racim's friend, the Islamic art specialist Georges Marçais:

> *The Rais: a master of a corsair ship, a member of the powerful corporation of the Rais on which the fortune of Algiers rests. Traditional rivals of the Turks, who comprise the militia, the Rais claim origins which are very diverse and sometimes far from exemplary. Among them one finds native-born Berbers, no doubt, and Levantines like Barbarossa...Spanish Muslims ejected by the Christian Reconquista...but also people from European countries who...thanks to a more or less sincere conversion, have embraced the adventurous but lucrative career of Barbary pirate.*[1]

According to Mustapha Orif, an old inscription by Racim identifies this Rais as Hamidou, 'one of the most famous Algerian corsairs' who was active in the early 19th century and of Berber origin.[2] His wheel-lock pistols and the relatively modern rigging of his tartan-style boat (the corsairs had converted to sail-power in the 17th century) bear this out.

Standing before an exact reconstruction of Algiers harbour (seen from the same angle as the Besnard, cat. 98), Hamidou is presented as a figure of great dignity, a dynamic leader acting with the legal imprimatur of the sovereign Algerian nation. Even as he reveals a nationalist aspiration, Racim employs a western iconography to express it: the full-length portrait for military leaders that originated with Renaissance masters such as Titian.[3]   RB

[1] Georges Marçais, *La Vie musulmane d'hier, vue par Mohammed Racim*, Arts et Métiers Graphiques, Paris, 1961, p. 29.

[2] Personal communication; on Hamidou and the corsair tradition see Peter Lamborn Wilson, *Pirate Utopias: Moorish Corsairs and European Renegadoes*, Autonomedia, New York, 1995, p. 31.

[3] The work is reproduced in *L'Afrique du Nord illustré* for May 1932; information from Mustapha Orif, Algiers, whose *catalogue raisonné* on Mohammed Racim is in preparation.

MOHAMMED RACIM

112 GALLEYS FLEEING THE STORM (Galères fuyant la tempête) c. 1937

Gouache heightened with gold 22.6 x 17.5 cm
Private collection, courtesy Lynne Thornton, Paris

A work of Racim's maturity, this nautical scene is one of many Racim devoted to reconstructing the golden age of Algiers in the era before the French occupation. The Regency of Algiers, established in a struggle against Catholic Spain led by the Barbarossa brothers in the 1510s and 1520s, became a major naval power whose corsair boats were the scourge of Christian shipping in the Mediterranean and beyond almost until the French landing of 1830.

As Racim's Arabic inscriptions reveal, we see here 'The Algerian Fleet' (top margin) 'Fleeing before the Storm' (bottom margin).[1] Racim, who had carefully researched his naval architecture, shows three galliots – smallish, twin-masted galleys with a single row of oars – whose speed and extreme manoeuvrability usually gave them the advantage over sail-powered merchantmen. The splendid leading galliot flies Turkish pennants (Algiers was under Ottoman protection), answered by the small Barbary Coast fort in the foreground. The galley-slaves, shown with shaven heads, were generally Christian captives whose freedom could be ransomed.

[1] Information from Mustapha Orif, Algiers, whose *catalogue raisonné* on Mohammed Racim is in preparation (information conveyed by Lynne Thornton).

[2] On Racim's art see *Mohammed Racim: miniaturiste algérien*, exh. cat., Musée de l'Institut du Monde Arabe, Paris, 3–29 March 1992, esp. essays by François Pouillon and Mustapha Orif (the latter reprinted from *Actes de la Recherche en Sciences Sociales*, no. 75, 1988, pp. 35–49).

Here Racim skilfully combines the materials and elaborate painted frame of the traditional Islamic miniature (the arabesques are Maghrebian in character) with a highly competent perspectival illusionism of the kind his supporter Dinet (q.v) suggested he adopt.[2] The result is a new hybrid Orientalism in which Racim's unique ability to synthesise the best of Islamic and European pictorial traditions is expressive of his identity as an Algerian of Turkish descent who moved adroitly in the French colonial and metropolitan art worlds.   RB

CHARLES DUFRESNE

113 EXOTIC COMPOSITION (Composition éxotique) c. 1912–14

Watercolour and ink 37 x 47 cm
Musée des Années 30 de Boulogne-Billancourt

Dufresne's Algerian gouaches and watercolours count, after Matisse's Moroccan canvases, as the most stylistically advanced images of North Africa by a French artist before the First World War. Already an habitué of the Salon des Indépendants familiar with Fauvism and the beginnings of Cubism,[1] Dufresne's 1910 scholarship to the Villa Abd-el-Tif gave him two years based in Algiers, where he made figure paintings on terrace rooftops, and watercolours in the Jardin d'Essai, the botanical gardens.

Dufresne would also visit the oasis town of Bou Saâda to see his friend Etienne Dinet (q.v.). A series of meticulous topographical line drawings (Musée National d'Art Moderne, Paris) were followed by synthetic compositions on the oasis motif. In *Exotic composition* he is attentive to the botanical forms of date-palms and cactuses, as well as women washing clothes in the stream (a motif common to Etienne Dinet and Ethel Carrick, qq.v.). The presence of oxen shows that Dufresne did not insist on the purity of 'African' fauna, but included a mark of colonial settlement and agriculture.

The two standing nudes in the centre of the composition are an unmistakable visual quotation of Henri Matisse's bronze sculpture, *Two negresses* of 1908, which had been exhibited with fanfare at the 1908 Salon d'Automne.[2] This calls attention not only to Dufresne's reworking of the fauve figure style, but also his departure from mere observation, the better to achieve a carefully balanced décor of intersecting lines, figures and colour patches. Eschewing the intense colour of both fauvist and Orientalist art, the subtle tonalities of this work increase its appeal. A harmony of tans, olive-greens and muted blues (including an upright 'blue nude' à la Matisse) is held in place by one piercing note of cherry red – the veritable bull's-eye of this superb composition. RB

1 See Louis Vauxcelles, 'Notes d'art', *Gil Blas*, 10 March 1905, in which he praises Dufresne's works on the modish subject of the café concert.

2 See *Société du Salon d'Automne*, exh. cat., Grand Palais, 1 October–8 November 1908, no. 922 (*Groupe de deux jeunes filles*); it is relevant that Matisse's model was a photograph of two Targui tribeswomen; see Isabelle Monod-Fontaine, *The Sculpture of Henri Matisse*, Thames & Hudson, London, 1984, p. 14.

CHARLES DUFRESNE

114 ALGERIAN OASIS (Oasis algérienne) c. 1912

Gouache, pastel, Chinese ink, pencil on cream paper 45 x 40 cm
Musée des Beaux-Arts de Bordeaux

This is the first in a set of three large colour drawings of the Bou Saâda oasis, purchased as a group by the leading patron of Orientalist art based in Algiers, the wine-producer Frédéric Lung. The three should be understood as constituting an informal triptych or decorative program based on the themes of tropical vegetation, running water and a low-key human presence. In this way they match other decorative works concerned with botanical exoticism, such as Matisse's three Moroccan gardens, or the Jardins d'Essai of Auguste Renoir, Jules Migonney, André Suréda or Emile Gaudissart.[1]

The three Bordeaux works must be similar to those Dufresne exhibited, to considerable acclaim, at the Société des Peintres Orientalistes Français in 1913 after his return to France:

> *M. Dufresne, who received the Algeria scholarship in 1910, is showing a suite of watercolours and canvases that are eloquent as biblical tales, vibrant with warm and muted tones in which purples play, and greens and pinks dominate. In his harmonies, in his sometimes unexpected perspectives, the magic of an Oriental dream unfurls: human bodies of the most diverse races, various stuffs, plants of capricious form.*[2] RB

[1] See Roger Benjamin, 'Orientalist excursions: Matisse in North Africa', in *Matisse*, exh. cat., eds Caroline Turner & Roger Benjamin, Queensland Art Gallery & Art Exhibitions Australia, Brisbane, 1995, pp. 79–80.

[2] René Jean, 'Petites expositions: les Peintres Orientalistes Français', *La Chronique des arts*, no. 7, 15 February 1913, p. 50; according to the *Société des Peintres Orientalistes Français*, 21st exh. cat., Grand Palais, 2–28 February 1913, Dufresne exhibited fifteen titled works and a suite of prints, gouaches, watercolours and drawings (nos 240–55).

CHARLES DUFRESNE

115 IMPRESSION OF BOU SAADA (Impression de Bou-Saâda) c. 1912

Watercolour on pen and pencil drawing 47 x 39.5 cm
Musée des Beaux-Arts de Bordeaux

Claude Roger-Marx, commenting on Dufresne's later excellence as a decorator of large surfaces, wrote of small works like this one: 'Each of his gouaches constitutes a sonorous and complete embryo; the richness of their colours and their proportions...gives them a character of immediate certitude'.[1] In this case Dufresne finds his motif in the juxtaposition of trunks of unlike trees: the massive bifurcated bole of an apparently deciduous European import, placed in contrast to the straight columns of two mature date-palms. Delicate palm-fronds, rendered in pen and in broad strokes of wash, overshadow the green canopy behind. Again Dufresne studies the melding of the indigenous and colonial scene at Bou Saâda, detailing the almost suburban forms of a picket fence enclosing a yard, in which the ghost-like outline of a dromedary can just be detected.

The rectilinear forms of the main tree-trunk and the almost magical assertion of its naked presence recall Picasso's forests from La Rue des Bois and Braque's of L'Estaque (in the summer of 1908). As the critic Waldemar George was to write, 'If Dufresne was able to adapt to cubist writing, it's because it gradually enabled him to move away from the plane of realism, while still safeguarding the rights of logic'.[2] RB

1 Claude Roger-Marx, 'Charles Dufresne', in *Peintures, pastels et gouaches de Charles Dufresne*, exh. cat. (Galerie Dru, 19–26 June 1931), Bourgeat & van Gelder, Paris, 1931, p. 4.

2 Waldemar George, 'Les grandes invasions: Charles Dufresne', *La Renaissance de l'art français et des industries de luxe*, vol. 10, October 1931, p. 293.

CHARLES DUFRESNE

116 LANDSCAPE AT BOU SAADA (Paysage de Bou-Saâda) c. 1912

Watercolour on pencil drawing 47 x 40 cm
Musée des Beaux-Arts de Bordeaux

In this third work from the Bou Saâda 'triptych' of Frédéric Lung, Dufresne is at his most naturalistic. The sense of three-dimensional space, looking across the rocky bed of the stream to the river-bank beyond, is pronounced. A canopy of palm-fronds casts sharp shadows onto the rock wall, and their forms are reflected in the pool of still water. The linear sensitivity evident in Dufresne's pure drawings is hinted at in the many lines describing the foreshortened arcs of palm-grove foliage. As in the other works, a few small figures of men and animals have been sketched in, but the artist seems to have sensed that to confirm them would detract from the overall impression of a floral décor. Before such imagery, memories of the Tahitian garden paradise of Paul Gauguin arose naturally in the minds of Dufresne's admirers.[1] RB

1 'M. Dufresne has good taste, and applies a very modern technique, somewhat influenced by Gauguin, to the land of the sun'; Gustave Kahn, 'Art: Exposition des Orientalistes français', *Mercure de France*, vol. 111, 1 March 1913, p. 198.

PAUL KLEE

117 ST GERMAIN NEAR TUNIS (MIDDAY, WITH THE YOUNG PALM IN THE FOREGROUND)
(St Germain bei Tunis (Mittags, mit der jungen Palme im Vordergrund)) 1914

Watercolour on paper 18.5 x 24 cm. Collection A. Rosengart

In 1914 Paul Klee made a journey to Tunisia with his artist friends August Macke and Louis Moilliet (q.v.). It was during that journey that Klee discovered the possibilities of colour and wrote jubilantly in his diary: 'Colour possesses me. I don't have to pursue it. It will possess me always, I know it. That is the meaning of this happy hour: Colour and I are one. I am a painter'.[1]

The group's host in Tunis was Dr Jäggi, a Swiss doctor who also owned an estate at St Germain (a small European settlement outside the city). Klee wrote: 'The country house is beautifully situated, close to the seashore, built on sand. A sandy garden with artichokes and so forth…Very hot during the day'.[2] The next morning he painted his first watercolours on the beach and from the balcony of the house, remarking on the dry desert air and the unfamiliarity of nature in Tunisia – the subtle definition of colours and the exotic plantings, here 'green-yellow-terracotta' and there 'a beautiful rhythm of patches'.[3]

Such diary entries highlight Klee's analytical perceptions and his tendency to read nature as pictorial possibilities. His Tunisian watercolours all utilise an informal grid structure which he derived from his admiration for Cubism and, more particularly, the translucent colour harmonies of Robert Delaunay. In *St Germain near Tunis* he fits the observed elements – palm trees, flowering bushes and fence palings as well as the roofs and windows of nearby houses – into this pictorial grid. These coalesce with crystalline zones of sky, colour-washed earth and areas of white paper, so that the whole image slowly blossoms into colour. Despite the work's abstraction, Klee was sensitive to light conditions: in the foreground the young palm tree referred to in the subtitle casts a sonorous shadow on the ground.   UP & RB

[1] Entry for 16 April 1914, *The Diaries of Paul Klee, 1898–1918*, ed. and intro. Felix Klee, University of California Press, Berkeley, 1964, p. 297.

[2] Entry for 10 April 1914, ibid., p. 289.

[3] ibid., pp. 287, 292.

PAUL KLEE

118 TWO ORIENTAL WATERCOLOURS (Zwei orientalische aquarelle) 1914

Watercolour on paper upper 8 x 7.3 cm lower 7 x 8.7 cm
Collection A. Rosengart

Next to the landscape and garden scenes exemplified by *St Germain near Tunis* (cat. 117), Klee's other great Tunisian theme was the image of Islamic architecture. Even as his boat approached the North African coast, he realised its pictorial potential: 'the first Arab town was clearly discernible, Sidi-Bou-Said, a mountain ridge with the shapes of houses growing out of it in strictly rhythmical forms. A fairy tale turned real'.[1] During his first days in the city of Tunis, hours spent rambling around the Arab quarter yielded sensations the painter would transform, by an almost alchemical process, into pictures: 'Art–nature – Self. Went to work at once and painted in watercolour in the Arab quarter. Began the synthesis of urban architecture and pictorial architecture'.[2]

[1] Entry for 7 April 1914, *The Diaries of Paul Klee, 1898—1918,* ed. and intro. Felix Klee, University of California Press, Berkeley, 1964, p. 286.

[2] Entry for 8 April 1914, ibid., p. 287.

[3] See the photo-essay on Klee's sites, Ernst-Gerhard Güse, 'Paul Klee–Wirklichkeit und Gestaltung', in *Die Tunisreise: Klee, Macke, Moilliet,* ed. Ernst-Gerhard Güse, exh. cat. (Westfälisches Landesmuseum für Kunst und Kultur-geschichte, Münster), Hatje, Stuttgart, 1982, pp. 56–9.

[4] See Prosper Ricard & J. Dalbanne, *Les Guides bleus: Algérie-Tunisie,* Hachette, Paris, 1930, p. 422.

It was in the holy city of Kairouan that Klee best achieved this synthesis of the two architectures.[3] Established in AD 670 during the first Arab conquest of the Maghreb by Okba Ibn' Nafâa, Kairouan and its classical Islamic monuments remains a place of pilgrimage to the present day. Together with Macke and Moilliet, Klee painted many views of the city's skyline, with its massive crenellated walls surmounted by floating cupolas, seen from the desert beyond. In *Two Oriental watercolours* he clearly depicts four of the five cupolas of the 'Mosque of the Sabres', constructed during the 19th century by a marabout or sainted man whose profession was blacksmith.[4]

Less popular with tourists and photographers than Kairouan's 'Grand Mosque', the Mosque of the Sabres excited Klee with its pictorial possibilities. Dividing up the surface of his tiny pictures like a chessboard, he gave these images an abstract dimension by making forms (including a Bedouin tent and minaret in the upper image) overlap. This both structures the picture and fractures the object into mosaics of charged, coloured pieces. The slabs of brilliant red and muted purple expressive of Klee's joyous response to the scene are offset by a sombre sage green. Klee's Orientalism also poses a challenge to traditional perspective drawing: viewers no longer stand outside the town looking in, but feel their way inside a magical world of eastern forms that float before their eyes like a mirage of heat and colour.   UP & RB

Fig. 39
GARRIGUES
Mosque of the Sabres at Kairouan
c. 1890
Collection Angela Tromellini, Bologna

LOUIS MOILLIET

119 COFFEESHOP IN TUNIS (Caféhaus in Tunis) 1920

Watercolour 23.1 x 28.3 cm
Kunstmuseum Basel

The Swiss artist Moilliet is best known as the companion of August Macke and Paul Klee, on that celebrated painter's journey to Tunis in April 1914. Although a progressive artist influenced by Macke, Moilliet painted rather little on the trip: one watercolour of a garden and two views of the holy city of Kairouan, which nevertheless approach the radical conception of Klee's cubistic colour compositions.[1] Moilliet recalled:

Klee was without doubt more intellectual than Macke and I, but Macke more powerful in creation. He was always practical about the solution to problems and painted, painted. We had watercolour boxes with us, it being so simple; Klee had a small black paintbox in which there were only seven colours. We lodged separately, but we saw each other at least once a day and talked over our painting…We tried out the effect of the juxtaposition of pure colours. Klee and Macke also had theoretical discussions. That was less interesting to me.[2]

Coffeeshop in Tunis dates to the post-war journey which marks the flowering of Moilliet's career as a watercolourist of the Orient. Shocked by the death of Macke in 1916, this image recreates one of the subjects they had admired together: the market stalls and street scenes of Tunisia. Klee had avoided the human element that Moilliet investigates here: four Arab men in fezzes seated at low tables, none in apparent conversation, but each absorbed in reverie or contemplation (as in Matisse's *Moroccan café* of 1913). The singing blue timbers of a painted door divide the interior scene from the vignette of an answering street café outside.

The basis of Moilliet's painting was the study of pure colour as a symbolic rendition of light – an approach indebted to the French 'Orphist' Robert Delaunay, whom Macke and Klee knew and admired. Moilliet skilfully controls the transparency of watercolours, drawing luminosity from the white of the paper. Although the café interior is sheltered, the artist conveys the impact of intense outside light on the men's bodies, and by extension on their consciousness. RB

[1] See Brigitte Kaul, 'Louis Moilliet und die Reise nach Tunisien', in *Die Tunisreise: Klee, Macke, Moilliet*, ed. Ernst-Gerhard Güse, exh. cat. (Westfälisches Landesmuseum für Kunst und Kulturgeschichte, Münster), Hatje, Stuttgart, 1982, pp. 158–67.

[2] Louis Moilliet, quoted in Werner Schmalenbach, 'Louis Moillet', in *Die Tunisreise*, p. 154.

ALBERT MARQUET

120 THE SOUKS (Tanger, les souks) c. 1913

Pen and Chinese ink 21.3 x 34.1 cm
Musée des Beaux-Arts de Bordeaux

1 A number of Marquet's Moroccan works were exhibited at the Galerie Druet, Paris, 31 March–12 April 1913.

2 'Marquet has been spending long days in Tangier. He has brought back from there three minuscule *Kasbahs*...He wants to return there: this first voyage was only prospecting'; 'Exposition Albert Marquet', *La Chronique des Arts et de la Curiosité*, no. 14, 5 April 1913, p. 107.

One of the rare drawings surviving from Marquet's first trip to Tangier in 1913,[1] *The souks* is certainly the most impressive. In it Marquet uses that summary, edgy, graphic expression that makes him one of the most admired of modernist draughtsmen. The walking figure in the foreground, swathed in the jellaba and broad straw hat typical of Morocco, has the kind of brevity and wit that made Matisse liken Marquet to the Japanese master Hokusai. Marquet uses the white of the paper in this unusual horizontal composition to indicate the intense sunlight of the foreground. To render the shade and the materials of the covered stalls, he employs a variety of pen-strokes: scribbled, swirled and evenly stroked.

Souks or covered markets were a favourite theme of painters in North Africa and Egypt. Lining narrow streets in the kasbahs or medinas, merchants and artisans seated among their wares occupy shallow shopfronts. The conviviality of this system is captured by Marquet: such stalls are a place for conversation between merchants and friends who drop by or customers who may enjoy debating the price of goods. Europeans regularly reconstructed Tunisian or Algerian souks as an attraction at the many Universal and Colonial expositions. But Marquet's version was directly experienced: on the spot in Tangier, he undertook a 'prospecting' for images and landscapes he was to pursue avidly in Algeria well into the 1940s.[2]   RB

ALBERT MARQUET

121 THE PORT OF ALGIERS IN THE MIST (Port d'Alger dans la brume) 1943

Oil on canvas 65 x 81 cm
Musée des Beaux-Arts de Bordeaux

Painted well after the other works in this exhibition, this exceptional landscape by Albert Marquet can be said to symbolise the passing of the era of exoticism beloved of Orientalists. Its subject, the port of Algiers, had long been a mirror of attitudes as well as change: from the romanticism of Besnard (cat. 98) or the historicism of Racim (cat. 111), to Marquet's frank acknowledgment of the march of modernity. A great painter of rivers, boats and ports, from 1900 Marquet had adapted his clear, uncomplicated landscape style to the Seine at Paris, to St Tropez, Rotterdam, Venice and, in the 1920s and 1930s, to Algiers and Aswan. Marquet spent the Second World War years of 1940–45 in Algiers rather than occupied Vichy France; an anti-fascist, he was active in aiding the Free French Forces there, and painted the Allied Squadron when it visited Algiers harbour.

In this picture, beyond a fringe formed by those signifiers of the exotic – palm trees – European-style buildings and then modern merchant ships rise from the mist. 'From the first light of morning, which veils the port in blue and violet tones, Marquet draws a surprising effect: cranes and ships take on a strange, almost phantom-like aspect...'[1] It is as if he were envisioning the arrival of the future, of the encroachment of Europe and that industrial modernity which was forcibly transforming the lives of people in North African cultures subject to colonisation and the vicissitudes of other peoples' wars. RB

1 *Albert Marquet, 1875–1947*, Galerie des Beaux-Arts, Bordeaux, and Orangerie des Tuileries, Paris, 1975, p. 120.

HENRI MATISSE

122 SEATED MOROCCAN, HAND ON CHIN (Marocain assis, main au menton) 1912–13

Pen and ink on paper 26 x 19.6 cm
Collection James Fairfax

Matisse's *Seated Moroccan* is one of the sixty-odd drawings with which the artist prepared his program of painting in Tangier. Sketching discreetly in the kasbah, the bulk of the drawings are spare line studies of Moorish architecture. Around his hotel Matisse made a dozen studies of men in traditional costume which resonate in canvases such as *Seated Riffian* and *Amido.*

Four drawings explore the composition seen here (but never realised as a painting): a seated and contemplative Moroccan, elbows and ankles crossed, stretched diagonally across the left of the picture space. The Fairfax drawing is the most detailed and accomplished of these; as Jack Cowart writes, in it Matisse achieves: 'a beautiful balance between all parts of the composition and the elegant draftsmanship. We see the Moroccan tribesman dressed in a costume common to Tangier, with a braided cord holding a sheathed dagger'.[1]

Comparison of this drawing with Delacroix's *Arab chieftain reclining on a carpet* (cat. 1) indicates how far the modernist Matisse had a traditional conception of the Oriental subject. Both stress the alert intelligence yet physical ease of the sitters and render the unfamiliar volumes of Moroccan clothing as a play of masterly curved lines which, in the Matisse, markedly stretch the norms of 'correct' drawing.   RB

[1] Jack Cowart, 'Matisse's Moroccan sketchbooks and drawings: self-discovery through various motifs', in Jack Cowart et al., *Matisse in Morocco: The Paintings and Drawings 1912–1913*, exh. cat., National Gallery of Art, Washington, 1990, p.131.

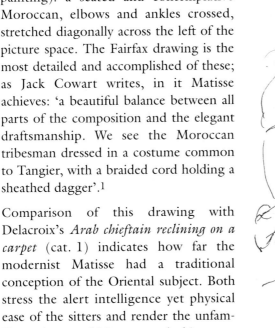

HENRI MATISSE

123 ODALISQUE IN RED CULOTTES, WITH EWER AND ROUND TABLE
(Odalisque à la culotte rouge, aiguière et guéridon) c. 1924

Oil on canvas 50 x 60 cm. Musée National de l'Orangerie. Collection Jean Walter et Paul Guillaume

Matisse's famous series of odalisques of the 1920s were painted in Nice, his Mediterranean home from 1918. They are nuanced studio constructions based on memories of masters like Renoir and Ingres, but also on his own experiences in Morocco a decade before: 'I do Odalisques in order to do nudes. But how does one do the nude without it being artificial? And then, because I know that they exist. I was in Morocco. I have seen them'.[1] Perhaps he refers to Zorah, the Moorish (or Jewish) teenager who posed for his best-known Tangier paintings and became a prostitute (see fig. 17).

Matisse's Nice 'odalisques' were, on the contrary, Frenchwomen feigning the Oriental, like his favourite, Henriette Darricarrère,[2] seen here posed in red harem pants and a cream *gandourah*. Coupled with the ornamental hangings Matisse has placed behind her, such studio props provide only minimal suggestions of a life of cloistered opulence in the East. The artist makes no unsustainable claims to ethnographic accuracy but, rather, finds a pretext for studying a profusion of light, colour and decoration, tracking themes of pale lime greens and more strident pinks and reds around the composition. Such works are a bridge between School of Paris painting of the 1920s and the comfortable exoticism of the emerging *art colonial*. RB

[1] Henri Matisse, 'Statements to Tériade, 1929–30', in Jack D. Flam (ed.), *Matisse on Art*, Phaidon, Oxford, 1973, p. 59.

[2] Darricarrère posed for Matisse from 1920 to 1927; on her life see Jack Cowart et al., *Henri Matisse: The Early Years in Nice, 1916–1930*, National Gallery of Art, Washington, 1987, pp. 26–7.

HENRI MATISSE

124 ODALISQUE WITH RED JEWEL-BOX (Odalisque au coffret rouge) 1927

Oil on canvas 51 x 65 cm
Musée Matisse, Nice

Painted two years before he turned sixty, this fine canvas was done as Matisse began to consider returning to Morocco, as if in recognition of a need to renew direct contact with the exotic (in the event, he travelled to colonial Tahiti in 1930).[1] His widely exhibited odalisques sometimes drew adverse criticism, of a kind rejected by the artist:

> *What I could never accept is that in reproaching me for a certain profusion of pictures, people felt able to employ in respect of them the words 'exoticism' or 'orientalism' in a pejorative fashion, as if for me the arts of the Orient, given the plastic use that I made of certain of their elements, could lead straight to mannerism, a facile decorativeness, if not a dubious rococo.*[2]

In fact Matisse's employment of the pictorial means of Oriental art – including the use of intense colour, arabesque patterning, the reduction of figures to outlines and a reliance on silhouette – was based on a serious study of Japanese prints, Persian miniatures, carpets and ceramics. His ability to reconcile the bright greens, golds and cherry reds in this *Odalisque* painting was enabled by years of adapting such lessons. But the interweaving curves of the woman's body and costume stem more from European precedents: Ingres's *Grand odalisque* (fig. 3) modernised, posed more naturally from the front, and imbued with the insouciance of a 1920s 'flapper'.   RB

[1] Letter of 1927, cited in Elizabeth C. Childs & John Klein, 'Oceanic escapes: travel, memory and decoration in the art of Henri Matisse', in *Matisse*, eds Caroline Turner & Roger Benjamin, Queensland Art Gallery, Brisbane, 1995, p. 124.

[2] Matisse, in André Verdet, *Entretiens, notes et écrits sur la peinture: Braque, Léger, Matisse, Picasso*, Galilée, Paris, 1978, p. 123.

BAYADÈRE

A word which excites the imagination.
All women of the Orient are bayadères
(see Odalisques)

DAGUERREOTYPE

Will replace painting (see Photography)

ODALISQUES

All women of the Orient are odalisques
(see Bayadère)

ORIENTALIST

A well-travelled man

PALM TREE

Adds local colour

PALMYRE

A queen of Egypt? Ruins? We aren't sure

RUINS

Add poetry to a journey

FLAUBERT, *Dictionary of Received Ideas*

THE ORIENT IN THE PHOTOGRAPHERS' MIRROR
FROM CONSTANTINOPLE TO MECCA

Mounira Khemir

THE IMPORTANCE ATTACHED TO TRAVEL IN THE 19TH CENTURY, TOGETHER WITH THE PROLIFERATION OF TRAVEL BOOKS FROM THE 1840s, CREATED IN THE EUROPEAN READER THE DESIRE TO VISUALISE DISTANT LANDS. AT A TIME WHEN TRAVEL WRITING INTERESTED SPECIALISTS IN MANY DIFFERENT DISCIPLINES – GEOGRAPHY, NATURAL HISTORY, ARCHITECTURE, ARCHAEOLOGY, PAINTING – THE ORIENT WAS A CONSTANT PRESENCE FOR THE BROADER PUBLIC.

It was the age of a western vision of the Orient expressed in diverse art forms. Orientalism was finally being coloured by actual journeys East, after two centuries of vision nourished by successive translations of the *Arabian Nights*, from Galland to Mardrus. But did this mediated East correspond to the real Orient, or indeed to the images brought back by the photographers?

THE 'MIRROR WITH MEMORY' AND THE EAST

A number of French and European painters visited North Africa after the conquest of Algeria from 1830, but the opening of the Suez Canal in 1869 finally brought the improved conditions of travel and accommodation that allowed photographers easy access to these lands. Many travellers hoped to find the Holy Land untouched since biblical times, a vision wonderfully illustrated by the photographs of the Englishman Francis Frith, made on his numerous voyages to Egypt and the Near East. Already, two months after Daguerre's invention of 1838, the painter Horace Vernet had left to photograph in Egypt and the Holy Land, accompanied by the daguerreotypist Frédéric Goupil-Fesquet. This first voyage was not without its symbolic dimension. That is to say, the history of photography and the Arabo-Islamic world then known as the 'Orient' are intimately linked.

Egypt, a land of light, witnessed multiple experiments in the development of the photographic process, such as those made by the German, Jacob August Lorent, or by the Briton, Charles Piazzi Smith, who attempted, very early on, to photograph in the interior of the Great Pyramid. The lands of the Middle East, with the Holy Land and, later, the Maghreb, became favoured destinations for European photographers.

From Daguerre's hopeful prediction that the intensity of Egyptian light would produce an image in two or three minutes, to Arago's endorsement before the members of the Institut de France, several official expeditions passed through the lands of the Near East. The first, led by Maxime Du Camp in 1849, included Flaubert. Du Camp, however, failed to translate his curiosity into the photographs he took. He was committed to his role as head of the expedition, but lacked the enthusiasm typical of later photographers, for some of whom, at least, it is possible to speak of a passion for photography. Du Camp's fame stems from his pioneering status rather than from his sensibility or originality.

At the historical moment of the first photographic voyages East there was a certain aura surrounding Orientalism and Orientalist painting, and when Francis Frith took his camera to the Middle East he was thinking not only of biblical sites but also of the pictures of the topographical watercolourist David Roberts. The links between painting and photography became more relevant still with the installation of photographers in residence in the 1860s. Beyond the painterly influence on photographers who tried to capture their own Orient, there was a thorough complicity between the arts as painters, in turn, used photographs to document figures and places and to detach the architectural and sartorial details that the camera recorded so well. The Orient reflected in photography's mirror offers images reminding us of a host of others.

The vast quantity of photographs produced in those lands evokes what might be described as a veritable photographic itinerary, beginning in a world inhabited by vestiges of the past. The human presence was initially used only as an accessory to measure the scale of the monuments. If the *Literary Souvenirs* of Maxime Du Camp are guilty of inventing meetings which never took place, the memoir *The Nile* (written at the instigation of his friend, Théophile Gautier), reveals the conditions in which Du Camp took his photographs, and leaves his prestigious travelling companion, Flaubert, in the shade.

> *Every time I went to inspect the monuments I had my photographic equipment carried with me, and was followed by one of my sailors named Hadji-Ismaël. He was a very handsome Nubian; I sent him clambering up on the ruins that I wanted to reproduce, and so obtained a consistent marker of proportion. The great problem was in keeping him completely still while I took the picture, and I managed it with the help of a Baroque deceit which will inform you, dear Théophile, of the credulous naïvete of those poor Arabs. The copper shaft of my lens, projecting from my camera, I told him, was a canon that would shoot grapeshot if he were unlucky enough to move while I pointed it in his direction; persuaded, Hadji-Ismaël did not budge more than once; you may verify it by leafing through my prints.*[1]

It should be noted, moreover, that Maxime Du Camp – who was well educated in Orientalism and who prepared for his journey with wide reading and research – thought he had captured the Orient more successfully in his writings than in his photographs. But, in an irony of history, the pairing of Flaubert and Du Camp prefigures the photographic fate of the Orient. The apparent divergence in their visions was to be brought together and confounded in an extravagantly Orientalised image of the East.

After those photographs which show an Orient inhabited by monuments, the properly Orientalist and exotic vision emerged. Between the first daguerreotype – taken by Goupil-Fesquet in Egypt in October 1839 and entitled *The harem of Mohamed-Ali in Alexandria* (but showing only a half-open door and two guards) – and the start of the 20th century, Europe viewed or held in its hands thousands of photographs of the Arab world in which Woman, after the monuments, was the subject of predilection. The desert had its place, too, among the dominant myths. The discovery of the desert at the foot of the pyramids reinforced the fascination of Egypt for English travellers while, for the French, the desert had long been synonymous with the Algerian Sahara. The sense of the void and a craving for distant shores obsessed generations and still exercises its fascination today. In the recent novel by Manuel Audran, *The Dreamer of the Orient*, the protagonist, Samuel, is haunted by the dream of the Orient that recurs from his Vendean childhood. He repeats the magical names to himself: Cairo, Damascus, Baghdad, Istanbul, Tripoli. I will go down there, he tells himself, where the sun emerges each morning, pure and yellow from the middle of the sands. Thus, the very word 'desert' impresses the western mind with images of solitude, retreat, meditation and serenity. Tourism and photographic albums would later come to favour this new pictorial sensibility and to perpetuate these myths.

At first, photographic techniques were impervious to the fleeting and the momentary, and models were obliged to strike extended poses before an image could be recorded. This technical exigency invariably accentuated the artificiality of adopted attitudes and poses. But the conditions of the medium were experienced differently by different sitters. For a European bourgeois of the 19th century, posing in a studio brought with it a desire for the most respectable image of oneself. The arrangement of the figure was decided by current cultural values: the back was straightened, the best clothes were worn, the subject turned to face the camera, stood up, leaned on a column, occupied the centre of the frame, held the desired attitude, and appeared dignified.

But what was the meaning of eastern photographic portraits, if not the representation of isolated individuals (without them having chosen the manner in which they were to be shown) by another society which, at the same moment was itself being represented? What meaning did the visiting card portraits of fellahs, of women or of dignitaries hold for those whom they would never reach, even when signed by Pascal Sébah or Arnoux? The gazes of these people often express fear, alarm or unease, traducing the inestimable value accorded the eyes in ancient Egypt. The eyes, above all, are vehicles of emotion.

In such cases, photography functions as a mirror reflecting one society as it shapes another through actions and habits that often reveal its own sense of superiority. The isolation of people photographed is always superficial, especially in a culture where the individual is rarely alone. A contradiction thus emerges between the fabricated context – abundantly reinforced by accessories – and the real situation of the sitter. In this game of substitutions between the imaginary and the real, the hermetic space of the studio fostered all kinds of compositions, many posing as private spaces. That which at first had seemed excluded by the photograph's role as an image of the real brought with it a variety of abuses. The emphasis placed on costume or race, and underlined by the caption, conspired to subvert the models' expression or appearance. *Moorish woman*, *Arab woman*, *Fellah woman*, figures drawn from the ordinary people, were consigned to anonymity while bourgeois men and women were frequently furnished with portraits recording their names as well as the date and place of the photograph. The so-called 'artistic' photographs of stock figures in which nothing is left to chance include mention, when reproduced on postcards, of 'Photographie véritable' or 'Photographed from life'. Whether signed by Bonfils, Zangaki, Pascal Sébah, Béchard, Arnoux or Lehnert and Landrock (qq.v.), such postcards were destined for a largely European public, and so appear variously captioned in French, in English, and sometimes in German or Italian. Colonialism and the diffusion of postcards went hand in hand with the multiplication of 'scenes and types' that effaced all differences in order to speak simply of the Arab and the Arab woman.

The first ethnographic photographs began to be made in the 1860s. They denoted a contempt, sometimes even a violence, acted out against these colonised populations. This fact would move the Algerian writer Malek Alloula to entitle his book on the postcards of Algeria – in which a multitude of 'Moorish women' display their naked breasts – *The Colonial Harem* as a sign of protest and resistance. A photographer such as Moulin, sent to Algeria on an ethnographic pretext, used his studio to invent scenes of the purest Orientalism. From 1850 certain photographers unhesitatingly began using the costumes and accessories lying around their studios to clothe Europeans posing as Arab figures.

The interest in Oriental costume nurtured by painting was perpetuated in photographs through the medium of disguise. The models who posed in Roger Fenton's studio in London in 1856, or the photographs taken by Lady Harwarden of her daughters in composite costumes are typical examples. They are reminiscent of the European women who posed as Algerians for Renoir (q.v.), or of the many postcards of the early 20th century in which Europeans of both sexes perform scenes of seduction in Oriental dress.

Photographers were put to the test by the question of how to record a society of the interior while respecting its principles of concealment and disclosure, and its separation of private and public spaces. Although the representation of religious subjects came late to Orientalist painting, it was necessary, according to the testimony of Dauzats, to take many precautions while drawing in a mosque, which had to be almost empty. The painter Fromentin wrote:

Perhaps I could have entered the mosque; but I didn't attempt it. To go further than permitted into Arab life struck me as a misconceived curiosity. One must observe these people from the distances at which they choose to show themselves: men up close, women from afar, the bedroom and the mosque, never.[2]

Fromentin did not want to adopt a false point of view – a predicament not feared by the many photographers who embraced the typically frontal, face-to-face characteristic of their medium.

Certain photographers at least give the impression of having experienced a pictorial delight equal to that of painters. The rich information of their images tends to be compromised, however, by false notes in the composition. Thus in certain photographs signed by Zangaki, scenes of prayer incorporated a variety of different postures, whereas collective prayer is in fact led in unison. The same error was committed by painters, and even by Gérôme, who made seven journeys to the Orient and became famous for his treatment of such subjects. Whether from contempt or through wonder and alienation, the symbolic and spiritual import of prayer was falsified.

While there were certain shots that remained, by definition, impossible to achieve – like the Moorish bath dear to Gérôme (q.v.) – others, like a number of photographs of men at prayer, are marred by unco-ordinated gestures. Many early photographers thought that their work needed to be manipulated to enhance its meaning. Falsehoods slipped into their compositions through errors and experiments, but also through the inherent difficulties of the medium. An example is a couple photographed in the middle of the South Tunisian desert whose muslin veil in the form of the Tunisian *malya* produced a proto-cinematic effect, a reminder of how Lehnert complained of missing his accessories when he went out to photograph in the desert.[3]

In a photograph signed Lehnert and Landrock and representing a young girl whose breast is bared (fig. 40)[4] Lehnert's picturesque interest extends to his studied depiction of every object: jewels – hands of Fatma and fibulas – jasmine blossoms hung in the hair (behind the ear, the famous jasmine bouquet), the bared breast. The stripes of the robe, *la malya*, accentuate the movement of the raised arms and contribute to the general allure of the model's compliant attitude. Such a subject was often the pretext for recording the play of light on the forms of the body. Lehnert, in fact, had a strong sense of composition and was influenced by Pictorialist photographers. This was one of many images produced by Lehnert and Landrock and distributed around the world. Printed in the form of postcards, captioned and recaptioned according to changing fashions and values, some were no doubt already shocking by contemporary standards, and remain so today.

PHOTOGRAPHS FOR THE SULTANS

Orientalist fashion did not spare the Abdullah brothers, any more than it did the Turkish painter Osman Hamdy Bey (q.v.). The photograph *Interior of a harem*,[5] bearing their signature, well illustrates the mythic atmosphere of the *Arabian Nights* that photographers, in their own way, attempted to render. Although the painted back-drop does not help to situate the scene precisely, the costume of the Turkish lady recalls those of a multitude of odalisques stretched out on their sofas. Signed Abdullah Brothers, this work presents a vision fashionable in the 19th century. When the Abdullah brothers were photographing for the archives of the Ottoman Sultan Abdul Hamid II (1876–1909) they usually worked in a documentary style (cat. 152), but they did not fail to submit to fashion when producing for the tourist market, for which the cultural origins of the photographer were of little import. These elaborate representations never fail to reflect the ideology of their epoch.

The Arab world also boasted sultan photographers, like Sultan Abdul-Aziz of Morocco who was intrigued by the progress of European science and technology. He took snapshots during his reign and, at the solemn audience in which he received the British ambassadors, regretted that he did not have his camera at hand to take a spontaneous portrait of the military attaché whose fur busby caught his attention. It appears in the collection of the *Archives of Morocco*.[6] The photographs included in works of this type often bear astonishing commentaries concerning Arabs and harems, advice on travel in the East, on how to become rich, and on remedies and charms. Such vulgarised productions are responsible for many errors concerning the sites of photographs, which have been perpetuated by the prestigious travel guides that continue to use these sources.

Certain photographs of the harem of Abdul-Aziz survive today, like the portraits of the women of the imperial harem, or the depictions of such distractions as a bicycle race conducted in a palace courtyard, in this case made from a cinematographic film by his Sherifian Majesty.[7] In the photograph, for example, representing *Two matrons of the harem of the Sultan Abdul-Aziz*, one is struck by the serious expression of the faces which produce a perfect consonance in the image. Luminous robes, draperies, coiffures, and the contrasts of light on the folds of the costumes lend a majestic character to this seemingly unique image.

Even earlier, Sultan Abdul Hamid II had wished to change the image of his empire by shunning all visions of the picturesque, to which he opposed a project of photographic documentation involving official photographers like the Abdullah brothers as well as the work of others. The sultan's gift to the United States and Great Britain of a self-portrait of the empire in the form of photographic albums was the first in history to be sent so far. A unique event, this visual report from the Islamic world already testified to its concern to offer an alternative self-image. Today it seems like a signature of modernity, appropriate to the sultans who cultivated the art of the signature as far back as Suleiman the Magnificent, as represented by the splendid collections of the *tugras* or imperial monograms of the Ottoman sultans in the Museum of Islamic Art in Istanbul.

Although painted portraits of sultans and dignitaries were fashionable even in the 18th century, the greater part of realist representation began at the start of the 19th century with Sultan Mahmud II (1808–39). His portraits were hung publicly in ceremonial fashion, as well as in military buildings. European aesthetic taste gained ground with the bourgeois Turks. In view of the importance of calligraphy in the education of the princes, a particular zeal would also be applied to photography, that other writing made with light. The aesthetic rupture defined by the uses of photography is thus in stark contrast to the Ottoman baroque which brought the Empire so close to western style.

The biography of her father, Sultan Abdul Hamid II, written by the princess Aïché Osmanoglou, reveals the importance of photography in the events of daily life, as well as on more official occasions. She testifies to the photographer's presence at each event. 'Papa had a great number of photographers sent but it was on the recommendation of Djevad Bey that I chose Ahmed Nâmi Bey.'[8] Or, later: 'Papa equally begged his brother to allow Mehmed Abid Effendi to attend one of the schools in Salonica, and, on this occasion sent him several photographs of the child then aged six years taken in the garden by the officers'.[9]

Presentation albums not only described the capital of the Ottoman Empire, but also revealed different aspects of its provinces. In the views of Constantinople may be seen mosques, houses, hospitals, factories, schools, banks, museums and foreign embassies. Other albums contain landscapes, *objets d'art*, sporting scenes, archaeological sites, farms and animals. In the same spirit, there are more pictures of the horses of the court than of the ladies of the palace.

VEILS, SACRED SITES, KNOWLEDGE

In Islamic tradition, the symbolism of the veil acquires particular importance; it represents either withheld knowledge (veiled) or communicated knowledge (unveiled, revealed). Revelation is in the opening of the veil.[10]

This quote defines but one aspect of the veil's function. We may question the attitude taken by Sadic Bey in about 1880 in concealing his camera to carry away the first image of the Kaaba from the most sacred site of Islam in Mecca, but his scientific approach to sacred sites reveals his acceptance of the photographic image as being no more than the product of a mechanical device. This was to be the interpretation made later by the sheikhs of El-Azhar University in Cairo, that great Islamic theological centre. Very early, a figure such as the Emir Abd-el-Kader had adopted the same attitude in his precious anthology, *Le Livre des Haltes*. A record of the photographic session that was devoted to taking the Emir's portrait has been left by Adrien Bonfils. The sitter was accompanied by a basket containing all of his decorations – and took a good hour to put them on.[11] Such examples encourage us to reconsider the incident – made much of in the history of photography – regarding the Viceroy of Egypt, Mohammed-Ali, who exclaimed at the sight of the daguerreotype produced by Goupil-Fesquet: 'It is the work of the devil'![12]

The following testimony appears in the chronicle of a medieval traveller: 'Inside the Kaaba there were images of angels and of prophets (grant them peace!), one of a tree, one of Abraham holding divining rods (*azlâm*), and an image of Jesus with his mother. At the taking of Mecca, the Messenger of God, may God bless and salute him, ordered them all destroyed, save that of Jesus and his mother'.[13] Today, photographs and pictures of Mecca can often be seen hanging on private walls. The two kinds of images exist together paradoxically. The interest accorded the portrait in Muslim societies defines the very essence of the photographic image and reveals an acceptance of images, as of other forms of modernity.

The fascination exercised by the Orient was concretised by the discovery of photography, which made it accessible to consumers or to 'armchair tourists' as they were known at the time. Writers of travel books would sometimes draw on the work of other writers, as, for example, Nerval drew on Lane. In such cases there appears to have been a resistance to direct observation. The same resistance can be discerned in 19th-century photographs. If the failure to observe went against the grain of the photographic medium, it did not prevent photographers from using their studios as laboratories where they experimented on indigenous people. Not until the 1920s or even the 1930s would images be produced in which it was apparent that photographers shared the cultural values of their subjects.

Flaubert, like other Westerners, had followed the general rule: on the one hand the mystery of the Orient – its exoticism, its secrecy, its unfathomable arcana; on the other, the commonplaces of ancestral vices – cruelty, indolence, corruption, backwardness, sexual abandon, neglect, fanaticism. The Orient was less important in itself than in its capacity to shape an artistic or literary vocation.

Thirty years later Mohammed Sadic Bey (q.v.), on the contrary, had the confidence and the secret determination to give an account of spiritual intimacy.[14] Of transparent faith, he never hesitated in choosing this role. Having the cultural identity of a Muslim, he was able to make the most of his proximity of vision and to reinvest in the mythic space of the Orient, through which Islam had been so badly served. Perhaps he sensed that the impenetrability of sacred places formed a constant barrier and induced a deviation from positive images of Islam towards caricature. This insight had been overlooked by the Romantics.

The photographic work of Clérambault (q.v.), a contemporary of Matisse and Klee, appears like a refutation of the bare-bathing Ouled-Nails who were photographed by Gustave de Beaucorps or are seen in the many negatives signed 'ND photographe'. Clérambault was fascinated by the script of Islam and by Islam's culture of signs. Among such signs and symbols is the cloth hung on the door of a hamman, still used in Cairo today, to signify the presence of women. It is lifted to announce the men's session. This sign, as simple as it seems, has a profound resonance.

Clérambault did not merely photograph veiled women, but was fascinated by the veil itself.[15] It is this that distinguishes his work from the production of commercial photographers. Moreover, Clérambault worked at a time when aesthetic research in the West was undergoing significant developments, and when the look addressed to the Other was becoming more positive. This was the case with Wassily Kandinsky, Paul Klee and Kees van Dongen, painters who, in pursuit of personal expression, turned to Arabo-Muslim architecture as towards the fabric of a different mental construction.[16] In Clérambault's case the attraction was to the fall of drapery, caressed by light – the Moroccan light so sensitive to detail. It is perhaps for this reason that he placed such little emphasis on the motifs of costumes. Light, lending its value to the drapery, is his sole subject (cat. 174).

Cultivating the exotic, or troubling to invent it when it was unavailable, clearly demonstrates the unequalled fascination that photographic realism held for its exponents from the dawn of photography. Photographers of the West must have felt comforted in being able to construct, through their medium, a little of that intimacy which so clearly escaped them in the reality of the colonial encounter. The failed painters among them (as numbers of them were) must have been doubly relieved at proving themselves adequate at last to the task of representation. But the alternative reality conveyed by non-western photographers such as Sadic Bey contributes to a new lesson: the ability of a medium to escape the confines of a cultural practice like Orientalism – to prove, in short, the openness of a visual technology as the generator of new meanings in new hands. ◆◆ TRANSLATED FROM THE FRENCH BY PETER RUDD
(with assistance from *Roger Benjamin*)

1 *Un voyageur en Egypte vers 1850, 'Le Nil' de Maxime Du Camp*, Sand/Conti, Paris, 1987, p. 81. See also Julia Ballerini, 'The invisibility of Hadj-Ishmael: Maxime du Camp's 1850 photographs of Egypt', in *The Body Imaged*, ed. Kathleen Adler & Marcia Pointon, Cambridge University Press, Cambridge, 1993, pp. 147–60 (editor's note).

2 Eugène Fromentin, *Un Eté dans le Sahara*, Michel Lévy, Paris, 1857.

3 Philippe Cardinal (ed.), *L'Orient d'un photographe Lehnert & Landrock*, Favre, Lausanne, 1987.

4 Mounira Khemir, *L'Orientalisme: l'orient des photographes au XIXème siècle*, Photopoche no. 58, Centre National de la Photographie, Paris, 1994, no. 41.

5 Collection Pierre de Gigord, Paris.

6 Interview cited in Jacques Borgé & Nicolas Viasnoff, *Archives du Maroc*, Editions Michèle Trinckvel, Collection Archives de la France, Paris, 1995 (first published in *Le matin*, 18 November 1901).

7 Photograph in the Collection Massiet, Bibliothèque des Arts Décoratifs, Paris.

8 Aïché Osmanoglou, Ottoman Princess (1887–1960), *Avec mon père le Sultan Abdulhamid de son palais à sa prison*, L'Harmattan, Collection Comprendre le Moyen-Orient, Paris, 1991, p. 175.

9 ibid., p. 205.

10 Eva de Vitray-Meyerovitch, *Anthologie du soufisme*, Albin Michel, Collection Spiritualités vivantes, Paris, 1995, p. 271.

11 Thomas Ritchie, 'Bonfils & Son: Egypt, Greece and the Levant, 1867–1894', *History of Photography*, no. 3, January 1997, pp. 33–46.

12 *Excursions daguériennes*, published by Lerebours from 1841 to 1844.

13 Abû l-Hasan, 'Ali Ibn Abï Bakr al-Harawî (died in 1215)', *Al Isârât ilâ ma'rifat az-ziârât (Le Guide des Lieux de pèlerinage)*, Institut français de Damas, Damascus, 1953.

14 Mustafa Amer, 'An Egyptian explorer in Arabia in the 19th century', *Bulletin de la Société Rotale de Géographie*, vol. 18; in the inventory (publication pending) of the principal public and private collections of photographs of the Maghreb and the Machreq, the single series of photographs by Mohammed Sadic Bey is that in the Bibliothèque de l'Institut de France in an album which previously belonged, among others, to the Schlumberger family; it assembles images of various world travels, probably purchased in Egypt.

15 The exhibition of Clérambault's photographs (see n. 16) began at the Centre Georges Pompidou in 1990. I lectured on the exhibition in several French and European cities, and the response to the photographs still remains enigmatic. Their installation in Edinburgh in 1992 next to some erotic photographs under the title 'Addressing the Forbidden' testifies at least to an attitude of provocation.

16 Mounira Khemir, in *Gaëtan Gatian de Clérambault, psychiatre et photographe*, Les empêcheurs de penser en rond, Paris, 1990, p. 49. See also Joan Copjec, 'The sartorial superego', *October*, no. 50, Fall 1989, pp. 57–95 (editor's note).

PHOTOGRAPHY CATALOGUE

No. 180. Intérieur de la Mosquée d'Amrou (Vieux Caire)   *H. Béchard*

125 HENRI BÉCHARD
Interior of the Amrou mosque (Old Cairo)
(*Intérieur de la mosquée d'Amrou*) c. 1870
Albumen print 22.5 x 28.5 cm
Collection Claude Philip, Orange

Perspectives, arcades and columns, whether at Cordoba,
Kairouan or Cairo, are representative spaces of Arab
architecture, inspiring calm and inviting meditation.
The photographer has deftly captured the interior
of a mosque in the city of a thousand minarets –
a rare photograph.

126 ERME DESIRE
Arab tailors, Cairo
(*Tailleurs arabes, le Caire*) c. 1870
Albumen print 25.1 x 19.8 cm
Collection Claude Philip, Orange

The practice of arts and crafts was usually
photographed by resident photographers.
Despite his brief stay in Egypt, Ermé Désiré
left a series of photographs of the handi-
crafts of Cairo which demonstrate that he
was not merely seeking the bizarre. Often
skilfully composed, privileging symmetry,
these photographs are precious documents.
In addition to one or two artisans
photographed at work, like these tailors,
they show that such shops were already
social spaces.

127 FELIX BONFILS
Dragoman tour guide, Lebanon
(*Dragoman, guide des voyageurs, Liban*)
c. 1865
Albumen print 28 x 22 cm
Collection Claude Philip, Orange

This famous photograph by Bonfils
represents a *dragoman* in a Syro-Lebanese
costume, proud of his elegance and
displaying a sabre and a rifle against a
backdrop of ruins. He sits as if on a halt.
Dragoman comes from the Arabic
torjoman and signifies a translator and
interpreter. His status as the intermediary
who acts as guide and interpreter to
travellers and photographers accounts
for his obliging attitude.

128 LEHNERT & LANDROCK
View of the desert (Vue du désert) c. 1910
Sepia print 17.5 x 23.6 cm
Collection Jacques Py, France

Rudolph Lehnert's views of the desert are
the most beautiful of his works. He often
took his photographs after a sand-storm
to obtain the desired smoothness of grain.
Such pictures communicate the feelings of
serenity and happiness that were to fascinate
the photographer for the rest of his life.
He stayed at the oasis of Redeyef until his
death. The impressions he left of it evoke
an entire poem, suggesting the loved one
who went away on a fine day with her nomad
tribe – a dominant theme of Arab poetry.
Lehnert's heart, devoted to the desert,
resounded with the echoes of this *qasida*.

129 LEHNERT & LANDROCK
Arab artisan (Artisan arabe) c. 1910
Sepia print 23.6 x 17.5 cm
Collection Jacques Py, France

Picturesque verve and a pronounced taste
for drapery contribute to this exercise in
antique imagery which harks back to Graeco-
Roman sources. Nothing is left to chance in
this composition, which aspires to perfection
even in the geometric decoration on the neck
of the jar fastidiously underlining the folds
of the drapery. The artisan's hand readily echoes
his bare shoulder.

130 PEDRA A TLEMCEN

Detail of a door, Algiers
(*Dètail de porte, Algérie*) c. 1890
Albumen print 27 x 21 cm
Collection Jean-Pierre Evrard, Maurepas

A detail of a door, with carved timber strap-work and metal door-knocker: this type of photograph is rare and belongs to the process of discovery of Arabo-Muslim art and architecture. Joseph Pedra seems to have profited more than anyone else from his stay in this city rich in architectural remains by documenting them down to the last detail. It was in the same city that Clérambault had a stele engraved in Arabic for his tomb.

131 PEDRA A TLEMCEN

Tlemcen, the Tower
(*Tlemcen, la Tour*) c. 1890
Albumen print 26 x 21 cm
Collection Jean-Pierre Evrard, Maurepas

Like a lament, the Tower of Tlemcen is the last vestige of a prestigious monument and the relic of a lost epoch. Today nothing remains of this tower beyond a piece of wall. Apart from its nostalgic effect, the photograph gains a definite documentary value from its sober viewpoint, which informs us of the changing state of the monument.

132 FELIX BONFILS
Caravan in the desert, Egypt
(*Caravane dans le dèsert, Egypte*) c. 1880
Albumen print 21 x 27 cm
Collection Jean-Pierre Evrard, Maurepas

This composition, showing a rest made for the camera,
is reminiscent of the paintings of Léon Belly or Joseph
Austin Benwell. Was the stop merely for the photographer
or, as suggested by the attitude of the man on the left,
was it a matter of necessity? He would seem to have been
preparing himself for prayer. This photograph reminds us
of an incident, famous in the history of photography, in
which Hammerschmidt was wounded while trying to
photograph a caravan on its way to Mecca.

133 ANONYMOUS

Studio portrait of a Moorish woman
(*Portrait de mauresque en studio*)
c. 1880
Albumen print 25 x 20 cm
Collection Jean-Pierre Evrard, Maurepas

This veiled Moorish woman is posed in the
studio, with palm branches evoking the oasis
on the painted backdrop. With her harem
pants and veil typical of the period, this
Algérienne also recalls the many photographs
of improperly unveiled women signed ND
Photographe or Lehnert & Landrock.

134 CAVILLA & MOLINARI

Woman in her interior,
Tangier, Morocco (*Femme dans*
son intérieur–Tanger, Maroc) c. 1890
Albumen print 18 x 14 cm
Collection Jean-Pierre Evrard, Maurepas

This is one of those photographs in
which the composition appears true to life,
and is a rare image of Morocco, the sherifian
kingdom long closed to photographers.
The photo is especially precious because
of the rarity of images of this period.
The costume, the pose, the coiffure and
the straw matting all denote the modest
status of the model, whose gesture and
attitude is so expressive as to recall Matisse's
Zorah on the terrace (fig.17).

135 GARRIGUES
Mosque of the Sabres at Kairouan
Photograph 26 x 26 cm
Collection Angela Tromellini, Bologna

This rare photograph of Kairouan well illustrates the space and the architecture whose particular scale seduced such travellers as August Macke and Paul Klee. White surfaces, arabesques thrown up by a luminous desert, the cupolas and the minarets rising like pictorial calligraphy. Beyond the sepia of the photograph, the most beautiful part of the image is reserved for colour.

136 J. P. SEBAH
Bedouin (*Bédouin*) c. 1885
Albumen print 27 x 21 cm
Collection Claude Philip, Orange

This beautiful Bedouin, holding a string of beads, realises a perfect composition with the folds of his burnous and draperies which offer balanced areas of light and shade. Even the left hand, cast in slightly deeper shadow, contributes to the composition. But the face is serious and does not appear completely consenting. The photo is distinguished by its *mise-en-scène*, the more so since its canvas backdrop was also employed for other scenes.

137 ANONYMOUS

Moorish women in a street of the kasbah, Algiers (Mauresques dans une rue de la Casbah) c. 1880
Albumen print 26.8 x 18.9 cm
Bibliothèque des Arts Décoratifs, Paris

Photographers of different types found rich material for study in the streets of the kasbah, where light and shade are accentuated by the depth of field. The kasbah of Algiers, with its stairs and covering arches in the Arab style, lodged 'between walls', is a world of its own. It offered photographers a multitude of scenes, such as the famous *yaouleds* or shoeshine boys of the postcards.

138 ANONYMOUS

Rue de la gazelle, Algiers (Rue de la gazelle (Alger)) c. 1870
Albumen print 26.8 x 19.9 cm
Bibliothèque des Arts Décoratifs, Paris

This image concentrates and celebrates a number of pictorial clichés: the man draped in his burnous, the shadowy street with its implication of mystery, the young man against the doorway lost in thought. The scene is quasi-cinematic. The site, even when empty, evokes the architecture of the Orient, as does that photo in the purest picturesque style, Frederick Holland Day's *In an eastern city*.

139 WILHELM HAMMERSCHMIDT
Karnak, Temple of Amon
(*Karnak, temple d'Amon*) c. 1870
Albumen print 31.2 x 23.6 cm
Bibliothèque des Arts Décoratifs, Paris

The proliferation of columns and the effect of light and
shade are what strike the visitor to Karnak in Upper Egypt,
the site of monumental remains of the Pharaohs. The length
of the shadows cast against the columns fixes the precise time
of the photograph. The Vicomte de Banville remarked of the
light: 'In Egypt, a subject, like a view, is never well lit for
more than ten or twelve minutes a day'.

140 HENRI BECHARD
Great Pyramid, eastern view
(*Grande Pyramide vue de l'Est*) c. 1875
Albumen print 21.2 x 39 cm
Bibliothèque des Arts Décoratifs, Paris

The multiplicity of views of the Pyramids and the Sphinx,
photographed from all angles, was one of the attractions
of millenary Egypt for travelling photographers.
This composition is of almost imaginary perfection,
but without the cold severity of the classical design of
the *Description of Egypt*. In time the framing of the image
became ever tighter, until Charles Piazzi Smith or August
Jacob Lorent experimented with photographing the interior
of the Great Pyramid by magnesium light to try and capture
a little of this Egyptian mystery.

141 HIPPOLYTE ARNOUX
*Tomb of the caliphs (Cairo), Egypt (Tombeaux des
califes
(Le Caire), Egypte)* c. 1880
Albumen print 21 x 27 cm
Collection Jean-Pierre Evrard, Maurepas

The tombs of the caliphs, with their cupolas and minarets,
were subjects highly valued by the photographers of this
period. As Emile Béchard wrote: 'Above the houses, neither
roofs nor chimneys…The square rooftop terraces give the
effect of a vast checkerboard on which, moving like colossal
figures…the 300 minarets glisten in the sun under the purest
sky. For a moment one is tempted to believe in the marvels
of the *Thousand and One Nights*'. Today Cairo is still
perceived as the city of a thousand minarets. Their sculptural
isolation evokes the poetry of many of Béchard's
photographs.

154 Anonymous
Turkish café, Istanbul (Café turc) c. 1870
Albumen print 21 x 27 cm
Collection Pierre de Gigord, Paris

Images of popular outdoor spots offering the chibouk
and the hookah, with straw seats for the customers, were
exploited and popularised by 19th-century photography.
Seemingly taken from life, such picturesque genre scenes
by certain photographers were reconstructed in the studio,
as in the photo of the *Wandering coffee-seller* by Pascal
Sébah. This type of café can still be found near the Grand
Bazaar in Istanbul.

155 ABDULLAH FRERES
Turkish lady (Dame turque) c. 1880
Albumen print 25.5 x 19.5 cm
Collection Pierre de Gigord, Paris

A divan, an inlaid table and a hookah were the indispensable
props for the Orientalist image *par excellence.* This one is
redolent of all the others devoted to Woman, the Odalisque,
the Lady of the Harem, and illustrates the vision of a world
seen in the light of the *Arabian Nights.*

Fig. 42
RUBELLIN
Turkish woman
(Femme turque) n.d.
Albumen print 26.5 x 20 cm
Collection Pierre de Gigord, Paris

Fig. 43
ABDULLAH FRERES
Turkish woman
(Femme turque) c. 1880
Albumen print 25.5 x 19.5 cm
Collection Pierre de Gigord, Paris

When she is not stretched out on
a sofa, all the coquetry of the
Turkish woman becomes
concentrated on her transparent
veil, which belongs to a world
between Occident and Orient.

156 ABDULLAH FRERES
A Turkish family outing, Istanbul (Dames turques
en promenade (Famille turque en promenade)) c. 1870
Albumen print 20 x 25.5 cm
Collection Pierre de Gigord, Paris

A picnic on the banks of the Bosphorus, evoking the 'sweet
waters' at the confluence of Asia and Europe, this prescient
snapshot would have charmed the Impressionists with its
tree, its cart, its sails, its little girl and its dog. Which is the
first and which the second image? Only the little girl seems
to have moved between the two poses (cf. the cover of
Photopoche no. 58 on *L'Orientalisme*). The sequence is
quasi-cinematic. Such an image, posed in the open air, is rare.

157 PASCAL SEBAH
Fellahin (women and children), Cairo
(*Fellahin (femmes et enfants), Caire*) c. 1870
Albumen print 27.1 x 21.2 cm
Collection Claude Philip, Orange

A painted backdrop, a laterally balanced composition,
a disruptive glance from the little girl, and a child carried
in the Egyptian manner are brought together in this over-
done studio photograph. The *borguoug*, a piece of metal used
to hold the veil in place, produced (and still produces)
many women who squint. Despite this, the photograph
is reminiscent of the Egyptian portraits of Emile Bernard.

163 LEHNERT & LANDROCK
Couple, Algeria c. 1911
Photograph 18 x 24 cm
Collection Angela Tromellini, Bologna

Couple, slave of love or *Abd-el-Gheram and Nouriel Ain*
evoke the same two Algerians. Photography makes their
existence real. This image embodies the complicity between
Orientalist painting and photography and exemplifies an
authentic encounter between painting and photography
that occurred in Biskra. It was used as a source by Etienne
Dinet and so contributed to his quasi-photographic realism.

164 ANONYMOUS

The santon, Egypt
(*Le Santon, Égypte*) c. 1880
Albumen print 24 x 18.5 cm
Collection Nabil Jumbert, Boulogne

The *santon*, somewhere between a dervish,
a saint and a tramp, lingers in the memory
of residents of Cairo. Only oral history can
elucidate this photograph, which recalls
traces of a lost past. Legend records that
sterile women would sleep with the santon to
cure their sterility – a scene which apparently
could even transpire openly in the street.

165 FELIX BONFILS

Group of running sais in Egypt
(*Groupe de Sais coureurs en Égypte*)
c. 1870
Albumen print 27 x 20.5 cm
Collection Nabil Jumbert, Boulogne

A group of *sais* such as these can be seen
running in the first film shot by the Lumière
brothers in Cairo. Sais were men who would
run in front of carriages to announce the
arrival of an important person – a peculiarly
Egyptian tradition that has long since
vanished. In height these men are
reminiscent of Nubians. The rather elaborate
costumes are in odd contrast to their bare
feet, especially as the sais are here posing for
the studio.

166 PASCAL SEBAH
Whirling dervishes (Derviches tourneurs) c. 1870
Albumen print 25.5 x 19.5 cm
Collection Pierre de Gigord, Paris

The mystic religious order of whirling dervishes was founded
by Jalal Eddine Errumi in Konya, still known today as the
city of whirling dervishes. Their dance involved a turning
which, like their music, could inspire a mystic ecstasy. This is
still one of the emblematic images of Turkey today. Often
well composed, such photographs evoke both mystery and
calm.

167 EMILE FRECHON
*'Bassour' for the new bride
(Ouled-Nail tribe, Algeria)* c. 1898
Photograph 23.1 x 29 cm
Collection Gérard Lévy, Paris

Apparently the third scene in a group of three
photographs signed by Frechon, this photograph, like a piece of reportage, shows the
preparation for the bridal procession in the *jehfa*,
a kind of litter affixed to a dromedary. The litter
serves to transport the bride in concealment to
her new home on the wedding night. The scene
is located in Algeria but represents a tradition
found all over the south of North Africa.

168 EMILE FRECHON
*Bride dancing (Ouled-Nail tribe,
Algeria)* c. 1898
Photograph 29 x 23.1 cm
Collection Gérard Lévy, Paris

The veil, the veil of modesty, and the
delicacy of the bride who, with eyes lowered,
holds the transparent veil, gives this
photograph a rare freshness and freedom of
pose. Despite the lowered gaze, the young
woman's character is clearly evident. Frechon
distinguishes himself here with his respect for
his subject and his effort to achieve the truth.

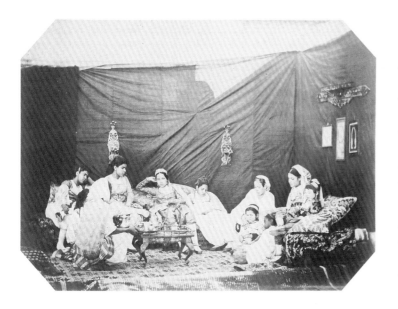

169 FELIX JACQUES MOULIN
Moorish women on a visit. Interior dress, Algiers (Mauresques en visite. Costume d'intérieur, Alger) c. 1857
Albumen print 16.2 x 22 cm
Collection Claude Philip, Orange

Tapestries, small shelves, rugs and cushions are used in a concerted effort to recreate a Moorish interior. The profile of the black servant is cast in deep shadow, while all the others face the camera. One notices the blurred movement of the face of the child seated on the left. Most interesting, however, is the attitude of the central figure, who strikes her pose and looks straight at the photographer like a professional model.

170 ABDULLAH FRERES
Interior of the kiosk of Baghdad (Intérieur du kiosque de Bagdad) c. 1869
Albumen print 25.6 x 19.5 cm
Bibliothèque des Arts Décoratifs, Paris

The pavilion of the Topkapi Palace was built at the command of Murad IV to commemorate the Baghdad campaign and is considered the most remarkable in the palace for its elegance. The faiences, mother-of-pearl, stained glass and geometric ornaments are fine examples of the Ottoman decorative arts.

171 ANONYMOUS
Cairo. Two hetaerae c. 1850–52
Photograph 21 x 14 cm
Collection Gérard Lévy, Paris

The sobriety of these two courtesans is in contrast to images conjured by written reports and to pictures of the women of the Ouled-Nail tribe in Algeria. The historical record is shaped by personal reminiscences such as this one from a nostalgic French officer:

> *My memories always lead me back there; to the poetry of the oasis and to the caresses of beautiful girls…for they are beautiful, those daughters of the desert, with their heavy silver bracelets and their clothes of dazzling colour; their bare feet shod in golden sandals; and when their burning eyes light up to the sound of the* derbouka, *when their supple and graceful bodies writhe below their naked arms in the wantonness of Arab dance, there is a thrill of admiration in the room.*

172 MOHAMMED SADIC BEY

The Kaaba, Mecca 1880
Albumen print 12.6 x 17.6 cm
Collection François Lepage, Paris

Mohammed Sadic Bey was the first to
photograph Mecca and Medina, to approach
this symbol of holiness and to carry away
its image. The Kaaba is covered with black
velvet, encrusted with gold calligraphy.
A place of fascination and of mystery for
non-Muslims, its inviolability by outsiders did
not prevent certain curious admirers from
penetrating it in disguise. One, in 1885,
was the Orientalist Snouck Hurgronje,
who left a photographic record of Mecca.

173 MOHAMMED SADIC BEY

*Sheikh of the Medina Mosque and the
eunuch servants of the tomb of the Prophet
(Cheikh de la mosquée de Médine)* 1880
Original albumen print 18.5 x 15.5 cm
Collection François Lepage, Paris

In this print the search for symmetry through
a carefully studied pose is striking. Its very
precision seems to suggest a great fastid-
iousness, even a respect. An inscription in
Arabic, in Maghrebian characters, gives this
title on the obverse side. It proves that this
photo changed hands, no doubt at a later date,
despite its apparently confidential nature.

231

174 GAETAN GATIAN CLERAMBAULT
Untitled (drapery)
Photograph
Collection Musée de l'Homme, Paris

On encountering Moroccan civilisation in 1915, Clérambault did not hesitate to learn Arabic, to have a stele carved for himself, and to take about 4000 photographs of draped costume. Passionate about fabrics and their folds, Clérambault produced a series of photographs which have an ethnographic value regarding habits of dress, as well as shots of veiled women in the open air. But his obsession with folds caused him to demand of his models poses which generated unexpected patterns of cloth: arms would be raised, lowered, placed to the left or right, opened and closed, while the head was turned to the same or the opposite side. Thus he juxtaposed dozens of almost identical poses which are sometimes differentiated only by the position of a shadow – so many snapshots of an improbable choreography.

ARTISTS' BIOGRAPHIES

LAWRENCE ALMA-TADEMA

1836 Dronrijp, Friesland – 1912 Wiesbaden
DUTCH (NATURALISED ENGLISH)

Lawrence Alma-Tadema was called 'the painter of the Victorian vision of the ancient world'. A fastidious technique, influenced by Gérôme and suited to the illusionistic representation of surfaces such as marble, combined with a flair for posing elegant females in archaeologically exact settings, characterise the artist's best works. After visiting Italy in 1863, Alma-Tadema became fascinated with the ancient world of Pompeii and Egypt, and the next year won a gold medal at the Paris Salon for *Pastimes in ancient Egypt: 3,000 years ago*, 1863 (Harris Museum and Art Gallery, Preston). In 1864 he met the influential Victorian art dealer Gambart, who put him under contract to produce a certain number of pictures each year. Gambart introduced his pictures to an English audience, and the artist settled permanently in London in 1870, when he was thirty-four.

Alma-Tadema quickly became one of the richest and most successful painters working in London and transformed his two homes, first Townshend House and then Tissot's former studio at Grove End Road, into elaborate Victorian palaces, decorating rooms in various styles, including Pompeian, Moorish and Japanese. He painted at home, using his antiquarian collections as props, and his second wife, the painter Laura Eps, and his two daughters as models. In spite of his fondness for Egyptian subjects, Alma-Tadema did not visit Egypt until the end of his career. In 1902 he was invited to go there by the engineer John Aird, whose company had built the Aswan Dam. When once asked why he painted Egyptian scenes Alma-Tadema answered, 'I don't know, but it seems to me that anyone who studies history always returns to the cradle of civilization, Egypt'.   UP

LEON BAKST

(Lev Samoilovich Rosenberg)

1866 Grodno – 1924 Paris
RUSSIAN

Bakst was unquestionably the greatest stage designer of all time. After a stay in Paris, he earned a reputation as a society portraitist and decorative muralist in St Petersburg. From 1898 he contributed to *Mir Iskustva* (*World of Art*), the influential magazine of the Russian impressario, Sergei Diaghilev, whose aim was to make Russia's great cultural heritage better known. Bakst also sent illustrations to other artistic and literary journals and began to design scenery for the Imperial theatres and ballet.

In 1909 Bakst contributed costumes for Diaghilev's first ballet season in Paris and, the following year, created *Carnaval*, *L'Oiseau de feu*, *Les Orientales* and the sensational *Schéhérazade*. By now permanently settled in Paris, his designs for Diaghilev's own, newly formed company, the Ballets Russes, included *Le Spectre de la rose*, *Narcisse*, *Le Dieu bleu* and *L'Après-midi d'un faune*. At the same time, he collaborated with Ida Rubinstein, who was also of Russian–Jewish origin. She had formed her own company after leaving the Ballets Russes, and Bakst continued to work with her after his breach with Diaghilev, with whom he often had angry quarrels.

Bakst's unforgettable, magical décors and sumptuous costumes stunned the public and made him a star. With bold juxtapositions of blazing colour, and inspired by a legendary Arabia, Persia and India, antique Greece and Egypt, Siam and traditional Russia, they combine exoticism and eroticism with daring modernity. Many of Bakst's superb designs, in watercolour and gouache, have been presented in exhibitions and auctions.   LT

LEON BELLY

1827 Saint-Omer – 1877 Paris
FRENCH

Belly is known above all for his imposing picture *Pilgrims going to Mecca* (Musée d'Orsay, Paris). His first journey to the Near East was in 1850–51, when he accompanied a scientific mission led by the archaeologist L. F. J. Caignart de Saulcy. After skirting the Dead Sea, Belly visited Beirut and then Egypt. While his rendering of the classical ruins of Baalbek in Lebanon is fairly conventional, other works, such as his views of the Dead Sea, have a more personal approach, and impart a disturbing appearance to the desolateness of this region.

Belly returned to Egypt in 1855, spending over a year in Old Cairo. In the spring of 1856 he ventured into the Sinai desert with the Orientalist painter Narcisse Berchère; his resulting empty landscapes have a strange atmosphere, their effect depending only on the configuration of the arid land. It was in the company of Berchère and Jean-Léon Gérôme (q.v.) that Belly explored the Nile that year. He painted a series of small pictures, astonished to find that the strong light rendered the sky pale, not a dazzling blue as it had so often been depicted. In his studies of Egyptians hauling a dahabiyah, fellah women, camels and water buffaloes, mass and forceful presence prevail over any anecdotal detail. In only two pictures did he paint stereotyped Orientalist themes: a dancer performing in a café, and the interior of a harem. Belly returned to Egypt once more in 1857, but then abandoned ideas of further journeys.   LT

Free, Renée. *Victorian Olympians*. Exh. cat., Art Gallery of New South Wales, Sydney, 1975.

Swanson, Vern. *The Biography and Catalogue Raisonné of the Paintings of Sir Lawrence Alma-Tadema*. Garton & Co., London, 1990.

Spencer, Charles. *Léon Bakst and the Ballets Russes*. Academy Editions, London, 1995 (1973).

Bénédite, Léonce. 'Léon Belly'. *Société des Peintres Orientalistes Français*. 5th exh. cat., Galeries Durand-Ruel, Paris, 19 February 1898, preface.

Léon Belly. Exh. cat., Musée de l'Hôtel Sandelin, Saint-Omer, November–December 1977.

Wintrebert, P. 'Léon Belly, premier essai de catalogue de l'oeuvre peint'. Dissertation, Université de Lille III, 1977.

BENJAMIN-CONSTANT
(François Jean-Baptiste Constant)

1845 Paris – 1902 Paris
FRENCH

Although remembered primarily for his Orientalist paintings, Benjamin-Constant was also a successful and accomplished portrait painter of international high society, who received many decorations and honours.

A former student of the Paris Ecole des Beaux-Arts, Benjamin-Constant left for Spain – then very much in vogue – in 1872. Like Clairin (q.v.), Mariano Fortuny y Marsal and other artists of that time, he was to use Hispano-Moresque architecture as a background for many of his works. Moving on to Morocco, he accompanied Charles Tissot, the French plenipotentiary minister, on a diplomatic mission from Tangier to Marrakesh, an official protection necessary in a country then unused to foreigners. After an eighteen-month stay he returned to Paris with a treasure-trove of Islamic artefacts which served as props for his pictures.

Many of the sumptuous eastern scenes Benjamin-Constant sent to the Salon over the following years, with their rich colours and lavish detail, are now in international museums. One of his favourite themes was languid women, accompanied by their servants, dreaming the time away on rooftop terraces or in ornate interiors. Another was Muslim rulers, whether of the sherifian dynasty of Morocco or of the Nasrid sultanates of Grenada, whom he showed as awe-inspiring, sensual and often cruel. Benjamin-Constant's taste for opulence and pomp led him to be interested in other regions and epochs, and in the late 1880s he turned to biblical and historical subjects before becoming a high-society portraitist. Rich and famous, he received many official commissions to decorate public buildings.   LT

EMILE BERNARD

1868 LILLE – 1941 PARIS
FRENCH

The products of Bernard's ten-year sojourn in Egypt, along with his later traditionalist works, have been all but forgotten in the wake of his precocious contribution to the symbolist avant-garde of the late 1880s and early 1890s.

Bernard travelled to Cairo in 1893 on a stipend from Antoine de la Rochefoucauld, a fellow participant in the first Rose + Croix Salon of 1892. His marriage to a Syrian woman, Hanenah Saati, in June 1894 is recorded in their striking wedding portrait (Musée des Beaux-Arts de Quimper) which mixes Byzantine hieraticism with a memory of Cézanne.

Bernard's painting in Egypt divides into two stages, separated by the death of his sister, Madeleine, after she contracted fever while visiting him in Cairo in 1895. Before 1896 he depicted a narrow range of subjects with simplified drawing and intense colour deriving from his symbolist experimentation in France. After 1896 and a six-month visit to Spain, where he met the fashionable painter Ignacio Zuloaga, he renounced his previous radicalism and moved to sombre figure studies, frequently painted from life, claiming inspiration from Renaissance Venice.

After returning to Europe definitively in 1904, Bernard wrote two influential essays on Cézanne as well as copious polemics attacking the 20th-century avant-garde. Although he exhibited with the Société des Peintres Orientalistes Français between 1902 and 1933, his idiosyncratic Orientalism, like the rest of his *oeuvre*, remained on the margins of accepted taste in a style seemingly out of its time.   PR

ALBERT BESNARD

1849 Paris – 1934 Paris
FRENCH

Winner of the Grand Prix de Rome in 1874, Besnard received many medals, honours and important posts. An illustrator and engraver, as well as painter of society portraits, genre scenes, nudes and large decorations for public buildings, he was a co-founder of the Société Nationale des Beaux-Arts in 1890, a group that broke away from the all-powerful Artistes Français, which it considered out of date.

Besnard was already appreciated for his broad brushwork, lyrical style and glimmering colours when he journeyed to Algeria via Morocco in 1893–94. As well as the Algiers harbour basin, he painted dancers and musicians of the Ouled-Nail tribe and a horse-market where men in white burnouses carry out their transactions. Among his portraits, that of a tattooed woman adjusting an earring is particularly interesting because, unusual for the time, he brings out the sitter's personality.

Besnard's most brilliant exhibition was a show of his Indian works at the Galerie Georges Petit, Paris, in 1912. During his trip, in 1910–11, he had covered enormous distances between the cities of that continent. The bayadères or temple dancers, the Brahmin priests, pilgrims praying and bathing in the river Ganges, a masked transvestite at a religious festival, the splendid court processions – these all were fascinating sights which had been recorded by writers and a long line of British painters. But Besnard's kaleidoscope of dazzling spectacles in explosive colours had such energy and vitality that the critics and public were overwhelmed. In 1913 excerpts from his Indian diaries were published in book form as *L'Homme en rose*.   LT

Cardis, Régine. 'Benjamin-Constant (1845–1902): peintre toulousain'. Dissertation, Université de Toulouse-Le-Mirail, 1985 (in which the often repeated error concerning the artist's first names is corrected).

Cardis-Toulouse, Régine. 'Benjamin-Constant et la peinture orientaliste'. *Histoire de l'Art*, no. 4, December 1988, pp. 79–89.

Luthi, Jean-Jacques. *Emile Bernard: catalogue raisonné de l'oeuvre peinte*. Side, Paris, 1982.

Rivière, Anne (ed.). *Emile Bernard: propos sur l'art*. 2 vols, Séguier, Paris, 1994.

Mille, Pierre. 'Le peintre Besnard dans l'Inde'. *L'Illustration* (Paris), Christmas number, 1911.

Mourey, Gabriel. *Albert Besnard*. H. Davoust, Paris, 1906.

Mourey, Gabriel. 'Albert Besnard aux Indes'. *Les Arts* (Paris), no. 127, July 1912.

LEON BONNAT

1833 Bayonne – 1922 Mouchy-Saint-Eloy
FRENCH

Bonnat was one of the outstanding personalities of the art world during the Third Republic, and one whose fortune allowed him to make a remarkable collection of drawings, now housed in the Musée Bonnat in Bayonne.

In 1847 Bonnat's family moved to Madrid, where the young man developed a life-long admiration for Spanish painting, particularly that of Velasquez. After completing his art training in Paris and Rome, Bonnat began his career as a painter of Italian peasant subjects and religious and historical scenes, popularised by lithographic and photographic reproductions.

In 1868 Bonnat travelled to Egypt, Sinai, Palestine, Lebanon and Constantinople, one of a party led by Jean-Léon Gérôme (q.v.), which included the photographer Albert Goupil. Gérôme and two other fellow artists, Paul Lenoir and Willem de Famars Testas, later published their accounts of this merry expedition. Interested in everything they saw, they all worked hard, either in groups or alone.

Many of Bonnat's loose but vigorous oil studies of landscapes and figures are now in French museums. Although he returned to Egypt in 1869 to assist at ceremonies for the opening of the Suez Canal, his Orientalist work formed only a small part of his repertoire. Bonnat's finished paintings – such as *Sheikh of Aqaba, Arabia Petraea* (Pushkin Museum, Moscow); *A fellah woman and her child* (Metropolitan Museum, New York); and *An Arab sheikh* (Walters Art Gallery, Baltimore) in this exhibition – with their dramatic lighting, subdued tones and the forceful realism of their figures, seen in close-up, divided the critics. LT

FREDERICK ARTHUR BRIDGMAN

1846 Tuskegee, Alabama – 1928 Rouen
AMERICAN

Among the first wave of Americans who came to study art in France after the Civil War, Bridgman studied under Jean-Léon Gérôme (q.v.). Summers were spent painting in Brittany, but journeys to Tangier and Algiers in 1872–73, and to Egypt in 1873–74, converted him to Orientalism.

In Cairo and on the Nile, Bridgman made hundreds of pencil sketches which he used to paint scenes of everyday life, but it was above all his reconstructions of ancient Egypt and Assyria which ensured his reputation. He returned to Algeria often, and articles about his stays, published in Harper's *New Monthly Magazine* in 1888, later came out in book form. Being rich, he did not need to sell, but exhibited in Paris, London, New York, Brooklyn and Chicago. After leading a brilliant – and extravagant – social life, he settled in Normandy.

Bridgman, who travelled to many different areas of Algeria, was always inquisitive about aspects of life usually unseen by Europeans. On one occasion he went to Blida for a Muslim religious festival and was vividly impressed by the spirituality and conviviality of the gathering. In the south he explored the villages and countryside on horseback and, during one winter stay, took up residence in a house situated in the Algiers kasbah, thus being able to observe the activities of the owner's family and neighbours. After having at first worked in a tight academic style, he loosened his brushwork and lightened his palette, but towards the end of his life these rich, attractive colours became sugary and unreal. LT

HENRIETTE BROWNE

(Mme Jules de Saux, b. Sophie de Boutailler)

1829 Paris – 1901 (unknown)
FRENCH

Sophie de Boutailler exhibited regularly at the Paris Salon from 1853 to 1878 under the professional name of Henriette Browne, a name adopted from her maternal grandmother. She began her career painting religious subjects, portraits and domestic narratives, exhibiting her first Orientalist paintings in 1861. Her marriage to Jules de Saux in 1853 (secretary to Comte Walewski, a diplomat for Louis-Napoleon) ensured that she moved in diplomatic circles and most likely facilitated her frequent travel. Browne travelled to Constantinople in 1860, to Morocco in 1865, and Egypt and Syria in 1868–69. She is one of a number of women Orientalists – including Sophie Anderson, Margaret Murray Cookesley and Elisabeth Jerichau-Baumann – whose role in the Orientalist tradition has been overlooked until recent years. Browne's first Orientalist works, harem paintings, generated considerable interest when exhibited at the Salon of 1861. The fact that Browne had crossed the threshold of a harem in Constantinople (something her male colleagues could not have done) fascinated the art critics and lent an authenticity to her harem paintings. Yet her work was considered threatening because it displaced cherished masculine fantasies of the harem by representing it as a social rather than sexualised space. After 1861 Browne regularly exhibited her Orientalist subjects, including pictures of children, eastern scholars, school scenes and representations of individual ethnographic types. While her harem paintings established her reputation in France, it was her convent pictures, in particular her *Sisters of Charity*, that secured her reputation in Britain.
MR

Ackerman, Gerald M. *Les Orientalistes de l'école américaine.* Les Orientalistes, vol. 10, ACR, Paris, 1994.

Bridgman, Frederick Arthur. *Winters in Algeria.* Chapman & Hall, London, 1890.

Fort, Ilene Susan. 'Frederick Arthur Bridgman and the American fascination with the exotic Near East'. PhD thesis, City University of New York, 1990.

Album de voyage: des artistes en expédition au pays du Levant. Exh. cat. (Musée Hébert), Association Française d'Action Artistique, Paris, 1993.

Lewis, Reina. *Gendering Orientalism: Race, Femininity and Representation.* Routledge, London & New York, 1996.

Yeldham, Charlotte. 'Henriette Browne', in *Women Artists in Nineteenth-century France and England.* Garland Publishing, New York & London, 1984, vol. 1, pp. 345–50.

RUPERT BUNNY

1864 Melbourne – 1947 Melbourne
AUSTRALIAN

A witty, cultivated and sensitive cosmopolitan, Rupert Bunny was married to French art student and model, Jeanne Morel, and felt very much at home in Paris. After training in Melbourne under George Frederick Folingsby, Bunny went to Europe and studied in London under P. H. Calderon and in Paris under Jean-Paul Laurens, who introduced him to the Société des Artistes Français in 1887. Always a decorative painter, Bunny was attracted to mythological subjects and painted a long series of pictures of quietly posed, graceful women in the period and spirit of the *belle époque.*

After visiting Australia in 1911 (for the first time in twenty-five years) Bunny changed his style. He exhibited his new works at the Salon d'Automne in 1913 – dynamic images of dancers influenced by Matisse, Orientalism, Primitivism and the Ballets Russes. These were not the result of travelling in North Africa, but belonged to the 1910s and 1920s fashion in France for an Orientalism characterised by vivid colours, swirling arabesques, and *Arabian Nights* costumes and décor. Orientalist figure subjects began to appear in Bunny's work around 1912 and his interest in such themes climaxed during the 1920s when he painted his self-portrait in Arab dress (c. 1928, private collection, Sydney). He exhibited in Paris with the dealer Georges Petit who had also shown Albert Besnard's Indian pictures in 1912. Their success may have stimulated Bunny to experiment with exotic, brightly coloured pictures. He continued to live in Paris and London until 1933, by which time he was chronically short of money, and returned to Melbourne following his wife's death. Exhibiting in Sydney and Melbourne, he gained his late reputation for a series of south of France landscapes, which he continued to paint from 1920s sketches long after his return to Australia. UP

ETHEL CARRICK

1872 Uxbridge, nr London – 1952 Melbourne
AUSTRALIAN (ENGLISH-BORN)

Ethel Carrick was born and trained in England. Between 1898 and 1902 she studied at the Slade School of Fine Art in London under Henry Tonks and Frederick Brown, then joined the artists' colony at St Ives in Cornwall. She met Emanuel Phillips Fox at St Ives and they married in 1905, settling in Paris. The only English woman to sit on the jury of the Salon d'Automne, Ethel Carrick exhibited in Paris at the Salon d'Automne from 1904 to 1930 and at the Salon de la Société Nationale des Beaux-Arts (New Salon) from 1906 to 1937. Her paintings of genre, flower and landscape subjects were influenced by Impressionism and Post-Impressionism.

In 1911 Carrick painted in North Africa for the first time, visiting Algeria and Morocco as well as southern Spain. With her husband she journeyed to Australia in 1908 and again in 1913, this time for an extended stay. Her North African pictures were favourably received by both French and Australian audiences. After her husband's death in 1915 she returned to Paris to work and teach. Throughout the rest of her long and active life she continued to travel and also painted again in the East, having become a Theosophist. She exhibited Tunisian subjects at the Salon d'Automne in 1921, and painted in India during the 1930s. Moving between her home in France and Sydney, where she stayed in Mosman at a Theosophical centre called The Manor, Carrick also spent time in Melbourne where Emanuel's family lived. From the 1930s she campaigned for Australian art institutions to acquire works by her late husband and by modern French artists. In later years Carrick returned to paint in the North African desert and, in 1950, two years before her death, shipboard letters (now in the Art Gallery of New South Wales archive and manuscript collection) record her once again looking forward to a stay in Morocco. UP

THEODORE CHASSERIAU

1819 El Limon, Santo Domingo – 1856 Paris
FRENCH

Painted with great intensity and sensibility, Chassériau's Orientalist paintings are among the most personal visions of the eastern world. The favourite pupil of the neo-classical master Ingres, he exhibited portraits and biblical scenes at the Salon from 1836. His early interest in Oriental subjects was certainly reinforced by his friendship with the artists Prosper Marilhat and Adrien Dauzats, who had both travelled to the East in the 1830s. In 1845 he was commissioned to paint a large equestrian portrait of the Caliph of Constantine, Ali ben Ahmed (Musée National du Château de Versailles). Having become quite friendly with the Arab ruler during his stay in Paris, Chassériau was invited to visit Constantine in north-east Algeria. This astonishing town, a natural fortress perched on top of a rocky plateau, had only recently come under French domination.

During his brief stay, from May to July 1846, Chassériau made many pencil and watercolour sketches of scenes which he found curious, primitive or moving. His first major work resulting from this trip, of the Sabbath in the Jewish quarter of Constantine, was destroyed in a fire. Obliged to finish a monumental mural decoration commissioned several years earlier, it was not until 1849 that he was able to return to Algerian subjects, by which time his fading memories had become distilled into idealised images. As well as pictures of dignified Arab horsemen, lion hunts and solemn, melancholy scenes of domestic life, Chassériau painted fantasy scenes of beautiful nude odalisques, for which he posed Parisian models. LT

Eagle, Mary. *The Art of Rupert Bunny.* Australian National Gallery, Canberra, 1991.

Thomas, D. *Rupert Bunny 1864–1947.* Lansdowne, Melbourne, 1970.

Turnbull, C. & Buesst, T. *The Art of Rupert Bunny.* Ure Smith, Sydney, 1948.

Pigot, John. *Capturing the Orient: Hilda Rix Nicholas and Ethel Carrick in the East.* Exh. cat.,Waverley City Gallery, Melbourne, 1993.

Rich, M. & Zubans, R. *Ethel Carrick Fox (Mrs Phillips Fox): A Retrospective Exhibition.* Geelong Art Gallery, Geelong, Vic., 1979.

Souter, D. H.. 'Parisian paintings in Melbourne: Ethel Carrick'. *Art and Architecture* (Sydney), vol. 5, 1908.

Bénédite, Léonce. *Théodore Chassériau: sa vie et son oeuvre.* Braun, Paris, 1931.

Sandoz, Marc. *Théodore Chassériau: catalogue raisonné des peintures et des estampes.* Arts et Métiers Graphiques, Paris, 1974.

GEORGES CLAIRIN

1843 Paris – 1919 Belle-Ile-en-Mer
FRENCH

Clairin, elegant and witty, was a well-known figure in Parisian literary and artistic circles. His painting was extremely varied: mural decorations, masked fêtes, portraits of opera singers and ballet dancers, Brittany landscapes and scenes inspired by his travels.

Clairin's first contact with the East was in the winter of 1869–70, when he stayed in Tangier with Henri Regnault (q.v.). This Moroccan idyll was cut short by the outbreak of the Franco-Prussian War. After Regnault's death, Clairin left again for Spain and Morocco, accompanying the diplomat Charles Tissot on a mission to the holy city of Fez, at the time rarely visited by Europeans. Obliged to copy antique inscriptions for Tissot, a fervent archaeologist, and hindered by the hostility of the population in Fez, he did little sketching, but the extraordinary sights he had seen remained engraved on his memory. Further journeys took him to Italy, Spain, Algeria and, in 1895–96, to Egypt. In Karnak he spent two happy months following the excavations of the Pharaonic ruins.

Clairin used his sketches and the photographs brought back from his trips as notes for years to come. Passionately interested in the theatre (he was a devoted admirer of the actress Sarah Bernhardt) his work became more fantastic and dramatic. Among his favourite themes were Napoleon Bonaparte in Egypt, jewel-laden women of the Ouled-Nail tribe, religious sects such as the Aissaouas, and historical battle scenes. He published his memoirs, written by André Beaunier, in 1906, under the title *Souvenirs d'un peintre*. LT

CHARLES CONDER

1868 London – 1909 Virginia Water, Surrey
ENGLISH-BORN
(ACTIVE IN AUSTRALIA AND FRANCE)

Conder's personal style was delicate, witty and nostalgic. Attracted to Whistlerian and Japanese influences, he combined them with evocations of warm summer light. As a child he spent time in India where his father was an engineer. His mother died in 1873 and he was sent back to school in England. In 1884 Charles Conder arrived in Australia to learn surveying with his uncle W. J. Conder. Taking art classes in Sydney at the Royal Art Society turned him from a career in surveying to painting. By December 1888 he had joined Roberts and Streeton in Melbourne where they spent memorable summers painting together at artists' camps near Heidelberg in Victoria.

Leaving Melbourne in April 1890, Conder returned to Europe, setting up a studio in Paris on the rue Ravignan where he quickly became a familiar figure in the bohemian art world. In Paris he admired the works of Puvis de Chavannes, Monet and Albert Besnard, and befriended Anquetin and Toulouse-Lautrec. In December 1891 he travelled to Mustapha near Algiers to recuperate in a friend's garden villa overlooking the sea. His Algerian pictures inaugurated a new sensitivity to symbolist colour and mood in his art, anticipating the 'faint mixed tints' and decorative fantasies for which he later became known. During the three months he spent in Algeria his health was poor and he only managed to complete a few pictures. He was inspired to paint the gardens and views of Mustapha looking over terraces onto the Bay of Algiers. On returning to Paris in the following spring he showed Algerian pictures at the Père Thomas gallery in March–April 1892 to positive reviews. Later, Conder would suggest harem themes in some of the imagery and titles of his decorative paintings on silk panels, but he never again painted in North Africa. UP

RICHARD DADD

1817 Chatham – 1886 Broadmoor, Berks
ENGLISH

Richard Dadd's life and career were remarkable. At the age of twenty-six he was arrested for the murder of his father. Judged to be criminally insane, he was sent to Bethlehem Hospital and ordered to be confined for life. In October 1843 the *Art Union* published a premature obituary: 'The Late Richard Dadd. Alas! we must so preface the name of a youth of genius that promised to do honour to the world; for, although the grave has not actually closed over him, he must be classed among the dead'. Thus Richard Dadd slipped from public view, but somehow over the next forty-three years continued to work, producing a number of Orientalist scenes based on his travel sketchbooks and fantasies.

The extended 'grand tour' of 1842–43, from which Dadd returned insane, was responsible both for the Egyptian content of his delusions (that it was the god Osiris who commanded him to kill his father with a knife), and for his life-long obsession with Near Eastern subjects. Recommended by the artist David Roberts, Dadd left England as travelling artist and companion to a wealthy barrister, Sir Thomas Phillips, in 1842. Crossing Europe, they travelled at an uncomfortable pace through Turkey, Syria, Palestine and Egypt, with Dadd forced to sketch picturesque sights from the back of a mule. However, Dadd's career did not begin as a travel painter. His first real success came in 1841, when he exhibited Shakespearian subjects. Later, he became notorious as the 'mad' painter, famous for his microscopically detailed masterpiece, *The Fairy Feller's Master-Stroke* (1855–64, Tate, London). His Orientalist works may be compared with those of John Frederick Lewis, whom he visited while in Cairo. What set Dadd's pictures apart was the peculiar intensity with which he worked, apparent in details like staring eyes, oddities of scale and tensely held gestures. UP

Arnold, Christel. 'Georges Clairin (1843–1919): un peintre voyageur'. Dissertation, Université de Paris IV Sorbonne, 1989–90.

Gibson, F. *Charles Conder: His Life and Work.* John Lane, the Bodley Head, London, 1914.

Hoff, Ursula. *Charles Conder.* Lansdowne, Melbourne, 1972.

Rothenstein, John. *The Life and Death of Conder.* Dent, London, 1938.

Allderidge, Patricia. *The Late Richard Dadd.* Exh. cat., Tate, London, 1974.

EDOUARD DEBAT-PONSAN

1847 Toulouse – 1913 Paris
FRENCH

Débat-Ponsan, laureate of the second Grand Prix de Rome in 1873, exhibited historical, religious and rural scenes, as well as portraits. This seemingly typical career was marked by two incidents. In 1887 he painted the portrait of the minister of war, General Boulanger, whose influential political movement threatened to topple the Third Republic. Two years later this portrait was withdrawn from the Universal Exhibition since the government feared disturbances. In 1898 a greater rumpus was caused by his picture *Truth will out*, an allegory of the famous Dreyfus case. It was purchased on subcription and offered to Emile Zola, who had publicly defended the cause of the Jewish artillery captain unjustly accused of spying by the army. Débat-Ponsan's unequivocal stand led to a break with his family, friends and clients who were, like many members of the bourgoisie, both anti-Dreyfus and anti-Semitic. He therefore turned to painting rural scenes, which he sold to North American collectors, and historical subjects, particularly appreciated in England.

Débat-Ponsan's only eastern visit was made in 1882, when he journeyed to Constantinople to make studies for a large panorama of the city. This commissioned work was shown in Paris the following year before being sent to Copenhagen. On his return home he painted a portrait of a seated woman surrounded by Islamic faience panels and textiles. But it was above all his 1883 exhibit, *Massage in the hammam* (Musée des Augustins, Toulouse), included in this exhibition, which marked his brief flirtation with Orientalism.   LT

ALFRED DEHODENCQ

1822 Paris – 1882 Paris
FRENCH

From an early age, Dehodencq had a moody, passionate personality, and was obsessed with the romantic writings of Chateaubriand. Wounded in the revolutionary uprisings of 1848, events which made him aware of the power of angry crowds, he went to Madrid. During his long stay in Spain he sent pictures back to France in which he depicted the Spaniards as being heroic, sanguinary and fanatically devout.

Dehodencq discovered Morocco in 1853 and over the next decade returned every year, making endless dynamic sketches – frenzied whorls that capture the movement of teeming street life. Largely dependent on the Jewish population for his models, he painted Sephardi concerts, weddings and festivities, but also violent, shocking scenes of the arrest and punishment of Jews, set in Morocco or in old Moorish Spain. Other works show caids and pashas, merchants, musicians, dancers and storytellers. Using strident and brutal colours, with a heavy use of black, he played on the contrast between Arabs, Jews and blacks from the Sudan. But what the critic Théophile Gautier saw as an astonishing ethnographic aptitude and a profound sensitivity to different races, today seems to border on caricature.

After Dehodencq's return to France in 1863 he found that his long absence had pushed him to the fringe of the current art movement; even his moving picture of Boabdil, the last Moorish king of Granada (Musée d'Orsay, Paris), was treated with indifference. He turned to more popular themes – sentimental paintings of children and narrative genre scenes – but, in poverty and despair, committed suicide.   LT

EUGENE DELACROIX

1798 Charenton-Saint-Maurice – 1863 Paris
FRENCH

Delacroix's famous six-month journey to Morocco and Algiers showed artists that North Africa held as much interest as the traditional Grand Tour of Europe. He was already interested in the eastern world in the 1820s, largely because of the Greeks' fight for independence against the Turks. The consternation caused by his harrowing painting of the Chios massacres drew him into the Romantic movement, until then led by writers such as Chateaubriand and Lord Byron.

In 1832 Delacroix was invited to travel in the suite of the Comte de Mornay, official envoy to the Sultan of Morocco, Moulay Abder Rahman, a journey which took them from Tangier to Meknès. Delacroix was struck by the dignified dress and bearing of the people from all walks of life, who were, he felt, living figures from classical times. He was impressed, too, by the dazzling colours and bright light, which reinforced his already masterly use of vibrant harmonies. The mission's brief stay in Algiers resulted in *Women of Algiers in their quarters* (Musée du Louvre, Paris), one of the best-known Orientalist paintings.

Until the end of his life, Orientalist scenes were part of Delacroix's vast repertoire. Using the wonderfully fluid and fresh pencil and watercolour sketches he had made on the spot in Morocco, he painted oils of the scenes he had witnessed. During the 1850s his odalisques and *pêle-mêles* of lions, horses and men, treated with a Rubenesque exuberance, evoked an imaginary eastern world such as that he had painted before his travels.   LT

Edouard Débat-Ponsan: portraits, scènes de genre 1900, paysages d'Orient, de Touraine et de Bretagne. Exh. cat., Musée des Beaux-Arts, Tours; Musée Municipal, Brest; Musée des Augustins, Toulouse, n.d. (1975).

Prat, Véronique. 'Alfred Dehodencq'. Dissertation, Ecole du Louvre, Paris, 1977.

Séailles, Gabriel. *Alfred Dehodencq: histoire d'un coloriste.* Ollendorf, Paris, 1885.

Séailles, Gabriel. *Alfred Dehodencq: l'homme et l'artiste.* Société de Propagation des Livres d'Art, Paris, 1910.

Constans, Claire (ed.). *La Grèce en révolte: Delacroix et les peintres français (1815–1848).* Exh. cat. (Musée des Beaux-Arts, Bordeaux; Musée national Eugène Delacroix, Paris; Alexandre Soutzos Museum, Athens; June 1996–April 1997), Réunion des Musées Nationaux, Paris, 1996.

Delacroix in Morocco. Exh. cat. (Institut du Monde Arabe, September 1994–January 1995), Flammarion, Paris, 1994.

Johnson, Lee. *The Paintings of Eugène Delacroix: A Critical Catalogue.* 6 vols, Clarendon Press, Oxford, 1981–89.

LUDWIG DEUTSCH

1855 Vienna – 1935 Paris
AUSTRIAN, NATURALISED FRENCH

Although Deutsch is today highly appreciated by collectors, he was almost totally ignored by critics of his time. A former student of the Vienna Academy of Fine Arts, he settled in Paris, where he met up with his compatriot and life-long friend, Rudolph Ernst (q.v.). He began to exhibit portraits and genre scenes at the Salon from 1879, but after 1883 his pictures were almost exclusively of everyday life in Cairo.

It seems clear that Deutsch travelled to the Near East, as a series of oil studies of Egyptian men and women have all the spontaneity of on-the-spot sketches. The architecture, the clothes, arms and armour in his oils are treated with breathtaking microscopic detail. Like many other artists of the time, he used as studio props the Islamic tiles, textiles and metalwork which decorated the houses in which he stayed, and very probably relied on photographs as well. Besides this exceptional technical ability, Deutsch had a keen eye for small gestures and individual expressions that give his people life and character. The themes he chose are quiet and peaceful: domino- and chess-players, Muslims at prayer, public scribes, armed guards, street entertainers and merchants and, in a very large and exceptional painting shown at the 1890 Salon, students in the sunlit courtyard of the University El-Azhar in Cairo.

Around 1909–11, Deutsch experimented with Post-Impressionism. In these pictures women sell watermelons, draw water from the Nile or keep watch over their goats. In one large canvas, an exuberant procession of pilgrims accompanies the Mahmal, or sacred carpet, on its way to Mecca.   LT

ETIENNE DINET

1816 Paris – 1929 Paris
FRENCH

Dinet opened the way to a better understanding of the traditions and customs in the Algerian desert towns. He had already begun to exhibit portraits and religious subjects when he made his first trip to Algeria in 1884. He was to spend every summer there and, in 1904, made the oasis town of Bou Saâda his second home. His first Orientalist paintings were above all investigations into vibrant luminosity; later, the depiction of human emotions was of prime importance. Many of Dinet's paintings are scenes of the everyday life of the Ouled-Nail tribe: women washing clothes or bathing naked in the wadi, children and adolescents playing, young couples flirting, men at prayer. Others interpreted more disturbing themes, which were never treated by other Orientalists: mourning, illness, imprisonment, repudiation and conscription.

It was through his friendship with the writer Sliman ben Ibrahim that Dinet learned about the ancient Arab legends of heroism and love. Their collaboration took the form of illustrated books, of which the first, *Antar,* was published in 1898. Dinet often made variations of his paintings and many of the book plates are adaptations of compositions in oils. Despite his renown, collectors in metropolitan France eventually found his realistic style old-fashioned, although his pictures continued to be highly regarded in Algeria.

Converted in 1913 (he undertook the hadj or pilgrimage to Mecca in 1929), he sought to show a philosophical and moral approach to Algerian civilisation and to the mysticism of Islam. It is for this reason that his work, which reaches beyond pictorial considerations, is so appreciated today.   LT

CHARLES DUFRESNE

1876 Milemont – 1938 La Seyné
FRENCH

A child of poor parents, Dufresne left school at eleven, but soon learned the techniques of engraving, sculpture and drawing. In 1908 he met the Egyptian-born translator of the *Arabian Nights*, Dr Mardrus, a friend of writers and Islamists such as Etienne Dinet (q.v.) and Léonce Bénédite, president of the Société des Peintres Orientalistes Français. In 1910 Dufresne won a travel grant to the Villa Abd-el-Tif in Algiers. During his two-year stay he visited Dinet in his oasis home and met Frédéric Lung and Louis Meley, important collectors who both bought his work.

On his return to Paris, Dufresne mixed with avant-garde literary and artistic circles and pursued a growing interest in Cubism and Fauvism. After the First World War, in which he was badly gassed, he painted battle scenes, then nudes, portraits, and religious and mythological subjects. In time, his dense, squared-off forms took on greater movement and evolved into a lyrical, baroque style. Ferociously independent, solitary, refusing honours and tributes, Dufresne exhibited rarely, but accepted a professorship at the Académie Scandinave, which was founded on anti-academicism.

Only a few of Dufresne's Algerian scenes – the Algiers port, a caravan, Ouled-Nail dancers – are realistic. Most of his poetic compositions of the 1920s and 1930s are dream-like journeys to the unknown or into the past. In these parade Amerindians, Blacks, spahis, naked women, sailors, Christopher Columbus or musicians, surrounded by wild animals, boats, dolphins, birds, serpents. Often big cats savagely attack their prey. Africa, the New World or the Garden of Eden – they are above all an imaginary, exotic world of Dufresne's own making.   LT

Juler, Caroline. *Najd Collection of Orientalist Paintings*. Manara, London, 1991.

Benchikou, Koudir & Brahimi, Denise. *La Vie et l'oeuvre d'Etienne Dinet. Catalogue raisonné*. ACR, Paris, 1991 (1984).

Pouillon, François. *Etienne Dinet*. Balland, Paris, 1997.

Casenave, Elisabeth. 'La Villa Abd el Tif et le mouvement artistique en Algérie, 1900–1962'. PhD thesis, Université de Paris IV Sorbonne, 1966.

Charles Dufresne. Exh. cats, Musée d'Art Moderne, Troyes, October 1987–January 1988; Musée Richard Anacréon, Granville, March–May 1988.

Fosca, François. *Charles Dufresne*. La Bibliothèque des Arts, Paris, 1958.

RUDOLPH ERNST

1854 Vienna – 1932 Fontenay-aux-Roses
AUSTRIAN, NATURALISED FRENCH

After having studied in his home town of Vienna and then Rome, Ernst settled in Paris in 1876. Until 1884 his paintings were essentially portraits, nudes and genre scenes of children and musketeers. During the 1880s he travelled to Spain, Morocco, Tunisia, Egypt and, probably in 1890, to Turkey. He took photographs, although in Constantinople, despite the fact that the city had many professional photographic studios, he was asked to move on by officials. He managed, however, to make quick sketches.

Besides Nubian palace guards, mosque interiors and street scenes, Ernst's favourite themes were the pastimes of Oriental women in their quarters. He was also fond of portraying tigers. Around 1900 he painted several pictures of Hindu temples, although he never travelled to India. His pictures always sold well, particularly to North Americans. His biggest success was a scene of people carrying and sorting piles of freshly picked pink roses. After it was shown at the 1908 Salon, where Ernst was a regular exhibitor, he was commissioned to paint numerous versions.

In all Ernst's highly coloured pictures, which often have touches of humorous realism, infinite attention is paid to details of architecture, costumes and works of art. Particularly interested in ceramics, Ernst painted faience tiles in the Islamic manner and was also a highly accomplished watercolourist.

Around 1900 Ernst left Paris for the nearby Fontenay-aux-Roses. A keen amateur violinist, he lived a quiet life looking after his flowers and bees, seeing few people except his childhood friend Ludwig Deutsch (q.v.). LT

HENRI EVENEPOEL

1872 Nice – 1899 Paris
BELGIAN

The work of Evenepoel, who died at the age of twenty-seven, has been written about many times, but usually in the context of *fin de siècle* art rather than in the context of Orientalism.

On his arrival in Paris in 1892 Evenepoel was immediately fascinated by the life of the capital, the Seine, the cafés, cabarets, errand girls, jugglers and street markets. From 1893 he studied painting under the symbolist artist Gustave Moreau (q.v.) and became friendly with Henri Matisse (q.v.), a co-disciple. A series of striking portraits followed, many in a subdued palette, others with daring and dazzling colour combinations.

In poor health, Evenepoel decided to go to Algeria. He arrived in Algiers in October 1897, then spent three months in Blida before moving to Tipasa. Some of his Algerian paintings are anecdotal and conventional. Others – *Announcement of the Negro fête in Blida* (Musées royaux des Beaux-Arts de Belgique, Brussels), *Negro fête in Blida*, *Negro dancing, Algiers* and *Women with narghile* – are extremely stylised and original. In these, the awkward angular position of legs and arms provides a sense of rhythm. The centring is asymmetric, the body cut by the edge of the image, a trick Evenepoel often used in his pictures and photographs.

Just when Evenepoel thought that his financial worries were nearly over and that at last he would be able to marry his mistress, Louise, and thus legitimise his son, he died of typhoid fever. LT

EMANUEL PHILLIPS FOX

1865 Melbourne – 1915 Melbourne
AUSTRALIAN

Having begun his training at the National Gallery of Victoria Art Schools, Melbourne, E. P. Fox went to Paris in 1887 where he studied at the Académie Julian and Ecole des Beaux-Arts. He took lessons with the famous Orientalist Jean-Léon Gérôme, but Fox was also attracted to Impressionism, Monet's work and *plein air* painting. He joined outdoor painting colonies in Brittany and Cornwall, and established contacts with the expatriate American art community in Paris through his American teacher, T. Alexander Harrison. By the turn of the century his academic training, coupled with a modified impressionist technique, had earned him some success in London, Paris and back home in Australia.

In 1905 Fox married fellow artist Ethel Carrick and they settled in Paris. Both were keen outdoor painters, interested in depicting the effects of sunlight. In search of sunlight, Fox followed the example of contemporary French and American artists, escaping the European winter by travelling to paint in North Africa. In February 1911 Fox, accompanied by his wife and one of his students, embarked on a six-week painting tour of Algeria, Morocco and southern Spain. He exhibited sixteen of the works he painted during this trip at the Société des Peintres Orientalistes in Paris in 1913 shortly before returning to Australia. Fox brought his North African pictures with him to Australia for exhibition and sale. In his last two years there he exhibited widely, painted portraits and landscapes, made a trip to Tahiti, and was active in the war effort to raise funds for the Red Cross, before his health failed. UP

Derrey-Capon, Danielle et al. *Henri Evenepoel*. Exh. cat. (Musées royaux des Beaux-Arts de Belgique, Brussels, March–June 1994), Crédit Communal, Brussels, 1994 (with a *catalogue raisonné* of the paintings).

Evenepoel, Henri. *Lettres à mon pére*. 2 vols, ed. Danielle Derry-Capon, Musées royaux des Beaux-Arts de Belgique, Brussels, 1994.

Juler, Caroline. *Najd Collection of Orientalist Paintings*. Manara, London, 1991.

Fox, L. P. *E. Phillips Fox: Notes and Recollections*. Sydney, 1969.

Zubans, Ruth. *E. Phillips Fox: His Life and Art*. Miegunyah Press, Melbourne, 1995.

EUGENE FROMENTIN

1820 La Rochelle – 1876 Saint-Maurice
French

A brilliant student, despite being stifled by an oppressive family atmosphere, Fromentin was sent to Paris by his doctor father to study law. He soon rebelled and opted for an artistic career instead. In 1846 he made a short visit to Algiers, without his parents' knowledge, then returned for eight months in 1847–48, this time travelling to the oasis town of Biskra and to Constantine in the north-east. In 1852–53 he spent nearly a year in Algeria, leaving his newly wedded wife in Algiers while he went south to Laghouat. Over the years, his Orientalist pictures received great critical acclaim at the Salon, while his illustrated travel notes, together with his romantic novel *Dominique*, and a work of art criticism, established his reputation as a literary figure as well as a painter.

Fromentin above all portrayed tribal life, horsemen and their splendid pure-blood mounts, nomads on the move or setting up camp, seen against sweeping plains and wide skies. He discovered that the intense light made everything seem grey, and that the shade was transparent, limpid and coloured, not obscure and black, as it was generally painted. In time, his pictures ennobled, idealised and beautified the reality. Feeling himself condemned to paint perpetual variations on the same – only too successful – themes, he made a short-lived attempt at mythological paintings. Invited to the opening of the Suez Canal in 1869, he painted excellent Egyptian scenes, but critical disapproval sent him back to the subjects which had made him renowned.   LT

JEAN-LEON GEROME

1824 Vesoul – 1904 Paris
French

Among the most famous painters of the world before his popularity declined, Gérôme is today considered one of the most influential and imaginative academic painters of the 19th century.

Gérôme first painted scenes of antique Greece and Rome – witty, erotic and trivial – but soon adopted a more serious, realistic approach. From 1856, when he first travelled to the East, he sent Orientalist pictures to the Salon as well as historical paintings, society portraits and genre scenes. He benefited enormously from the commercial sense of his father-in-law, Adolphe Goupil, an influential dealer who not only organised a world-wide distribution of photo-engravings of Gérôme's painting and sculpture, but obtained the patronage of European and American collectors. This largely explains the dearth of works by Gérôme in French museums, except for early State commissions and the collection in his home town of Vesoul.

Gérôme loved travelling and visited Turkey, Egypt, Palestine, Greece, Spain and Algiers in the 1860s and 1870s. A particularly observant man, with a keen eye for the differences in people's features and costumes, he was fascinated by the extraordinary ethnic diversity in the Ottoman Empire. While many of his pictures show scenes of traditional everyday life which were already familiar in Europe, others show aspects which were recorded by writers but rarely by painters.

A professor for nearly forty years, Gérôme not only encouraged his pupils – many of whom came from all over the world to study with him – to travel but also instilled in them a passion for accurate detail.   LT

EMIL GLOCKNER

1868 Dresden – (date and place of death unknown)
German

Glockner was born and brought up in the Saxon city of Dresden, famous for its palaces and fine museum collections, and once renowned for its cabinetmakers and silversmiths. The visionary landscape painter, Caspar David Friedrich, had settled there in 1798 and his work had strongly influenced the Dresden Romantics; since that time, artists from various European countries had been attracted to the city. In was in this prevailing cultural climate that Glockner decided to train at the local school of arts and crafts before entering the Dresden Academy of Fine Arts. Four years later he enrolled in the studio of the Belgian history painter, Ferdinand Pauwels. Glockner left his professor in 1896, but in the meantime had already been working with open-air landscapists such as Paul Baum and Carl Bantzer, whose pictures encouraged him to use stronger colours.

Like many 19th-century artists, Glockner had a varied repertoire: Saxon landscapes, allegorical subjects and portraits, as well as Orientalist themes. He was awarded two gold medals by the Dresden Academy.   LT

Fromentin, Eugène. *Une Eté dans le Sahara.* Michel Lévy, Paris, 1857.

Fromentin, Eugène. *Une Année dans le Sahel.* Michel Lévy, Paris, 1859.

Thompson, James & Wright, Barbara. *Eugène Fromentin.* ACR, Paris, 1987.

Wright, Barbara. *Correspondance d'Eugène Fromentin, 1839–1876.* CNRS, Paris, 1995.

Ackerman, Gerald M. *The Life and Work of Jean-Léon Gérôme.* Sotheby's, London & New York, 1986 (PocheCouleur series, 1997).

Field Hering, Fanny. *The Life and Works of Jean-Léon Gérôme.* Cassell, New York, 1892.

Juler, Caroline. *Najd Collection of Orientalist Paintings.* Manara, London, 1991.

GUSTAVE GUILLAUMET

1840 Paris – 1887 Paris
FRENCH

Guillaumet's work was a turning-point in 19th-century Orientalism, not only because of his interest in light and atmosphere, but because of the manner in which he depicted the Algerian people.

While on his way to study in Rome, Guillaumet made a snap decision to go to Algeria instead. Despite a first bout of recurrent malaria, this decisive journey was to be the first of ten trips to North Africa. During the 1860s his Salon paintings tended to be melodramatic: scenes of prayer in the Sahara; desperate people wasted by famine (a familiar disaster in Algeria at the time); a camel's skeleton in the scorched, empty desert; a raiding party.

The early 1870s marked a new phase in Guillaumet's work. Attracted to the southern oasis towns of Biskra, Bou Saâda and Laghouat (less tainted by the presence of Europeans than the coastal towns) he showed the unchanging and impoverished existence of the desert people whose life he shared. Besides austere fortified villages or *ksars* burned dry in the sun, he painted the interiors of humble rammed-clay dwellings in which women weave, prepare couscous or look after their babies. In these, masterpieces of chiaroscuro, shafts of filtered light fall on the bare earth floors. Other works show scenes of rural labour, a theme dear to the realist school in Europe, but applied to North Africa for the first time. In all Guillaumet's paintings and drawings the religious leaders, peasant women, children, horsemen and chiefs are portrayed with respect. Each person is accorded their individuality and their dignity.   LT

OSMAN HAMDY BEY

1842 Constantinople (Istanbul) – 1910 Constantinople (Istanbul)
TURKISH

Painter, archaeologist, architect, poet, writer and musician, Hamdy Bey was one of the leading figures of Turkish artistic life of his time. Sent to Paris by his father, the Grand Vizir Müsir Ethem Pasha, he studied painting with Gustave Boulanger and Jean-Léon Gérôme (q.v.). After a twelve-year absence he returned to Constantinople. He was director of the Imperial School of Fine Arts and founder of the short-lived Stamboul Salons, to which Turkish and European artists contributed. Named director of the Imperial Ottoman museum, he was active in preventing the illegal export of antiquities from Turkey. Married to a Frenchwoman, Hamdy Bey played host to visiting Orientalists such as Paul Leroy and Rudolph Ernst (q.v.) and formed a renowned collection of Islamic carpets and works of art.

Hamdy Bey's paintings, which he exhibited in Paris, Vienna, Berlin, London and Constantinople, show the high finish and academic discipline of his professors. Among his favourite subjects were fashionable Turkish women strolling outdoors, muslin yashmaks covering their mouths, their rich clothes hidden by *feraces* or coats. Other pictures show believers in mosques or reading the Koran, portraits of his family, elegant domestic scenes, and arms and carpet merchants. As Hamdy Bey was passionately interested in both architecture and works of art, the details in these paintings are impeccable. His religious paintings too are faultless since, being a Muslim, he did not commit the errors so often made by western Orientalists. Examples of his work can be seen in museums in Istanbul, Ankara, Liverpool and Paris.   LT

WALTER CHARLES HORSLEY

1855 London – 1934 London
ENGLISH

Walter Charles Horsley worked as a portrait painter, illustrator and a painter of Orientalist genre scenes. He was the son of the historical genre painter John Callcott Horsley, who was appointed rector of the Royal Academy from 1875 to 1890, where his prudish objections to the use of nude models earned him the nickname of 'Clothes-Horsley'. Walter Charles Horsley was also related (by marriage) to another eminent Victorian, the engineer Isambard Kingdom Brunel. Horsley's London studio was located in Kensington, and between 1875 and 1911 he successfully exhibited fifty-five works at the Royal Academy, over half of which were Orientalist subjects set in Egypt, Turkey and India.

In 1873 Horsley entered the Royal Academy Schools as a student and while there gained a silver medal for figure painting from life. In 1875, aged twenty, he was sent to India via Turkey by the *Graphic* as one of its special artists recording the visit of HRH the Prince of Wales to that country. While he was in India, Horsley was also commissioned by the Nawab of Bahawalpour to paint a series of sporting portraits. Three years later Horsley visited Egypt and it is notable that, after 1879, the majority of his Orientalist genre scenes were set in Cairo. His sharp eye for details of costume, characteristic gestures and animated expressions gave an engaging liveliness to his figures. Horsley's work was also distinguished by its focus on scenes which illustrated, often humorously, the confrontation between divergent cultures, Oriental and Occidental, that he observed in the cosmopolitan streets of Cairo.   UP

Chabour, Anne-Marie. 'Gustave Achille Guillaumet: peintre et écrivain de l'Algérie'. Dissertation, Université de Paris IV Sorbonne, 1985.

Guillaumet, Gustave. *Tableaux algériens*. Ed. Eugène Mouton, Plon, Nourrit et Cie, Paris, 1888.

Cezar, Mustafa. *Sanatta Bati'ya Açilis ve Osman Hamdi*. Erol Aksoy, Istanbul, 1995.

Ackerman, Gerald M. *Les Orientalistes de l'ecole britannique*. Les Orientalistes, vol. 9, ACR, Paris, 1991.

'The French in Cairo'. *Art Journal* (London), 1885, p. 368.

Graves, A. *The Royal Academy of Arts: A Complete Dictionary of Contributors and their Work from its Foundation in 1796 to 1904*. vol. 2, S.R. Publishers & Kingswood Reprints, (London), 1970 (1905).

JEAN-AUGUSTE-DOMINIQUE INGRES

1780 Montauban – 1867 Paris
FRENCH

A brilliant draughtsman, whose highly finished paintings represent a search for ideal beauty, Ingres was the most distinguished and influential exponent of 19th-century classicism. After having lived in Italy from 1806 to 1824, he was elected to the Institute, opened a successful atelier, and was later named president of the Paris School of Fine Arts and director of the French Academy in Rome. He was frequently pitted against Eugène Delacroix (q.v.) and other members of the Romantic movement in the controversy of line versus colour. His themes were as varied and exotic as those of his opponents, ranging from classical mythology, portraits, and ancient and modern history to religion and the eastern world.

Ingres's exploration of the theme of the female nude in Oriental settings began with *The Valpinçon bather*, 1808 (Musée du Louvre, Paris), a chaste and modest picture in which the naked woman is seen in a silent and private world. More sensual paintings followed, such as *The grand odalisque*, 1814 (Musée du Louvre, Paris), in which the artist has transformed a classical nude into an Orientalist subject by adding eastern accessories. In *Odalisque with slave*, 1839 (The Fogg Art Museum, Cambridge) and the 1842 version (Walters Art Gallery, Baltimore), a languorous woman exposes her body to the viewer, conveying abandon and acquiescence. This series culminated in what is probably the best known of all hammam scenes, *The Turkish bath*, 1862 (Musée du Louvre, Paris). Here, a profusion of nudes are shown in provocative and lascivious poses, an open evocation of eroticism. LT

PAUL KLEE

1879 Munchenbuchsee nr Berne – 1940 Muralto nr Locarno
SWISS

A painter, draughtsman, printmaker, teacher and writer, Paul Klee was a major theoretician of 20th-century art. While studying art in Munich, Klee began to recount his experiences in a diary he kept from 1898 to 1918. By 1911–12 he was part of the Blaue Reiter circle of artists in that city, sharing with Wassily Kandinsky and Franz Marc a belief in the spiritual nature of artistic activity. His involvement with the Blaue Reiter also stimulated his interest in the international avant-garde. He saw the work of the Cubists and the Italian Futurists in German galleries and in 1912 travelled to Paris, where he called on Robert Delaunay and was profoundly affected by Delaunay's Orphism.

Klee's nearly exclusive concentration on graphic work changed in 1914 when he visited Tunisia. He spent two weeks in North Africa with the painters August Macke and Louis Moilliet, travelling from Tunis to nearby St Germain and visiting Kairouan and Hammamet. During this trip he produced a number of extraordinarily beautiful watercolours that were to be important sources for his work for the rest of his life. Some were naturalistic impressions, others were based on abstract structures of coloured squares related to Delaunay's work. In his journal Klee recorded the most important breakthrough of this trip: 'Colour and I are one. I am a painter'.

After the First World War, Klee became a Bauhaus master nicknamed the 'Bauhaus Buddha', with a major part of his teaching devoted to colour theory. In 1928 he travelled to Egypt and was again inspired by the landscape and the light he encountered there. His last years were spent in Switzerland, an exile from the Nazi regime and plagued by an incurable skin disease. In this period he developed a meditative pictorial language with the distilled simplicity of ancient runes or Egyptian hieroglyphs, and explored powerful themes, including death. UP

GEORGE LAMBERT

1873 St Petersburg – 1930 Cobbity, New South Wales
AUSTRALIAN

Lambert lived for a period in Europe before emigrating to Australia in 1887. He trained under Julian Ashton in Sydney before studying in Paris at Colarossi under Delécluse. Influenced by Spanish art, especially Velasquez and aspects of Manet's style, he achieved some sucess living and exhibiting in London from 1902 to 1921. A portraitist, illustrator, and painter of bravura figure subjects, towards the end of the First World War Lambert was asked to serve as Australian official war artist in Egypt and Gallipoli. As a result of his service he produced a series of sparkling Middle Eastern landscapes, rhythmically curved and subtly coloured, as well as idealised soldier portraits and battle pictures.

Lambert returned to live in Australia in the 1920s when his Palestine landscapes became very well known, and influenced a number of local painters, including Hans Heysen. Lambert's interest in Orientalism continued into the 1920s via the contemporary fashion for fancy-dress balls, for which he liked to dress himself as a Persian prince. In 1922 he designed the costumes, sets, colour and movements for an Oriental pageant that was staged in Sydney that July, called *The Persian Garden*. It consisted of a series of tableaux accompanying a performance of Liza Lehman's song cycle. The curtain rose to reveal Omar and his muse reclining in a Persian garden at dawn. UP

Ockman, Carol. *Ingres's Eroticized Bodies: Retracing the Serpentine Line*. Yale University Press, New Haven & London, 1995.

Vigne, Georges. *Ingres*. Trans. John Goodman, Abbeville Press, New York, London & Paris, 1995.

Wildenstein, Georges. *The Paintings of J. A. D. Ingres*. Phaidon, London, 1954.

The Diaries of Paul Klee 1898–1918. Ed. and intro. Felix Klee, University of California Press, Berkeley, 1964.

Die Tunisreise: Klee, Macke, Moilliet. Exh. cat., ed. Ernst-Gerhard Güse (Westfälisches Landesmuseum für Kunst und Kulturgeschichte, Münster), Hatje, Stuttgart, 1982.

Gray, Anne. *Art and Artifice: George Lambert, 1873–1930*. Craftsman House, Sydney, 1996.

Lambert, A. *The Career of G. W. Lambert: Thirty Years of an Artist's Life*. Society of Artists, Sydney, 1938.

MacDonald, J. S. *The Art and Life of George W. Lambert*. Alexander McCubbin, Melbourne, 1920.

Motion, A. *The Lamberts: George, Constant and Kit*. Chatto & Windus, London, 1986.

FREDERIC LEIGHTON

1830 Scarborough – 1896 London
ENGLISH

Frederic Leighton, 1st Baron Leighton of Stretton, painter and sculptor, was one of the leading figures in the Victorian art establishment. He achieved renown for his monumental, finely crafted and choreographed figure compositions. A tireless worker on behalf of the Royal Academy, and its president from 1878, almost his last words were, 'my love to the Royal Academy'. A well-travelled and cultured artist, Leighton studied in Germany under the Nazarene artist E. von Steinle and worked for a time in Italy, based in Rome. Between 1855 and 1859 he was in Paris, where he met Ingres and Delacroix and was influenced by Scheffer and Fleury. On his return to London he continued to show at the Royal Academy and established links with the Pre-Raphaelite circle.

As well as his interest in the classical world and in Renaissance Italy, Leighton was attracted to the East and made five trips to North Africa and the Near East. In 1857 he visited Algiers, in 1867 Constantinople, in 1868 Egypt; in 1873 he was in Damascus and in 1882 he returned to Egypt. While in Damascus he sketched buildings, which he used as backgrounds, and decorative accessories for Orientalist scenes completed in his studio in London. He also painted a series of direct oil sketches of desert landscapes in Egypt and Syria. However, the most notable result of his trip to Damascus was the 'Arab Hall', designed by Aitchison and added to Leighton's Holland Park home between 1877 and 1879. An austere man who never married, Leighton's best work was imbued with a sense of poetic melancholy. His late works were influenced by the Aesthetic movement and notable for their brilliant colouring. UP

LUCIEN LEVY-DHURMER

(Lucien Lévy)

1865 Algiers – 1953 Paris
FRENCH

Formerly a student at the Paris Ecole des Beaux-Arts, Lévy-Dhurmer worked for Clément Massier, renowned for his lustre faience, from 1887 to 1895. The shimmering glazes of these ceramics, like the wings of the butterflies of which Lévy-Dhurmer had a collection, are closely linked to the colour effects he sought to obtain in his pastels.

Lévy-Dhurmer's first exhibition in 1896 at the Galerie Georges Petit in Paris revealed his symbolist pictures, from which emanate a sense of mystery and a dream-like atmosphere. He soon became greatly appreciated by leading art critics, who wrote long essays on his work. In time, the avant-garde circles turned away from him, but *nouveau riche* clients commissioned their own and their family's portraits. From 1906 he painted a series of pictures using a pointilliste technique – inspired by the music of Beethoven, Fauré and Débussy – which later included idealised nudes in monochrome colours.

Lévy-Dhurmer was an indefatigable traveller and often visited the French provinces, Italy, Spain and Holland. From 1901 he made his first journey to Morocco and, around 1906, to Constantinople. North Africa in particular inspired striking portraits of Arab men and tattooed and bejewelled Berber women with limpid, soulful eyes. In other works, Muslim women covered in white haiks flit through streets and oases like moths. His empty land- and town-scapes in mauves, pinks, blues, violets and greens, luminous and evocative, often verge on non-figuration. His Moroccan sketches, in turquoise and sepia ink, are generally less romanticised, while his *Blind men of Tangier* shows a ferocious realism. LT

JOHN FREDERICK LEWIS

1805 London – 1876 Walton-on-Thames
ENGLISH

Exotic cultures were a source of inspiration for Lewis's art early in his career, and he painted numerous Spanish subjects after he lived in Spain in 1832–34. However the Orientalist paintings for which he is best known were produced after he spent the decade from 1841 to 1851 in Cairo. In the absence of Lewis's own accounts of his life in Cairo a mythology about the artist has developed around Thackeray's laconic description of Lewis as a 'languid, Lotus-eater' living a 'hazy, lazy, tobaccofied life in the most complete oriental fashion'.[1] Describing him as dressed like a 'Turkified European' and living in a traditional Islamic house, Thackeray delighted in the possibility that Lewis had his own harem. Thackeray constructed the familiar Orientalist myth of the western artist–traveller 'going native', which was later taken to be evidence of Lewis's authority as an Orientalist painter. Lewis completed very few paintings during this period. He returned to England in 1851 and brought back an extensive collection of costumes, hundreds of sketches and Oriental objects which were to be used in his paintings for the rest of his career. Desert encampments, street scenes and harem interiors were Lewis's favourite Orientalist subjects. His most popular works were *The hhareem*, 1849, and *A frank encampment in the desert of Mount Sinai*, 1856. Lewis's extraordinarily detailed paintings were often interpreted as accurate chronicles of the scenes they portray and visual equivalents of contemporary ethnographic texts. His paintings of the 1850s seemed closely allied with the symbolic realism of early Pre-Raphaelitism; although Lewis was never a member of the Pre-Raphaelite Brotherhood, Ruskin noted the parallels.[2] MR

[1] William Makepeace Thackeray, *Notes on a Journey From Cornhill to Grand Cairo*, Smith Elder & Co., London, 1869 (1844), p. 508.

[2] John Ruskin, 'Pre-Raphaelitism' (1851), in *The Works of John Ruskin*, eds E.T. Cook & A. Wedderburn, George Allen, London, 1903–12, vol. 12, pp. 363–5.

'British artists: their style and character, no. XXXII – John Frederick Lewis'. *Art Journal*, vol. 220, 1858, pp. 41–3.

Lewis, Major-General Michael. *John Frederick Lewis R.A. 1805–1876*. F. Lewis Publishers, Leigh-on-Sea, 1978.

Barrington, Mrs R. *Life, Letters and Work of Frederic Leighton*. 2 vols, George Allen, London, 1906.

Corkran, A. *Frederic Leighton*. Methuen, London, 1904.

Jones, Stephen et al. *Frederic Leighton 1830–1896*. Exh. cat., Royal Academy of Arts, London, 1996.

Autour de Lévy-Dhurmer. Exh. cat. (Grand Palais), Editions des Musées Nationaux, Paris, 1973.

EDWIN LONG

1829 Bath – 1891 London
ENGLISH

Edwin Long began his career as a portraitist and painter of Spanish subjects. A careful and industrious worker, he was inspired by his travels, first to Moorish Spain, then to Egypt and Syria, and by his reading of the Bible and books documenting 19th-century archaeological discoveries. His largest paintings, often combining antiquarian research with Near Eastern settings and religious sentiments, appealed to Victorian taste, making him both rich and successful. He was the only other artist of the era who came close to Alma-Tadema and Edward Poynter as a painter of grand historical subjects set in the ancient Near East.

After his first visit to Egypt and Syria in 1874, Long painted his most famous picture, the *Babylonian marriage market*, 1875 (Royal Holloway and Bedford New College), which he exhibited at the Royal Academy. He was elected ARA in 1876 on the strength of it, and RA in 1881. This picture was also sold at a record price for the work of a living artist at Christie's in 1882, where the then National Art Gallery of New South Wales was among the unsuccessful bidders. Long's financial success enabled him to commission fashionable architect Richard Norman Shaw to design two houses for him, both in Hampstead. Orientalist pictures by Edwin Long to enter Australian collections in the 19th century included a replica of his famous *Queen Esther*, which was commissioned for the National Gallery of Victoria. UP

AZOUAOU MAMMERI

1892 Taourirt-Mimoun – 1954 Taourirt-Mimoun
ALGERIAN

Mammeri was one of the first North Africans to break with the tradition of non-representation of the human figure, proscribed by Islam. Born in Kabylia, a member of the Ath-Yenni tribe, he was an itinerant teacher when he met the French artist Léon Carré, who gave him painting lessons. In 1916 Mammeri left Algeria for Morocco, where he became professor of drawing in Fez, then Rabat. In 1922 he returned to Kabylia to take up the post of caid, or local governor, of the Benni-Yenni douar. At the same time as carrying out his official functions, he continued to paint and draw landscapes, portraits and family scenes, which aroused the curiosity and admiration of the local population.

In 1927 Mammeri returned to Morocco, where he was appointed to successive official posts in Fez, Rabat and, from 1929 to 1948, Marrakesh. As regional inspector of Moroccan Art and Arts Industries, he created workshops and a museum in the 18th-century palace Dar Si Saïd, as well as a school of traditional music and dance.

With an extreme simplification of form, Mammeri's paintings, in which the architecture is accorded as much importance as the people, transmit inward-looking emotions and a contemplative, serene atmosphere. Encouraged from the start by personalities such as General Lyautey, the Resident-General of France in Morocco, and Léonce Bénédite, curator of the Musée du Luxembourg in Paris, he had a *succès d'estime*. Although Mammeri was never particularly commercial, his widely exhibited paintings were purchased by museums in Paris, Cleveland, Brooklyn and Algiers. LT

ALBERT MARQUET

1875 Bordeaux – 1947 Paris
FRENCH

A painter and draughtsman, Albert Marquet met and befriended Henri Matisse during their student days together, between 1894 and 1898, at the Ecole des Beaux-Arts under Gustave Moreau. In 1900 Marquet was hired, with Matisse, to paint the art nouveau ornaments of the Grand Palais for the Exposition Universelle. Like Matisse, Marquet began to use the strong colours and separate brushstrokes identified with Fauvism. However, he was the most subdued of the Fauves as a colourist, preferring to use more tonally quiet colours – greens and greys and purple – to express the play of light over water viewed from the quays of the Seine, his most typical subject. Marquet also travelled and painted the coastal regions of France, and spent time in England, The Netherlands, Germany, Italy, Spain and Russia. His Orientalist views recorded visits to Morocco in 1911 and 1913, and inspired Matisse to make two painting journeys to Tangier. In 1920 Marquet made his first visit to Algiers, where he met Marcelle Martinet, whom he married in 1923. He spent several successive winters in North Africa, painting in Algeria and in Tunisia. In 1928 he also made a journey to Egypt. During the Second World War, Marquet spent the years from 1940 to 1945 in Algeria, where his wife had relatives. A quiet, self-effacing personality, near-sighted and with a limp, Marquet shied away from official honours. However, his late works, including views of the harbour at Algiers, continued to demonstrate his keen observation and fresh handling of the port subjects and urban waterways that had inspired him since moving into Matisse's old studio on the Quai Saint Michel in 1908, where, when not travelling, he worked until 1931. UP

Bills, Mark. *Edwin Longsden Long RA*. London (in press).

Free, Renée. *Victorian Olympians*. Exh. cat., Art Gallery of New South Wales, Sydney, 1975.

Quick, Richard. *The Life and Works of Edwin Long RA*. Exh. cat., Bournemouth Art Gallery and Museums, Bournemouth, rev. edn 1970 (1931).

Angéli, Louis-Eugène. 'Azouaou Mammeri'. *Algéria* (Algiers), May–June 1955.

Tharaud, Jean & Tharaud, Jérôme. 'Si Azouaou Mammeri: peintre de Rabat'. *Art et Décoration* (Paris), no. 40, 1921.

Albert Marquet. Exh. cat., ed. Jean Cassou (Galerie des Beaux-Arts, Bordeaux), Musée de l'Orangerie, Paris, 1975.

Albert Marquet. Exh. cat., ed. François Daulte, Fondation Hermitage, Lausanne, 1988.

Freeman, Judi et al. *The Fauve Landscape*. Exh. cat. (Los Angeles County Museum of Art), Abbeville Press, New York, 1990.

HENRI MATISSE

1869 Le Cateau-Cambrésis – 1954 Nice
FRENCH

Matisse is the most celebrated 20th-century artist to have contributed to the Orientalist tradition. The instigator of the Fauve movement which liberated colour from its descriptive function (1905–07), Matisse pushed painting to an art of sheer surfaces bounded by arabesque lines in the years before the First World War.

Matisse travelled to the East three times: to French Algeria as a tourist in 1906, when he visited (but scarcely painted in) the oasis resort of Biskra; and then twice to Tangier in the new French protectorate of Morocco (winters of 1912 and 1913). His twenty canvases painted in Morocco mark the fruitful encounter of experimental abstraction and a traditional conception of Orientalist themes: kasbah architecture, exotic gardens, Maghrebian ethnic types resplendent in traditional costume. Matisse's admiration for the Islamic decorative arts and miniature painting had a distinct impact on his art of pattern and curvilinear form: 'Persian miniatures…showed me all the possibilities of my sensations…By its properties this art suggests a larger and truly plastic space…Thus my revelation came from the Orient'.[1]

In the 1920s, as a resident of Nice, Matisse painted his long series of odalisques, which combine a homage to Ingres and Courbet with memories of his favourite Moroccan model, the prostitute Zorah. These odalisque pictures, posed for by French models draped (like Delacroix's or Regnault's) in the artist's own studio props, produce a playful profusion of pattern and bright colour, and an unabashed eroticism that helped seal the artist's new popularity with a middle-brow public.   RB

LOUIS MOILLIET

1880 Berne – 1950 La Tour-de-Peilz
SWISS

Moilliet was born one year after his famous compatriot Paul Klee, with whom he went to school in Berne. Initially trained as a decorative painter, Moilliet studied at the Worpswede artists' colony, and at the Düsseldorf and Stuttgart academies. In 1905 he and Klee went to Paris to observe avant-garde painting. A great traveller, in 1907–08 Moilliet worked in Rome and made the first of many excursions to Tunisia.

His friendship with August Macke, who had a decisive influence on Moilliet's art, began in 1909. Moilliet's Tunisian landscapes of 1910 are loosely brushed divisionist paintings, but by 1912–13 his contact with the Blaue Reiter artists in Munich, who exhibited Robert Delaunay's Orphist paintings, revolutionised his style. His major canvas, *In the circus* of 1913–14, created a sensation when it was acquired by the Basel Kunstmuseum.

Moilliet's Tunisian contacts facilitated the trip he, Klee and Macke made to Tunisia in 1914. Although he painted very little there, the group's radical watercolour style was the foundation for the many watercolours he painted in Tunisia, Morocco, Algeria and Spain in the 1920s. Distressed by the deaths of Macke and his first wife during the war, Moilliet became an inveterate traveller whose 'rucksack was his studio', as his friend Hermann Hesse observed. The last two decades of Moilliet's life were dedicated to stained-glass design for religious buildings.
RB

GUSTAVE MOREAU

1826 Paris – 1898 Paris
FRENCH

One of the best-known symbolist painters, Moreau's allegorical, biblical and mythological subjects combined sensuality and sumptuous richness. His early work was strongly influenced by Eugène Delacroix (q.v.) and his friend and mentor Théodore Chassériau (q.v.), whose premature death inspired *Young man and death* (The Fogg Art Museum, Cambridge).

Over the years, Moreau developed variations in oils and watercolours on the theme of the *femme fatale* (Salome, Delilah, Helen, Messaline), and also of the hero (Hercules, Orpheus, Jason, Prometheus). Fascinating and exotic, these paintings strongly appealed to the élite and inspired writers and poets. Only a few intimates saw his audacious oil and watercolour sketches which, with slashes of pure broken colour, verge on abstraction. An exceptional and unusual teacher, Moreau played an important role in encouraging young artists such as Matisse (q.v.), Evenepoel (q.v.), Albert Marquet (q.v), Odilon Redon and Georges Rouault, who were to become bold innovators.

Moreau did not need to sell his work and exhibited only intermittently at the Salon until 1880. A man of private means and vast culture, unmarried, looked after by his beloved mother, he lived in semi-reclusion, working relentlessly. On his death he left to the State his Paris home and its contents, including over 10,000 drawings, which now form the Musée Gustave Moreau.

Although he never travelled to the East, Moreau was certainly influenced by the vogue for Orientalism in both literature and painting. He also copied Persian miniatures and, at the end of his life, became fascinated with Indian civilisation, architecture and painting.   LT

[1] Henri Matisse, 'The path of colour' (1947), in Jack D. Flam (ed.), *Matisse on Art*, Phaidon, Oxford, 1973, p. 116.

Cowart, Jack et al. *Matisse in Morocco: The Paintings and Drawings 1912–1913*. Exh. cat., National Gallery of Art, Washington, 1990.

Flam, Jack. *Matisse: The Man and his Art, 1869–1918*. Cornell University Press, Ithaca, NY, 1986.

Ammann, Jean Christophe. *Louis Moilliet: Das Gesamtwerk*. DuMont Schauberg, Cologne, 1972.

Die Tunisreise: Klee, Macke, Moilliet. Exh. cat., ed. Ernst-Gerhard Güse (Westfälisches Landesmuseum für Kunst und Kulturgeschichte, Münster), Hatje, Stuttgart, 1982.

L'Inde de Gustave Moreau. Exh. cat., Musée Cernuschi, Paris, February–May 1997.

Mathieu, Pierre-Louis. *Gustave Moreau, with a catalogue raisonné of unfinished paintings*. Flammarion, Paris, 1995.

ALBERTO PASINI

1826 Busseto – 1899 Cavoretto
ITALIAN

Finding it difficult to earn his living in Italy, Pasini moved to Paris in 1851. There he met the French diplomat Prosper Bourée, who invited him on an official mission to Nasser-al-Din's court in Persia. Since it was on the overland route to India, Persia – of key importance to France, Russia and England – was the centre of endless political manoeuvres. Bourée's task was to counteract Russia's influence, particularly strong at that time.

In March 1855 Pasini set off through Egypt, Yemen and Oman, finally arriving in Teheran, where he spent eighteen months. Not only were many of his trips around Persia made in the company of the shah, but the sovereign commissioned a number of paintings. Pasini returned to Paris in 1856, this time by the more usual route via the Black Sea and Constantinople. He visited the Turkish capital again in 1868–69, and travelled to Syria and Lebanon in 1873. After a successful career in Paris, he finally settled down in Italy.

Pasini was struck by the delicacy of the light in the East. His treatment of the play between shadow and sun, and his quasi-photographic representation of architecture and figures, are a world apart from the artificial exoticism of early Orientalists. In his charming and meticulous drawings and paintings the individuality of the people portrayed is not emphasised. The mounted horsemen, modestly veiled Turkish women, merchants selling their wares and street musicians are an integral part of his perfectly balanced compositions.   LT

EDWARD JOHN POYNTER

1836 Paris – 1919 London
ENGLISH

Edward Poynter's name is associated with the revival of classical painting in Britain during the second half of the 19th century. His reputation was established by his large, scholarly reconstructions of antiquity, illustrating biblical events (such as *Israel in Egypt*, 1867) or classical myth, history and genre (*Atlanta's race*, 1876; *On the terrace*, 1889). Having trained in Paris during the 1850s, at the atelier of the academic painter Charles Gleyre, Poynter played an important role in the introduction of French art-teaching methods to England. He became the first Slade Professor at University College, London, in 1871, and then headed the National Art Training Schools in South Kensington. His career as an arts administrator culminated in his appointment as director of the National Gallery, London, in 1894 and his election as president of the Royal Academy two years later. In spite of this involvement in public office, Poynter's considerable artistic *oeuvre* extended across a range of subjects and media. Alongside his paintings of the ancient world, he executed portraits and landscapes throughout his life, participated in the illustration revival of the 1860s, and was a fine academic draughtsman and watercolourist. His activities as a decorative artist were equally significant and included major interiors (such as the tiled Grill Room at the South Kensington Museum) as well as smaller commissions for painted furniture and stained glass. Knighted in 1896, he was created a baronet in 1902.   AI

MOHAMMED RACIM

1896 Algiers – 1975 Algiers
ALGERIAN

Variously considered in the colonial period as craftsman or artist, Racim was honoured as a national painter by the Algerian Republic. Racim's father and uncle, from an old Algiers family of Turkish origin, were well-known artisans. Familiarised with drawings in their workshop, Racim showed an early artistic aptitude. At that time, French settlers wanted to marginalise the Algerian population, so certain politicians, feeling this could lead to a clash between the two communities, sought to form an Algerian élite. Prosper Ricard, in charge of the preservation and renewal of Algerian arts and crafts, suggested that the young Racim should join his service. To Racim's disappointment, he was given the tedious task of copying models of carpets and textiles.

Racim had already begun to paint portraits and illuminations when he met Etienne Dinet (q.v.) and received a commission by the publisher Henri Piazza for the ornamentation of Dinet's book *La Vie de Mohammed*. Piazza was particularly interested in Oriental miniatures, and soon Racim had access to both private and public collections.

After travelling to Spain, London and Venice, Racim introduced figures into his miniatures for the first time. Many of these were historical scenes of the old city of Algiers and its fast-disappearing traditions. Others, in a European, Turkish or Persian manner, treated heroic themes: sovereigns, fighting warriors, lion hunts. Another project with Piazza kept Racim in Paris on a prolonged stay. From 1934 he taught at the Algiers National School of Fine Arts, training generations of illuminators and miniaturists but, as his sight failed, turned to painting oils of popular images.   LT

Alberto Pasini, da Parma a Constantinopoli via Parigi. Exh. cat. (Fondazione Cassa di Risparmio di Parma; Palazzo Bossi Bocchi, Parma), STEP, Parma, 1996.

Calderini, Marco. *Alberto Pasini.* E. Calanza, Turin, 1916.

Cardoso, Vittoria Botteri. *Pasini.* Sagep, Genova, 1991.

Monkhouse, Cosmo. 'The life and work of Sir Edward J. Poynter P.R.A.'. *Easter Annual,* extra no. of the *Art Journal,* 1897.

Wood, Christopher. *Olympian Dreamers.* Constable, London, 1983.

Baghli, Sid Ahmed. *Mohammed Racim: miniaturiste algérien.* 5th edn, Entreprise Nationale du Livre, Algiers, 1984 (SNED, Algiers, 1971).

Bouabdallah, Malika, Orif, Mustapha & Pouillon, François. *Mohammed Racim: miniaturiste algérien.* Exh. cat., Musée de l'Institut du Monde Arabe, Paris, 3–29 March 1992.

Orif, Mustapha. 'Mohammed Racim: *catalogue raisonné'* (forthcoming).

HENRI REGNAULT

1843 Paris – 1871 Buzenval
FRENCH

Regnault's patriotic death at the age of twenty-seven, which immortalised his name, is the reflection of his life and his career – brilliant and dynamic.

After a stay in Rome as winner of the coveted Grand Prix, he left for Spain in 1868, where he witnessed the revolution which overthrew the monarchy. The following year he rented a house in Tangier with Georges Clairin (q.v.). At that time it was difficult for Europeans to paint in Morocco, although the Tangerines, used to foreigners, were less hostile to infidels than their co-religionists inland. Since images were considered blasphemous by Islam, Regnault and Clairin were obliged to use Jewish models before meeting a young Muslim woman who, though risking reprisals from the population, sat for the young men. The following year, Regnault's provocative *Salome* (Metropolitan Museum, New York) was exhibited with enormous success at the Paris Salon. Planning to spend the rest of his life in Tangier, Regnault moved into an immense studio where he painted his vast, spectacular and violent *Summary execution under the Moorish kings of Grenada* (Musée d'Orsay, Paris). 'My aim is to depict the real Moors in the way they used to be', he wrote, 'rich and great, both terrifying and voluptuous, the ones that are to be found only in past history'.[1]

At the outbreak of the Franco-Prussian War, Regnault left for Paris, where he painted three brilliant, atmospheric Orientalist watercolours, including the one in this exhibition. He was killed during the battle of Buzenval.   LT

[1] Arthur Duparc (ed.), *Correspondance d'Henri Regnault*, Charpentier, Paris, 1872.

Henri Regnault. Exh. cat., Musée Municipal de Saint-Cloud, October 1991–January 1992.

AUGUSTE RENOIR

1841 Limoges – 1919 Cagnes
FRENCH

Renoir, the celebrated painter, was originally associated with the Impressionist movement, and his early works were scenes of real life, where the vibration of the atmosphere was suggested by small brushstrokes of contrasting colour. By the mid-1880s, however, he had broken with the Impressionists to apply a more disciplined technique to portraits and figure paintings, particularly of women.

Renoir's first Orientalist pictures were painted long before he visited Algeria. He deeply admired Eugène Delacroix (q.v.) and an 1870 picture of a reclining odalisque (National Gallery of Art, Washington) has the scintillating colours and loose brushwork of the romantic master. Renoir's 1872 oil of Parisian women dressed as Algerians (National Museum of Western Art, Tokyo) is clearly inspired by Delacroix's famous *Women of Algiers*.

His paintings being difficult to sell, Renoir often had serious financial worries but, with commissions for portraits, and purchases by his dealer, Paul Durand-Ruel, he was able to travel. During his first month-long trip to Algiers, in March 1881, he painted landscapes, with figures seen only in the distance. Shimmering light fused with colour is the dominating factor in these works: the lush vegetation of the Jardin d'Essai, panoramic views of the bay of Algiers, people outside the Sidi Abd er Rahman mosque, the crowd gathered during a religious festival. When he returned to Algiers a year later he was able to paint portraits of Algerian women and a mocking *yaouled* or shoeshine boy. An oil of sketches of heads and a man was acquired in 1931 by the Algiers Musée National des Beaux-Arts.   LT

Carnet de dessins: Renoir en Italie et en Algérie. Pref. Albert André; intro. Georges Besson, D. Jacomet, Paris, 1955.

White, Barbara Ehrlich. *Renoir: His Life, Art and Letters*. Abrams, New York, 1984.

HILDA RIX NICHOLAS

1884 Ballarat – 1961 Delegate, NSW
AUSTRALIAN

Hilda Rix Nicholas studied at the National Gallery School in Melbourne between 1902 and 1905 and, accompanied by her mother and sister, left Australia in 1907 bound for London and Paris where she studied with several well-known artists. In 1910 she joined the artists' community at Etaples and worked there for a part of each year until 1914.

In late January 1912 Rix Nicholas travelled to Morocco for the first time with the African–American Salon painter Henry Ossawa Tanner and his wife, and returned two years later with her sister, Elsie. On both occasions she stayed at the Hotel Villa de France on the edge of the Grand Soko. She remained in Tangier and its immediate environs for most of the time, although the opportunity to join an excursion by donkey to the Rif city of Tétouan was too good to refuse. Some of her Moroccan works were shown at a solo exhibition at the Galerie Chaîne and Simonsen in Paris in 1912 and at the Société des Peintres Orientalistes Français in 1913 and 1914. The *Studio* published an article about her pictures and *Notre Gazette* ranked Rix Nicholas among the best French Orientalist painters.[1] The Musée du Luxembourg purchased one of her drawings for the State,[2] and her Moroccan work was an outstanding success in Paris.

The First World War saw the deaths of Rix Nicholas's mother, sister and first husband. After her return to Australia in 1918 she began painting Australian bush scenes and showed her new work in Paris and London in 1925. Rix Nicholas never returned to North Africa, although Dinet's *The snake charmer*, one of her favourite works in the Art Gallery of New South Wales, always rekindled memories of its life and colour.   JP

[1] Hilda Rix, 'Sketching in Morocco', *Studio*, vol. 63, 1914, pp. 35–41; P. Marcel, 'Silhouettes d'artistes', *Notre Gazette*, April 1914, p. 19.

[2] The Musée du Luxembourg purchased a drawing, now lost, called *Grand marché, Tangier*.

Pigot, John. *Capturing the Orient: Hilda Rix Nicholas and Ethel Carrick in the East.* Exh. cat. Waverley City Gallery, Melbourne, 1993.

Stevens, Bertram. *The Art of Hilda Rix Nicholas*. Anthony Hordern & Sons, Sydney, 1919.

TOM ROBERTS

1856 Dorchester – 1931 Kallista, Victoria
AUSTRALIAN (ENGLISH-BORN)

Tom Roberts, whose artist nickname was 'Bulldog', achieved recognition as 'the father of Australian landscape painting' and as a pioneer of the Heidelberg School. He was also an accomplished studio figure and portrait painter. After beginning his art studies in Melbourne, he returned to England in 1881 and enrolled at the Royal Academy Schools, recommended by Edwin Long. In 1883 he interrupted his studies to travel through Spain with the painter John Peter Russell. They both learnt something of French Impressionism from two Spanish art students they encountered in Granada, Ramon Casas and Loreano Barrau.

Impressed by the picturesque beauties of Moorish architecture, especially the Alhambra at Granada, Roberts painted his first known Orientalist pictures. He later joined Jean-Léon Gérôme's painting classes at the Académie Julian in Paris. Returning to Australia in 1885, Roberts, with Frederick McCubbin, established the first artists' camp at Box Hill (on the outskirts of Melbourne), painting impressionist landscapes *en plein air*. However, his admiration for academic masters such as Long and Gérôme also inspired Roberts with an ambition to paint allegorical or historical pictures. This led him to paint a series of 'fancy portraits' of women such as *Jephtha's daughter* (Long had painted a series on the biblical theme of *Jephtha's vow*). Other of Roberts's titles, such as *Eastern princess*, *A rose of Persia* and *Snake charmer* (c. 1920) indicate the persistence of his interest in eastern themes. Over a period of eight years he also worked on an ambitious *Arabian Nights* inspired picture of dancing female figures, which was finally accepted for exhibition at the Royal Academy in 1913 but was not the success he had hoped. In 1923 Roberts returned to Australia and spent his last years at Kallista, painting landscapes. His most famous pictures were those which celebrated Australian pastoral life and sunlit landscapes. UP

Croll, R. H. *Tom Roberts: Father of Australian Landscape Painting*. Robertson & Mullens, Sydney, 1935.

Spate, Virginia. *Tom Roberts*. Lansdowne, Melbourne, rev. edn 1978.

Topliss, Helen. *Tom Roberts, 1856–1931: A Catalogue Raisonné*. 2 vols, Oxford University Press, Melbourne, 1985.

ARTHUR STREETON

1867 Mt Duneed, Victoria – 1934 Olinda
AUSTRALIAN

A largely self-taught painter, Streeton was influenced by his older friend Tom Roberts and the young Charles Conder to paint poetic landscapes *en plein air*. His early success, like theirs, came as a member of the so-called Heidelberg School. In 1897 he sailed for Europe, hoping to achieve a reputation overseas and ambitious to show his works at the centre of the Empire, London. En route he travelled to Cairo where he stayed for five or six weeks painting small Orientalist views on the spot, as well as making sketches, taking photographs and gathering inspiration for paintings he planned to complete later in his London studio. His Egyptian works were spontaneously painterly, directly observed and instinctively decorative. Like the best of his Australian landscapes inspired by hot, summer light, they were small poems of sunshine and colour.

Arriving in London, Streeton sought to remake this painterly style, forsaking the directness of manner that had been his earlier strength. In England the academic success he craved eluded him, and he struggled with loneliness, the climate and commercial neglect. He did not repeat his Cairo experience as an Orientalist travel painter. However, like his friend Roberts, Streeton had ambitions to succeed as a painter of allegorical and historical subjects, and during the early 1900s attempted a series of decorative pictures inspired by Omar Khayyám and themes from the *Arabian Nights*. In 1905 he exhibited his *Allegory from Omar* at the Royal Academy, with limited success. After serving as a war artist in France during the First World War, he finally settled in Victoria, consolidating his reputation as one of Australia's best-loved painters of imposing vistas of blue-and-gold landscape. UP

Eagle, Mary. *The Oil Paintings of Arthur Streeton in the National Gallery of Australia*. National Gallery of Australia, Canberra, 1994.

Galbally, Ann. *Arthur Streeton*. Lansdowne, Melbourne, rev. edn 1979 (1969).

Galbally, Ann & Gray, Anne (eds). *Letters from Smike: The Letters of Arthur Streeton 1890–1943*. Oxford University Press, Melbourne, 1989.

WILLIAM STRUTT

1825 Teignmouth – 1915 Wadhurst
ENGLISH

William Strutt worked as a painter and illustrator. He trained in Paris under Paul Delaroche and Horace Vernet. While in Paris, possibly influenced by his teacher Vernet, he was impressed by the Orientalist works of Chassériau and Delacroix's *Sultan of Morocco* at the Salon of 1845. In 1850 he travelled to Australia and later spent time in New Zealand. While in the Colonies he painted portraits, scenes of pioneering life and pictures of Maoris and Aborigines. After his return to England in 1862 he exhibited with the Royal Academy, becoming well known for his religious paintings, which often included animals. He shared a passion for depicting lions (studied at London zoo) with the French Orientalist Jean-Léon Gérôme. In 1885 General Gordon was killed at Khartoum and the British press published many articles on the war and rebellion in the Sudan. In the same year, Strutt exhibited a lion subject titled *Stolen children: a scene in the Soudan* at the Royal Academy. In 1890 he showed *The Nubian hunter,* and in 1891 a large oil of an Arab on horseback being attacked by lions, titled *A terrible scare,* at the Royal Society of British Artists. He died aged ninety, ultimately disappointed in his attempts to be recognised as a painter of great history pictures. UP

Curnow, Heather. *The Life and Art of William Strutt: 1825–1915*. Alistair Taylor, Martinborough, New Zealand, 1980.

Curnow, Heather. *William Strutt*. Exh. cat., AGDC, Sydney, 1981.

ANDRE SUREDA

1872 Versailles – 1930 Versailles
FRENCH

Suréda, from a family of Spanish origin, had already travelled to North Africa before being awarded a travel grant in 1904. From 1910 his work was almost exclusively of the Maghreb, where he made long stays every year. In 1926 he visited the Middle East – Jerusalem and Aleppo – a journey full of joy but from which he returned fatally ill.

Although he took part in the Paris Salons, Suréda did not care about worldly success. He was, however, highly appreciated by the élite of artistic circles, who saw in him both a poet and an ethnographer of closed societies which were undergoing radical transformation. He observed scenes usually ignored by other Orientalist painters: the Jewish communities of Tlemcen and the Ile de Djerba; members of the Aiassaouas sect, who inflicted injuries on themselves during their religious ecstasy; beggars and the blind; processions of Arab mourners and Armenian priests; Muslim women praying in a shrine or taking a nap in the heat of the day; the ritual dance of the whirling dervishes.

In time, Suréda's spontaneous, energetic drawings became more simplified and synthetic, while his paintings – often in tempera – took on a deceptive air of naiveté. From the 1920s he began to use unusual colour combinations – acid tones of orange, green, pink and blue – outlined flat tints which reduced his subject matter to the essentials. Suréda was also an accomplished engraver and his plates illustrate books by Guy de Maupassant, Louis Bertrand and Jean and Jérôme Tharaud. LT

HENRY OSSAWA TANNER

1859 Philadelphia – 1937 Paris
AMERICAN

Henry Ossawa Tanner was the first child of the black activist Benjamin Tucker Tanner. The family were not artistic and they were sceptical about their son taking up a career in the arts, but in 1879 they relented and allowed him to enrol at the Pennsylvania Academy of Fine Arts, Philadelphia, where he studied with Thomas Eakins and Thomas Hovenden. Racial problems and the lack of opportunities for a black artist eventually forced Tanner to leave the United States in 1891. In Paris he found a more congenial artistic and political environment and, while he returned to the United States on a number of occasions, he made France his permanent home. In the early years of the 20th century Tanner became famous for his biblical pictures. The Musée du Luxembourg acquired three works, and several articles were published in both France and the United States, making Tanner the first black artist to achieve an international reputation.

Travelling to Egypt and Palestine for the first time in 1897, Tanner was fascinated by the grandeur of Cairo's monuments, but 'from a picturesque point of view many smaller things pleased me more', he noted in his diary.[1] He returned to the Holy Land in 1898 for a more extended trip in search of background material for his paintings of biblical life. In 1908 he worked in Algeria for a short time and in 1912 he travelled to Morocco with his wife and a party of friends that included the young Australian painter Hilda Rix Nicholas.

Following the First World War Tanner's career continued to expand and in 1923 he was awarded the Cross of the Légion d'honneur by the French government. During the late 1920s his health deteriorated and he painted fewer pictures. JP

PAUL-DESIRE TROUILLEBERT

1831 Paris – 1900 Paris
FRENCH

Trouillebert's Salon exhibits were at first genre scenes, portraits and voluptuous, sensuous nudes. For many academic artists, white and waxily perfect female bodies were an ideal; pictures of these improbable creatures were reproduced in such publications as *Le Nu au Salon* and, for photographs, in *Le Nu Artistique*. Very often, artists, in order to avoid censure over overt eroticism, placed these nudes in a remote and exotic eastern setting or in a historical context. Trouillebert transformed his beautiful women into nymphs, captives, Judith, Diana the Huntress, Ariadne, Cleopatra or Danae.

In one of his rare Orientalist pictures, *Harem servant* (Musée des Beaux-Arts Jules Chéret, Nice), the slave is both submissive – her two bracelets are linked by a chain, and she performs a menial task – and, with her naked breasts and piercing stare, provocative. Gold jewellery, palm and banana trees, a narghile – nothing has been left out to persuade the viewer that his Parisian model was indeed Oriental. A snake-charmer is the subject of another large oil. Here, a young and beautiful naked woman plays castanets to attract the cobra, which, rearing up, flickers its tongue in the direction of her thighs. With less overt sexual overtones, Trouillebert's picture of a seated Oriental woman holding a sword is nevertheless ambiguous, evoking the implacable *femme fatale* ready to use her irresistible power of fascination to kill or maim.

From the 1880s Trouillebert painted landscapes, above all of French riversides, in subdued colours in the later manner of Camille Corot. LT

[1] Diary kept by Tanner during his trip in 1897; quoted in Marcia Mathews, *Henry Ossawa Tanner: An American Artist*, University of Chicago Press, Chicago, 1969, pp. 82–6.

Gendre, Catherine. *André Suréda (1872–1930): designs-estampes-illustrations.* Exh. cat., Musée Lambinet, Versailles, 7 June–7 July 1983.

Vuillemot, Gustave. *Centenaire d'André Suréda.* Exh. cat., Musée Rolin, Autun, May–October 1972.

Mathews, Marcia. *Henry Ossawa Tanner: An American Artist.* University of Chicago Press, Chicago, 1969.

Mosby, Dewey F. et al. *Henry Ossawa Tanner.* Exh. cat., Philadelphia Museum of Art, 1991.

Marumo, Claude. 'Paul-Désiré Trouillebert: *catalogue raisonné*' (forthcoming).

PHOTOGRAPHERS' BIOGRAPHIES

HIPPOLYTE ARNOUX

(dates unknown)
FRENCH

A photographer resident in Port Said, Arnoux was active around 1865. He photographed the building of the Suez Canal. In order to document the largest construction site in the history of photography, he transformed his boat into a dark room. A selection of his photographs was published in the *Album du Canal* in 1869. After that, however, he devoted himself to studio portraits and genre scenes.

HENRI BECHARD

(dates unknown)
FRENCH

Béchard was a photographer who worked in Egypt between 1869 and 1880. His studio was situated in the gardens of the Ezbekiya district in Cairo. He photographed landscapes and monuments, artisans at work, and also took portraits.

BONFILS

Félix Bonfils 1831–1885 Lydie Bonfils 1837–1918 Adrien Bonfils 1861–1929
FRENCH

Félix Bonfils learned the art of photography from Nièpce de Saint Victor. He installed himself in Beirut with his wife, Lydie Bonfils, in 1867. She took studio portraits and kept the accounts while Félix took photographs across the Middle East. In 1871 he submitted his prints of Egypt, Palestine, Syria and Greece to the French Photographic Society and received their medal. In the same year his stock comprised 15,000 prints and 9000 stereoscopic views. In 1872 Bonfils published with Ducher an album of 100 photos of the Near East and in 1876 settled in Alès, where he published a series of albums titled *Souvenirs d'Orient*. He received a medal at the Paris Exposition Universelle of 1878 and, in the same year, handed over his business in Beirut to his son, Adrien.

A. CAVILLA

(dates unknown)

Cavilla worked with Molinari, signing his works Cavilla & Molinari. Both were active around 1880 and took photographs in Morocco and Algeria.

GAETAN GATIAN DE CLERAMBAULT

1872–1934
FRENCH

A psychiatrist and photographer, Clérambault, after taking courses in law and art, decided (against the advice of his family) to study medicine. He specialised in mental illness and pursued two parallel projects after 1915 – psychiatry and the photographing of a single subject, namely traditional Moroccan dress. He would connect these two parts of his work in two texts devoted to the erotic passion for fabrics in women. He probably produced 4000 photographs of costumes, of which only about 400 survive in the collection of the Musée de l'Homme in Paris. Shown for the first time in 1990, these works were never exhibited in his lifetime. Lacan said of Clérambault that he was his only master in psychiatry.

ERME DESIRE

(dates unknown)
FRENCH

The photographer Ermé Désiré produced photographs in Egypt between 1864 and 1867. Although situated in Cairo, his studio advertised 'Parisian photography'. Désiré is noted for the very high quality of his series of artisans at work, taken in Cairo. He was appointed 'photographer to his majesty the King of Egypt and to the Princes, Cairo, Egypt'.

EMILE FRECHON

(dates unknown)
FRENCH

A photographer active in 1890, Frechon worked in France and made journeys to Algeria, Holland and Palestine. Influenced by the pictorialist vogue, his images were mainly of ethnographic figures, landscapes and animals.

ABDULLAH FRERES

Kevork Abdullah 1839–1918 Hovsep Abdullah (?)–1902 Vichen Aliksan Abdullah
(dates unknown)
ARMENIAN

These three brothers of Armenian origin were to produce the most important photographic *oeuvre* of Istanbul and of the Ottoman Empire. Their fame rose steadily from the 1860s onwards. They became photographers to royal guests visiting Istanbul. Named official photographers to Sultan Abdul Aziz in 1863 and, later, to Sultan Abdul Hamid II, they became members of the French Photographic Society in 1870. In 1886, at the request of Tewfik Pacha, Kevork Abdullah established himself in Cairo. He was joined there by his brother, Hovsep, but they returned to Istanbul two years later. They sold their studio to Sébah and Joaillier in 1899.

GARRIGUES

(dates unknown)

A French photographer established in Tunis, Garrigues stopped working around 1889, as mentioned in the Tunisian *Indicateur*, when his business was taken over by Marichal. He was the official photographer to the Bey of Tunis and photographed Tunisia from north to south. He won several medals at the expositions of Toulouse and Tunis in 1889, as well as at the Paris Exposition Universelle of 1889. His studio advertisement at the entry to the Medina of Tunis announced: 'Kodak – Cameras – Supplies for amateurs – Indigenous costumes – Enlargements – Postcards'.

JOHN BEASELEY GREENE

1832–1856
AMERICAN

Born in Paris of American parents, Greene died very young. An amateur archaeologist, he made voyages to Egypt and Algeria. From 1853 to 1854 he was authorised by Said Pacha to conduct archaeological excavations. He then crossed the Nile and visited Beirut, Jerusalem and Damascus. In 1854 he became a founding member of the French Photographic Society. His photographs of Egypt were published by Blanquard-Evrard under the title *The Nile: Monuments, Landscapes, Photographic Explorations*. In 1854 and 1855 Greene made a second trip to the Near East sponsored by Ferdinand de Lesseps. His died in an accident in Egypt.

WILHELM HAMMERSCHMIDT

(dates unknown)
GERMAN

Hammerschmidt was a professional photographer who opened a studio in Cairo around 1860. In 1861 he showed his Egyptian views at the French Photographic Society, becoming a member in 1863. In 1867 he contributed to the Exposition Universelle with a series of views and costumes of Egypt and Syria. His photographs are well preserved and are considered among the most interesting of those by resident photographers.

LEHNERT AND LANDROCK

Rudolph Lehnert 1878–1948
Ernst Landrock 1878–1966

Rudolph Lehnert, who came to Tunisia via Italy and Sicily, discovered a familiar Orient. He fell in love with the country that would shape his whole life, setting himself up in Tunis in 1904 by opening a shop on the avenue de France with his friend Ernst Landrock. Each of them lived in an Arab palace in the Medina and together they created a business whose scope is announced on the back of a postcard as: 'Artistic photographs – Types – Landscapes (Oasis-Sahara) – Artistic studies of the Nude – Engravings – Albums – Postcards – Arab Oriental costume scenes – Studies for amateurs'. In 1914 one of them was imprisoned and the other fled the country. In 1920 they decided to restart their enterprise in Egypt. By 1930, missing the Tunisian desert, Lehnert returned to Tunisia and remained there until his death at the oasis of Redeyef. The business they founded in Cairo still operates at no. 44 rue Sherif Pasha.

FELIX-JACQUES MOULIN

c. 1800–after 1868
FRENCH

Assisted by his wife and daughter, Moulin had a flourishing business in Paris where he traded in his own photographs as well as in those of other photographers. From 1852 the journal *La Lumiere* paid tribute to this artist who, as well as producing portraits, was a specialist in genre scenes and artistic nudes. In 1856–57, with a letter of recommendation from the minister of war and accompanied by Achille Quinet the younger, he travelled to Algeria. The images he took on this trip were published in *L'Algérie photographiée* in 1860.

CHARLES NAUDET

(dates unknown)
FRENCH

A photographer active around 1890, Naudet produced portraits in the pictorialist style.

JOSEPH PEDRA

(dates unknown)

Joseph Pedra was active in Algeria around 1860 and signed his work 'Photo Pedra à Tlemcen'. He primarily photographed landscapes and architecture.

RUBELLIN

(dates unknown)

Very little is known about this photographer, the author of very fine portraits of Turkish gentlewomen. Established in Smyrna, he photographed widely throughout Turkey before and after 1870. He signed the back of his photographs: 'Rubellin Père & Fils, Edouard Rubellin, succ. Smyrne'.

MOHAMMED SADIC BEY

(dates unknown)
EGYPTIAN

The photographer Mohammed Sadic Bey was a colonel in the Egyptian army. He was the first to photograph Mecca, accompanying the Mahmal or sacred carpet during the pilgrimage of November 1881. He signed his photographs in Arabic and French (Sadic Bey) and at times would note the year according to the Muslim calendar. He was also an explorer, since he made the first record of the exact measurements of the plan of the Haram and of the tomb of the Prophet. The thirteen photographs conserved in the library of the Institut de France in Paris may be a complete collection of his photographs of Mecca and Medina.

PASCAL SEBAH

(?)–1890
MIDDLE EASTERN

Pascal Sébah was a photographer whose studio, named El-Chark, was in the rue Postacilar in the Péra quarter of Istanbul, formerly Constantinople. He received medals and prizes at the Universal Exhibitions of Paris, Vienna and Philadelphia. His success led him to open a second studio in Cairo in 1873. He worked in close collaboration with Béchard. In 1884 the photographer Policarp Joaillier of Istanbul became his partner. In 1888 the new name of Sébah and Joaillier was given to the studio. At seventy years of age, Pascal Sébah sold his studio to Agop Iskender and Perpanyani, but his fame endures in Istanbul.

NORTH AFRICA AND THE NEAR EAST 1900

FRANCE

Marseilles •

ITALY

• Rome

SPAIN

GREECE

• Cordoba

• Seville

• Granada

Tangier •   • Tetouan
Rabat •   • Moulay-Idriss   Blida •   • Algiers
Casablanca •   • Fez   Oran •   • El-Asnam   Constantine   Tunis •
        Meknès •   • Tlemcen   TUNISIA
                                             Bou Saâda •   Kairouan •
MOROCCO   • Biskra

• Marrakesh   MEDITERRANEAN

ALGERIA   • Laghouat

                   • Ghardaia   • Tripoli

                                                                LIBYA

SAHARA DESERT

BLACK SEA

CASPIAN SEA

Istanbul ● (Constantinople)

TURKEY

PERSIA

● Izmir   ● Konya

● Aleppo

SYRIA

LEBANON   ● Baalbek
Beirut ●   ● Damascus

CRETE

PALESTINE

● Jerusalem

Alexandria ●

Suez Canal

Giza ▲ ● Cairo

● Mt Sinai

EGYPT

SAUDI ARABIA

● Aswan Dam   ● Medina

● Mecca

RED SEA

Select Bibliography

(See Artists' Biographies for monographs)

Ackerman, Gerald M. *Les Orientalistes de l'école britannique*. Les Orientalistes, vol. 9, ACR, Paris, 1991.

— —. *Les Orientalistes de l'école américaine*. Les Orientalistes, vol. 10, ACR, Paris, 1994.

Alazard, Jean. *L'Orient et la peinture française au XIXe siècle*. Plon, Paris, 1930.

Alloulah, Malek. *The Colonial Harem*. University of Minnesota, Minneapolis, 1986.

Coloniales 1920–1940. Exh. cat., ed. Emmanuel Bréon, Musée Municipal de Boulogne-Billancourt, 7 November 1989–31 January 1990.

Graham-Brown, Sarah. *Images of Women: The Portrayal of Women in Photography of the Middle East*. Quartet, London, 1988.

Jammes, André & Janis, Eugenia P. *The Art of the French Calotype*. Princeton University Press, Princeton, NJ, 1983.

Jullian, Philippe. *The Orientalists: European Painters of Eastern Scenes*. Phaidon, Oxford, 1977.

Khemir, Mounira. *L'Orientalisme: l'orient des photographes au XIXème siècle*. Photopoche no. 58, Centre National de la Photographie, Paris, 1994.

Lewis, Reina. *Gendering Orientalism: Race, Femininity and Representation*. Routledge, London & New York, 1996.

Lowe, Lisa. *Critical Terrains: French and British Orientalisms*. Cornell University Press, Ithaca, NY, 1991.

MacKenzie, John. *Orientalism: History, Theory, and the Arts*. Manchester University Press, Manchester, 1995.

L'Orient des provençaux. Series of 7 exh. cats, Marseilles, November 1982–February 1983.

Les Peintres orientalistes (1850–1914). Exh. cat., ed. Philippe Comte & Françoise Baligand, Musée des Beaux-Arts, Pau; Musée des Beaux-Arts, Dunkirk; Musée de la Chartreuse, Douai; May–October 1983.

Peltre, Christine. *L'Atelier du voyage: les peintres en Orient au XIXe siècle*. Gallimard, Paris, 1995.

Rosenthal, Donald. *Orientalism: The Near East in French Painting, 1800–1880*. Exh. cat., University of Rochester Memorial Art Gallery, Rochester, NY, 1984.

Said, Edward W. *Culture and Imperialism*. Chatto & Windus, London, 1993.

— —. *Orientalism*. Routledge & Kegan Paul, London, 1978; repr. with an afterword, Penguin, Harmondsworth, 1995.

Stevens, MaryAnne (ed.). *The Orientalists: Delacroix to Matisse*. Exh. cat., Royal Academy of Arts, London, 1984.

Sweetman, John. *The Oriental Obsession: Islamic Inspiration in British and American Art and Architecture 1500–1920*. Cambridge University Press, Cambridge, 1987.

Thompson, James. *The East: Imagined, Experienced, Remembered*. Exh. cat., National Gallery of Ireland, Dublin, 1988.

Thornton, Lynne. *The Orientalists: Painter–Travellers 1828–1908*. Les Orientalistes, vol. 1, ACR, Paris, 1983.

— —. *La Femme dans la peinture orientaliste*. Les Orientalistes, vol. 3, ACR, Paris, 1985.

Visions of the Ottoman Empire. Exh. cat., Scottish National Portrait Gallery, Edinburgh, 1994.

Lenders to the Exhibition

The Art Gallery of New South Wales

Art Gallery of South Australia, Adelaide

Auckland City Art Gallery

Philip Bacon Galleries, Brisbane

Ballarat Fine Art Gallery

Bibliothèque des Arts Décoratifs, Paris

Bibliothèque Nationale de France, Paris

Dr Joseph Brown

Conseil International de la Langue Française, Paris

Jean-Pierre Evrard

James Fairfax AO

Fine Arts Museums of San Francisco

Galerie Jean-François Heim, Paris

Galerie Gérard Lévy, Paris

Galerie Rosengart, Lucerne

Pierre de Gigord

Harris Museum and Art Gallery, Preston

Hearst Castle™/Hearst San Simeon State Historical Monument™

Hiroshima Museum of Art

Institut du Monde Arabe, Paris

Nabil Jumbert

Kunstmuseum Basel

The Leicester Galleries, London

François Lepage

M. Alain Lesieutre

Mr Frank McDonald

Manly Art Gallery and Museum, Sydney

Musée des Augustins, Toulouse

Musée des Beaux-Arts de Bordeaux

Musée des Beaux-Arts, Nice

Musée des Beaux-Arts, Reims

Musée de Cambrai

Musée de la Chartreuse, Douai

Musée de l'Homme, Paris

Musée Ingres, Montauban

Musée Lambinet, Versailles

Musée du Louvre, Paris

Musée Matisse, Nice

Musée National des Arts d'Afrique et d'Océanie, Paris

Musée de l'Orangerie, Paris

Musée d'Orsay, Paris

Musées Municipaux de Boulogne-Billancourt

Musées Royaux des Beaux-Arts de Belgique, Brussels

Museum of Fine Arts, Boston

The Najd Collection, courtesy of the Mathaf Gallery, London

National Gallery of Australia, Canberra

National Gallery of Victoria, Melbourne

National Museum of American Art, Smithsonian Institution, Washington DC

Nippon Life Insurance Company, Osaka

Claude Philip

Jacques Py

The Russell-Cotes Art Gallery and Museum, Bournemouth

Savill Galleries, Sydney

Sterling and Francine Clark Institute, Williamstown, Mass., USA

Tate Gallery, London

Toowoomba Regional Art Gallery

Angela Tromellini, Bologna

UCLA at the Armand Hammer Museum of Art and Cultural Center, Los Angeles

Victoria and Albert Museum, London

The Walters Art Gallery, Baltimore

The Whitworth Art Gallery, The University of Manchester

Rix Wright

and a number of private collectors in Australia, France and Switzerland who wish to remain anonymous

CREDITS